SERGEI PROKOFIEV

DISCARDED

PROGRESS PUBLISHERS 1978

SERGEI PROKOFIEV

MATERIALS
ARTICLES
INTERVIEWS

Compiled by *Vladimir Blok*
Designed by *Grigory Dauman*

Сергей Прокофьев

МАТЕРИАЛЫ, СТАТЬИ, ИНТЕРВЬЮ

На английском языке

The illustrations in this book are reproduced from newsreels and documentaries.

Printed in the Union of Soviet Socialist Republics

$$\text{П } \frac{90103 - 194}{014\,(01) - 79} \;\; 117 - 77$$

CONTENTS

COMPILER'S NOTE

The many-sided work of Sergei Prokofiev with its rich variety of genres is of great interest to musicians and musicologists alike. His music, in which the pulse of the age beats so intensely, is loved far and wide. It has, indeed, conquered the world. According to official UNESCO statistics, Prokofiev is the most widely performed composer of the 20th century.

Soviet musicology has produced many works about Prokofiev, ranging from detailed studies and specialised articles to popular brochures. The reminiscences of the composer's close friends and eminent musicians who were personally acquainted with him well are of special interest.

The present volume contains material previously published in other Soviet collections devoted to Prokofiev's work. These include articles, interviews and notes by Prokofiev himself (with the exception of his article "The Years of Wandering"), extracts from his correspondence with Nikolai Myaskovsky, reminiscences by David Oistrakh, Emil Gilels, Svyatoslav Richter and Galina Ulanova published in the book *S.S. Prokofiev; Materials, Documents, Reminiscences* (edited and compiled by S. Shlifshtein), second edition, Moscow, State Music Publishers, 1961; Prokofiev's article "The Years of Wandering"; L. Danko's article "S. Prokofiev in His Work on *The Duenna* (The writing of the libretto)" from the collection *Features of S. Prokofiev's Style* (edited and compiled by L. Berger), Moscow, Soviet Composer Publishers, 1962. V. Blok's monograph entitled *Prokofiev's Music for Children* appeared as a separate edition (Moscow, Music Publishers, 1969).

Most of the other material first saw the light of day in Soviet periodicals. In all cases references to their first publication are given in the material itself.

Nearly all the material and reminiscences about Prokofiev included in the present volume, and all the special studies, are published here for the first time in English.

V. Blok
Moscow, March 14, 1976

SOVIET COMPOSERS
ABOUT PROKOFIEV

Dmitry Shostakovich

Sergei Prokofiev is the pride and glory of Soviet music. It would be difficult to find a modern composer whose name is more widely recognised throughout the world. Unlike other composers, about whom much is said and written but whose works are rarely played, Prokofiev has become firmly established in the repertoire of the finest orchestras and soloists and in opera and ballet theatres throughout the world. His musical legacy stands in direct contrast to reactionary, modernist rubbish and the empty theories of the "reformers" of music fashionable in the West.

Prokofiev's music is loved both in our great country and abroad. I stress the word "loved" for true love of a modern composer's music is comparatively rare for a variety of reasons. In spite of all its innovatory daring and originality, its uncompromising approach to the important and complex tasks of developing a modern musical idiom and style, Prokofiev's music is loved deeply by audiences and performers alike. It can be heard throughout the world, bringing people the great joy of contact with the powerful humanism of Soviet art.

In one of his articles Sergei Prokofiev wrote: "The music we compose must be, first and foremost, great music, that is, music in which both the idea and its technical execution correspond to the sweep of the times."

Great music. To my mind this definition by Prokofiev of the modern composer's task is most characteristic. This was the aim of all his work: whether it was the fine miniatures of *Fugitive Visions*, the great epic of *War and Peace*, the wise tale of *The Ugly Duckling*, or the pensive lyricism of his First Concerto for

Violin and Orchestra—it was always great music, music endowed with unusual inner energy, vitality, always forging ahead "towards new shores".

Prokofiev's creative legacy is immense, all-embracing, in respect of theme, genre, form, means of expression, artistic aims and purposes. I think there is no sphere in the art of composition which Prokofiev left untouched. Like Mozart, Beethoven and Tchaikovsky, he was proficient in all genres—from the mass song to opera, from the instrumental ensemble to the symphony. And in everything he was a new, bold, original, inspired, national artist, his roots firmly embedded in Russian music, Russian culture.

Prokofiev is a model of complete devotion to his art. He was an indefatigable worker. I do not remember who said that genius is talent plus hard work. This certainly applies to Prokofiev, a composer who was brilliant at organising his work, composing every day, systematically and painstakingly to the point of self-oblivion. In the last years of his life, when he was seriously ill, he persuaded his doctors to allow him to work for an hour each day. And he certainly made the most of this hour. When one recalls the many splendid works he composed within these strict time limits—the Seventh Symphony, the ballet *The Stone Flower*, the oratorio *On Guard of Peace*, the revision of *War and Peace*, and the Symphony-Concerto for violoncello and orchestra—one cannot but marvel at the remarkable power of this brilliant musician's creative spirit. He made use of this *one hour* even on his last day, working on the score of *The Stone Flower*.

Prokofiev strove to compose an opera based on a modern subject. He achieved a great deal. His two operas *Semyon Kotko* and *A Story of a Real Man* record the features of our age. His *Betrothal in a Nunnery* belongs to the classic works of Soviet operatic art. And *War and Peace*, a profoundly patriotic work written during the war, occupies a special place in Soviet music and world music in general. Yet this list does not exhaust his operatic legacy. And it is good that our theatres are showing an increasing interest in him. It is to be hoped that it will not be long before all his operas, including *The Flaming Angel, The Gambler*, and *The Love for Three Oranges* are performed on the Soviet stage.

A great Soviet composer, Prokofiev was also an ardent patriot, an honest, high-principled artist, who sincerely sought contact with a mass audience. He was a great optimist, who believed in his people and its radiant future. And he strove with all his might to serve the people with his art. Prokofiev wrote: "The time is past when music was written for a handful of aesthetes. Today vast crowds of people have come face to face with serious music and are waiting with eager impatience.... The masses want great music, great events, great love, lively dances. They understand far more than some composers think, and want to deepen their understanding."

I am proud and happy to have had the good fortune of witnessing the splendid flowering of Prokofiev's genius, to have been closely acquainted with this remarkable musician and have benefited from his advice. I shall never tire of listening to his music and studying his most valuable experience.

Sovietskaya Muzyka,
No. 4, 1961

Dmitry Kabalevsky

It would be hard to find a composer whose works provoked such impassioned and sharp disputes as those which centred round Sergei Prokofiev throughout his life. These disputes were the natural result of the composer's striking talent and originality, and the novelty of the tasks which he set himself and sought to solve in his work.

His very first piano concerto—written at the age of twenty—produced a storm of criticism such as Russian music had not known for a long time. Admiring voices mingled with flat condemnation of both the work and its young composer. The concerto was too unusual, not so much in form, idiom and piano technique (although here too there was much that was novel), as in the explosive force of its content which contrasted strongly with the anaemic music of the decadent salons of the day. Life itself has resolved this dispute, slowly but surely: for more than forty years now Prokofiev's first concerto has been performed throughout the world, attracting the attention of celebrated pianists and invariably enjoying great success with audiences.

There was also the most bitter dispute which flared up in the mid-1930s when Sergei Prokofiev—already an artist of world repute—composed the ballet *Romeo and Juliet*. For the first time Shakespeare appeared on the Russian ballet stage—without simplification, without that conventional ballet "sweet-wrapping" in which Cervantes and Byron had been presented to the public in *Don Quixote* and *Le Corsair*. It was new, daring, unusual. So unusual that the management of the Bolshoi Theatre rejected the ballet composed on their own initiative and did not produce it until eight years later, after it had been performed with great success at the Kirov Theatre in Leningrad. The debate on *Romeo and Juliet* continued for a long time. Some critics argued that it was a pantomime, not a ballet, and as such did not blaze any new paths. Others attributed the ballet's success to the unique art of Galina Ulanova. Yet ... *Romeo and Juliet* now adorns the repertoire of many of the world's finest ballet stages ... and audiences, unaware of the critics' scholastic debates, have come to love the work as a ballet, while prima ballerinas covet the part of Juliet so vitally and poetically embodied by Prokofiev in his music.

Life, the supreme judge which passes sentence on works of art, is no abstraction, nor is it necessarily a time factor. Life means people who accept or reject the art which has been created for them. And an artist must not rely only on the "judgement of history" fifty or a hundred years hence, although it cannot, of course, be denied that historical perspective corrects a great deal in earlier evaluations.

Many of Prokofiev's works gained world recognition during his lifetime. The patriotic cantata *Alexander Nevsky* with its great epic sweep, the symphonic fairy-tale *Peter and the Wolf* charming in its childlike spontaneity; the ballets *Cinderella* and the *Tale of the Stone Flower* distinguished by their lyrical warmth; the publicistically sharp oratorio *On Guard of Peace* and the *Lieutenant Kizhe* suite with its brilliant wit of the characterisation; Prokofiev's finest symphonies, concertos, sonatas and many other of his works in various genres constitute the pride not only of the composer himself, but of Soviet music as a whole. These works are performed by eminent musicians throughout the world. They have become the possession of civilised humanity as a whole.

An optimistic attitude towards life, unbridled energy and, at the same time, a most poetic lyricism and an inexhaustible wealth of melody and perfection of artistic form—all these features determine the power and appeal of Prokofiev's music, which is uniquely individual as well as an organic development of Russian classical music.

...To the end of his days Sergei Prokofiev remained the same eagerly questing artist, striving tirelessly for novelty, as he was when he began his career. With time his youthful ardour was replaced by the wisdom of the mature artist and master, who was enriched by vast experience of life and was profoundly aware of his ideological tasks as a composer.

Before he had completed one work, Prokofiev was already deeply absorbed in plans for new ones. Before he had exhausted the possibilities of this or that creative discovery, he was already searching for something that would give fuller and more perfect embodiment to his ideas of the great realistic art of our day, which were crystallising with ever-increasing clarity. This is why the creative legacy bequeathed by Prokofiev, which embraces the most various themes and genres, from simple children's songs to the heroic pages of *Alexander Nevsky*, is so important, rich and many-sided.

From the preface to Volume 1 of Prokofiev's *Collected Works*, State Music Publishers, Moscow, 1955

An inspired bard of life, the sun and youth, he gave the people of the troubled, harsh and cruel 20th century the joy and radiance which they so often lack. The courage, optimism, and dignity of Prokofiev's music personify for the whole world the ideals of Soviet art in its advance towards the future, towards noble humanistic ideals.

From the preface to Sergei Prokofiev's *Autobiography, Sovietsky Kompozitor* Publishers, Moscow, 1973

Kara Karayev

When you really love someone it is hard to speak of love. Particularly during an anniversary.

But, nevertheless, I shall attempt to talk about my very first love, a constant and undying one, my love for Sergei Prokofiev. It began when I was still at school. At that time (as today, incidentally) Prokofiev was the centre of much dispute. I accepted him at once, totally, completely, without dividing his work into the "indisputable" and the "contradictory". I remember being struck by the remarkable novelty in this music, by a special blend of radiance and daring, which at one time I tried frankly to imitate. I can say without exaggeration that the awareness of art as the main ideal and aim of existence entered my life with the music of Prokofiev. And therefore I regard myself as his "indirect" pupil....

Many years have passed since the day in Baku when I first heard the Third Piano Concerto in the composer's "volcanic" rendering. I have written many works, experienced success and failure, and long realised the old truth that, unlike youthful infatuation, mature love is exacting because it is based not only on emotion, but also on sober analysis. Naturally, as a composer I have studied almost all Prokofiev's scores. I have made a long, careful examination of his dramaturgy, of the delightfully laconic intonation of his portraits, the features of the form. I can say that I now *know* Prokofiev, with all his magnificent achievements, and his occasional miscalculations. Does my present love differ from that in my youth? Yes, it does. It is greater. The

Fourth, Fifth, and Sixth symphonies, the piano pieces, *War and Peace, Semyon Kotko, The Duenna, Romeo and Juliet,* and the completely Mozartian *Cinderella*—without these works my life would in some respects probably be poorer, duller, less interesting. I mean my life, not only music. For Prokofiev's art, like all great art, is of great *ethic* as well as aesthetic power; it extols beauty in man and nature. This is why I dedicated *The Path of Thunder*—a ballet about human striving for happiness and freedom—to Prokofiev.

Sergei Prokofiev's music is so original that it is easy to imitate. At first glance it even seems fairly easy to write like Prokofiev in general: all one needs do is compose, for example, a slow, very plastic, yet at the same time intonationally slightly "prickly" theme in C major, an *ostinato* accompaniment or a cadence with a major seventh instead of the usual dominant. Yet the more "authentic" the imitation of Prokofiev, the farther removed it is from him, a composer who recognised one path only in art—the path of tireless quest, radical transformation. Prokofiev never followed familiar paths; and those who see themselves as his followers should not take them either.

Like all true reformers, by reinterpreting some traditions and sweeping aside others, Prokofiev created *his own* traditions in art. He became one of the classics of socialist musical culture, whose artistic experience must be studied on an equal footing with the work of the great composers of the past. Without assimilating Prokofiev's heritage one cannot progress further. Here I must reproach the critics: whereas Prokofiev the theatre dramatist has been "studied inside out", the same, unfortunately, cannot be said of Prokofiev the symphonic composer. At any rate I have never come across a single thorough, more or less exhaustive study of his symphonies. It is high time that one appeared!

Prokofiev is such a profuse and versatile artist that occasionally very different creative personalities meet on the trails which he blazed. In teaching students I see that one is more attracted to his "careful", pent-up lyricism, another to his powerful, "sharp" dynamism, a third to the inimitable precision of his genre imagery.... But for all these natural differences, the younger generation of Soviet musicians is unanimous in its love for Prokofiev's work: it regards him as a perfect artistic example. And, therefore, when I need to divert a pupil from abstruse experiments, I always turn to Prokofiev—to the deep popular spirit, the unique melodic charm of his imagery.

Prokofiev's art belongs to the people. And my love as an individual and a musician for this magnificent art is but a wave in the vast sea of popular love for him, which is growing constantly....

Sovietskaya Muzyka,
No. 4, 1961

Albert Leman

The process by which an artist gains wide and firmly-established recognition is a most complex phenomenon.

Why is a great deal of time sometimes required before art which is truly sublime, important and vital to people is fully appreciated? What is it? A genius who has rushed too far ahead? Or perhaps a certain sluggishness on the part of his contemporaries, who are more used to assimilating the vast spiritual legacy of the past? Perhaps there is, in general, a strong and justified tendency not to admit anyone to Olympus without the thorough and lengthy test of time? The answer is probably—all three.

Mankind adds to the treasure store of eternal values only that which has passed the examination and judgement of a multitude of impressions and opinions, that which has been selected with the greatest possible objectivity. This is probably why those who greet everything unusual with rapturous admiration and those who accept the new only with time, soberly, after the most scrupulous testing, as if they are resisting it, are equally right and useful. With the passage of time the gullible renounce their excessive enthusiasm, and the sceptics gradually give way. Sergei Prokofiev has now passed through both extremes of criticism. But evidently the latter had more, if not arguments then force of inertia, due to which the complete recognition of Prokofiev as a great Russian, Soviet composer was somewhat postponed. This was all the more regrettable, because for a while the public at large could not play a proper part in the appreciation of Prokofiev's work. What a good thing that Prokofiev, like the legendary Orpheus, has now won the attention of millions with his remarkable art.

How strange it would be today to hear: "Prokofiev lacks melody...." For now we can say: Prokofiev is almost complete melody! It is everywhere: in Juliet, Cinderella, and Natasha Rostova, it flows broadly and endlessly in *Semyon Kotko*, in *A Story of a Real Man.* It astounds us in the First and Second violin concertos, in the Second Piano Concerto and the Symphony-Concerto.... And how many marvellous melodic themes there are in *Fugitive Visions* and the piano and violin sonatas! Thematic melodism is the basis of the whole psychological structure of images in the composer's symphonic, cantata-oratorial, operatic, ballet and instrumental work.

And what about harmony? As a rule, it fully complements and "serves" the melody. At times Prokofiev invests the harmony with a completely independent function, but again in the interests of the *imagery.* His discoveries in melody and harmony—these fine qualities of the artist, traditionally Russian features of musical composition—are truly invaluable.

As an artist Prokofiev was immense and all-embracing. He loved his homeland, breathed with its breath, fought and suffered for it. *Alexander Nevsky* is full of the staunchness and invincible spirit of the Russian people in its struggle against a mortal enemy. "Arise, Men of Russia!"—this music has become a kind of "injection" of stamina! The whole cantata was a precursor of the crucial test of loyalty to the homeland. To an even greater extent *War and Peace* developed this most popular and vital patriotic theme on a grandiose scale. It would be hard to find another ideological-artistic phenomenon of such magnitude in the whole of our culture after Glinka or Tolstoy....

The war ended but the great patriot again reminded people of the possibility of the resurgence of evil with the oratorio *On Guard of Peace.*

How much light, kindness, reverie, humour and magic there is in this Russian genius' work! How children love Prokofiev! I once heard a six-year-old boy ask for *Peter and the Wolf* to be replayed several times in succession. Each time the record finished he said: "Play it again" and his face lit up with joy. How many children play Prokofiev at music schools! Prokofiev is to be heard in all classes at schools and conservatoires. He is performed on all the concert stages of the world.

There is a marked growth of interest in the composer's opera and ballet works. The most progressive theatres included them in their repertoire a long time ago. It can hardly be necessary to remind people yet again of the remarkable theatricality of Prokofiev's music, of his rare "producer's" gift for intoning his characters, and their vivid characterisation.

Listening to this music, you can always hear the author's commentary on what is taking place on the stage; he has the knack of visualising everything that occurs there as if he were a member of the audience....

One of Prokofiev's greatest qualities is a profound understanding of the way in which his art is perceived. It is this quality—the ability to take account of the logic of this perception in the process of the vigorous development of the idea—that we should call artistry or a sense of form. In some mysterious way (intuitively!) the genius knows what is *still* interesting and what is *already* not, *where* and *when* to make the action take this or that turn, to introduce a contrast, in a word, how to keep it effective. I am convinced that talent, vitality, artistry, a sense of form are synonyms. They all have the same basic root.

The performance of Prokofiev's music (as of all real music) is usually accompanied by a growing interest in the inner processes of the development of artistic thought. To return to the composer's operatic works, however, we must mention a few "buts"....

This work is still comparatively rarely put on in our theatres, particularly in the provinces. According to some theatre managers Prokofiev's scores are still difficult for performers and audiences alike. They also claim that his operas are not a good box-office attraction. This is a passive attitude, which is most *active* in its *passivity!* It has existed for years and many people have become used to it. Special efforts must be made to ensure that the pinnacles of Soviet spiritual culture, to which Prokofiev's operatic works undoubtedly belong, are made available to the people. It is essential that these values be equated with *enlightenment*, and enlightenment, as we know, requires material and moral expenditure which is recouped by the most important thing of all—the education of man.

Semyon Kotko and *A Story of a Real Man*, to say nothing of *War and Peace* and, in fact, all Prokofiev's operas should be actively and constantly popularised and should eventually be shown in all theatres throughout the country.

From the very beginning Prokofiev introduced much that had

not previously been known or experienced into the world of art. But even in his period of "bitter" searching, the period of youthful "violent creativity", he was clearer than many of his contemporaries. Prokofiev was a peculiar sensor of revolutionary mood, of the impending revolution. He retained this remarkable sensitivity to the age, the brilliant ability to "run on ahead", to the end of his life. In music, he was a forerunner of the revolutionary epoch. And he absorbed the spirit of the post-revolutionary years deeply and authentically, creating a musical monument of the Soviet age. This links him closely with Mayakovsky.

Prokofiev, his immense power of artistic expression, his fidelity to the finest ideals of the age, his original musical idiom, his vast range of themes and imagery, his remarkably universal mastery of and interest in all forms and genres, has a tremendous instructive influence today on the whole of Soviet music. Everything Prokofievian, special and unusual is now gradually becoming a norm for *creative thinking* and is bound to become soon a universally accepted standard for audiences too.

Prokofiev is the great son of a great people, for whom he traversed his arduous creative path. He was a happy gift of nature, of the generous Russian soil. And his art, like a true fount, will live on to tell our descendants about our turbulent and creative age, about all the finest things we were capable of achieving and strove for.

Sovietskaya Muzyka,
No. 4, 1966

Tikhon Khrennikov

It was Sergei Prokofiev's good fortune to return to his native land at the right time. After his state of crisis in the late 1920s and early 1930s (clearly evident in his *Symphonic Song* and *Things in Themselves*), the great artist realised his need for new impressions of life. And these impressions he got from his Soviet homeland. It was in the Soviet period of his life that Prokofiev gave the world such brilliant works as *War and Peace, Semyon Kotko, Romeo and Juliet, Alexander Nevsky, Ivan the Terrible*, the Fifth, Sixth and Seventh symphonies and all the fine compositions that he ever wrote.

Published in the collection *I.F.Stravinsky. Articles and Materials* (compiled by L.S. Dyachkova), *Sovietsky Kompozitor* Publishers Moscow, 1973

2

SERGEI PROKOFIEV

ARTICLES
INTERVIEWS
NOTES

CLARITY AND LACONISM

...I have always felt the need for independent thinking for pursuing my own ideas. I was always in conflict with my professors at the Conservatoire as I never wanted to do anything just because the rules demanded it....

...When I completed the composition class at the Conservatoire I found that I had too many ideas and not enough technique to carry them out. However, I decided that it was better this way than the other way round. And every year I composed at least one large orchestral work until I felt that after five or six years of tenacious struggle I had earned my "salvation" in composition.

And I am not ashamed to admit that in essence I am the student of my own ideas. In everything I write I adhere to two main principles—clarity in expressing my ideas, and laconism, avoiding everything superfluous in their expression.

From an interview published in the magazine · *The Musical Observer* by Frederick Martens, New York, 1918. (Retranslated from the Russian.—*Ed.*)

ON THE GAMBLER

...I paid special attention in my new work to the stage flexibility of opera, for of late we can see in Russian operas the decline of the composer's interest in the stage aspect, as a result of which an immobility and a mass of boring conventionalities appeared in opera. This gave some of the leading musicians, for example Stravinsky and Diaghilev, grounds for predicting the degeneration of the operatic form.

27

The plot of Dostoyevsky's *The Gambler* had interested me for a long time, especially since that story, apart from its thrilling subject, consists almost entirely of dialogues, which gave me the opportunity of preserving Dostoyevsky's style in the libretto. I concerned myself a great deal with the stage aspect of the opera and tried wherever possible not to burden the singers with unnecessary conventionalities so as to give freedom to the dramatic presentation of their roles.

For that same reason the orchestration will be transparent so that every word could be heard. This is especially desirable when you take into account Dostoyevsky's incomparable text. I think that the custom of writing operas on rhymed texts is a completely absurd convention. In this case Dostoyevsky's prose is more vivid, more expressive, and more convincing than any poetry.

In *The Gambler* the dramatic tension gradually increases as the end draws near. It seems to me that I was successful in conveying the grandmother's appearance on the stage. The "hit" of the opera is, without doubt, the last but one scene, which takes place in the gambling-house. This scene is without a choir as a choir is not versatile, nor is it amenable to staging. However it does call for a large number of participants—gamblers, croupiers, onlookers—and each one of them has his own specific character. All this, in addition to the extreme quickness and complexity of action, results in a confused tangle which will demand a great deal of work in staging.

I make bold to believe that the scene in the gambling-house is totally new in operatic literature both in idea and structure. And I feel that in this scene I succeeded in accomplishing what I had planned....

MORE ABOUT *THE GAMBLER*

"And there will be no extravagance in your *Gambler*?

"None at all. I am striving only for simplicity...." *Vecherniye Birzhevye Vedomosti*, May 12, 1916.

...In view of the fact that the dramatic action is considerably declining towards the end of Dostoyevsky's novel and turns into psychological emotional experiences, and that this would have affected the closing scene and weakened its effect and that of the whole opera, I thought it better to end the opera at the point where Polina leaves the main character.

The entire opera is written in a declamatory style. ...I feel that the greatness of Wagner had a pernicious effect on operatic development and, as a result, even the most progressive-minded musicians began to consider opera a dying form. And yet, given an understanding of the stage, the flexibility, freedom, and declamatory expressiveness, opera should be the most vivid and powerful of the scenic arts.

THE YEARS OF WANDERING

Letter to the editors of the journal *K Novym Beregam*

You are interested in knowing what has become of me since I left Moscow on May 7, 1918, and set off for America in the Siberian Express. I am happy to comply with your request.

My journey to Vladivostok was a somewhat slow one—eighteen days—but quite safe. This was particularly surprising because Siberia was seething with unrest at the time, with Czechoslovak detachments, the Ataman Semyonov and so on, so that the express before reached Vladivostok after some serious adventures and the one after did not reach it at all. By June 1, I was in Japan, where I stayed for two months waiting for an American visa. During this time I gave three concerts, two in Tokyo and one in Yokohama, with a mixed programme, half classical and half consisting of my own works. Thanks to the fact that books about modern music had already appeared in Japan, and one of them, belonging to the pen of M. Otaguro, contained a chapter about me, I was given the Imperial Theatre for my concerts in Tokyo. The audience was entirely Japanese in Tokyo and European in Yokohama. Neither knew much about music, but I will not conceal the fact that I enjoyed playing to the Japanese more. They listened attentively, sat extremely quietly and ... applauded my technique.

From Japan I sailed to San Francisco via Honolulu, then crossed the continent to New York. It was not so easy to begin musical activities here, for I hardly knew anyone in New York. An American conductor to whom I showed my Classical Symphony exclaimed: "Splendid! It's real Kalinnikov!" I left in a rage, but later it was explained to me that he had meant this as the highest compliment, for he was a great admirer of Kalinnikov's symphony and had travelled all over America with it.

My first concert took place in New York in November and was well received by both the public and the press which devoted long articles to me without, incidentally, any great understanding of the essence of my music. My next appearance, however, in a symphony concert of Altschuler's, a Russian conductor who has done a great deal of work for Russian music in America, but is not talented and not liked by the Americans, resulted in a number of attacks on my compositions. Chicago, where I conducted the Scythian Suite and played the First Concerto, behaved much better. The orchestras in America are excellent, they managed the Scythian Suite easily, after three rehearsals (there were six in the Mariinsky Theatre in 1916), and the press quite earnestly called it "Bolshevist" music. The whole management of the Chicago Opera attended the concert, and as a result I was invited to put on *The Gambler*. Since the score of *The Gambler* was somewhere in Petrograd, I suggested that instead of *The Gambler* I should write them a new opera based on Carlo Gozzi's play *Love for Three Oranges*. This subject was recommended to me by Meyerhold just before I left Russia, and I gave it considerable thought on the way to America.

The director of the opera, the Italian Campanini, was very pleased to have an Italian subject, and so a contract was signed. This was the first case in America of a composer being officially commissioned to write an opera which had been accepted in advance.

I worked on *Love for Three Oranges* for nine months, taking only a few weeks off to have scarlet fever and diphtheria, and by October 1, 1919, the score was completed. Anisfeld was commissioned to do the sets, and the enormous sum of $ 80,000 was allocated for them. But in the autumn of 1919, on the eve of the rehearsals, Campanini, who had been the heart and soul of the Chicago Opera, suddenly died. The management was taken unawares, could not cope with the repertoire, and *Three Oranges* was postponed.

I found myself in an extremely unpleasant position, because working on the opera for almost a year had made me completely neglect my concerts. What is more, the style of the American concert system was not to my liking, for the American audience was not used to hearing a whole evening of works by one composer: it wanted a varied programme with a sprinkling of popular pieces. Rachmaninov made this concession, and his programmes were often blotted by waltzes by Johann Strauss—Tausig, Liszt galops or Mendelssohn's *Spinnrocken*. I could not help dreaming of the tremendous success of his concerts. In despair I embarked on a new five-act opera, wrote the libretto and composed two acts of the music..

In the spring of 1920 I went to London to talk to Diaghilev about the ballet *Tale of the Buffoon (Who Out-Buffooned Seven Buffoons)*. Diaghilev had commissioned me to write this ballet in 1915, and I had made sketches of it in the same year, Larionov designed the sets and costumes, but for some reason the production kept being postponed. My talks with Diaghilev were successful and, after settling down near Paris, I spent the summer of 1920 finishing the *Buffoon* and its orchestration.

I returned to America that autumn to find the Chicago Opera willing to put on *Three Oranges*. However, I demanded that they reimburse me for breaking the contract according to which the opera should have been produced the year before. The new director refused, I forbade the production, and so the *Oranges* was again postponed, this time through my fault. During the winter I made a concert tour in Canada and California, not so important from the artistic point of view, as interesting from the tourist and financial angle. In addition, there were several performances of my Overture for Sextet (clarinet, two violins, viola, cello and piano) on Hebrew themes, which had been brought to me by my fellow-students at the Petrograd Conservatoire.

In the spring of 1921 I arrived in France to direct the production of the *Buffoon*. Rehearsals began in Monte Carlo, but the première took place on May 17 in Paris. Working with French orchestras is less pleasant than with American ones, because although French musicians themselves are good, they have the most anti-artistic rule that any musician may find another to take his place if it is inconvenient for him to attend a rehearsal or performance. Orchestral players abuse this right terribly, and, for example, during the rehearsals and four Paris performances of the *Buffoon* I saw three different leaders of the orchestra.

In June the Diaghilev company moved to England, and I conducted the first performance of the *Buffoon* in London. In Paris and London the public gave the ballet a very warm reception, the Paris press too, but the English press produced about 120 reviews, of which 119 were scathing. Nevertheless the *Buffoon* was performed six or seven times in London.

31

During the summer, which I again spent in France, on the shores of the Atlantic Ocean, I wrote my Third Piano Concerto which I had already sketched, partly in Russia, partly on the way to America.

In the meanwhile the Chicago director with whom I had quarrelled had been replaced by Mary Garden, the famous performer of the parts of Melisande and Salome, a most progressive and energetic woman. She gave me a new contract for the production of *Three Oranges,* invited me to conduct it, and allowed me as many rehearsals as I wanted (16 orchestral ones alone), and the opera was put on most impressively on December 30, 1921. Nina Koshitz in the part of Fata Morgana. Chicago gave *Three Oranges* a splendid reception. New York, where the Chicago company went next, an even better one. The same with the Third Concerto, which after Chicago and New York I went to play in Paris (with Koussevitzky) and London (with Coates). The Third Concerto was a particular success in London, where the critics were now apologising for the hostile reception given a year ago to the *Buffoon.*

In the summer of 1922 Diaghilev revived the *Buffoon* in Paris, and I moved to Bavaria where I continued work on the five-act opera begun in America and also read the proofs of many of my works which are being published by the Gutheil publishers in Leipzig....

(Journal K Novym Beregam, No. 2, 1923)

EGYPTIAN NIGHTS IN THE KAMERNY THEATRE

In the art of writing music for the stage the following point of view can serve as a criterion: if the presence of music in the given scene strengthens its drama or lyricism then the music is in place here, that is, it is the kind of music needed. If the given scene can be dramatically performed, without the music, with no less effect, then either the music is poor or the scene does not require any music at all, as is the case with various "naturalistic" moments from contemporary operatic literature. In an opera of one of my French colleagues, the words "give me an umbrella" are sung. In that moment it is very difficult for music to add anything to the action which would unfold even without it.

SERGEI PROKOFIEV

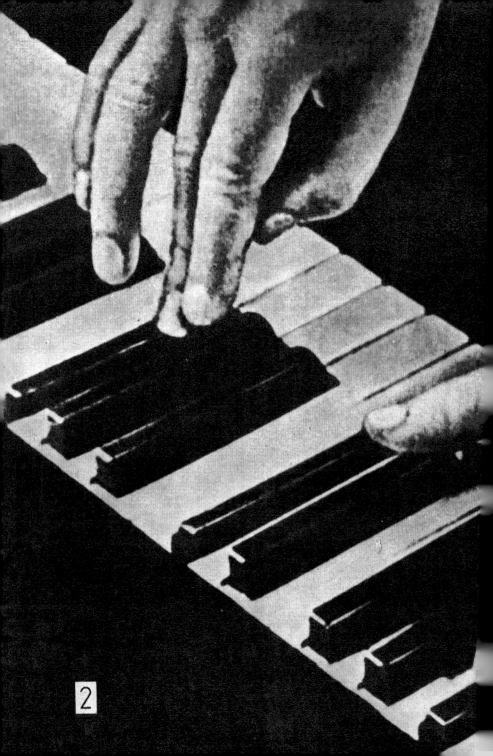

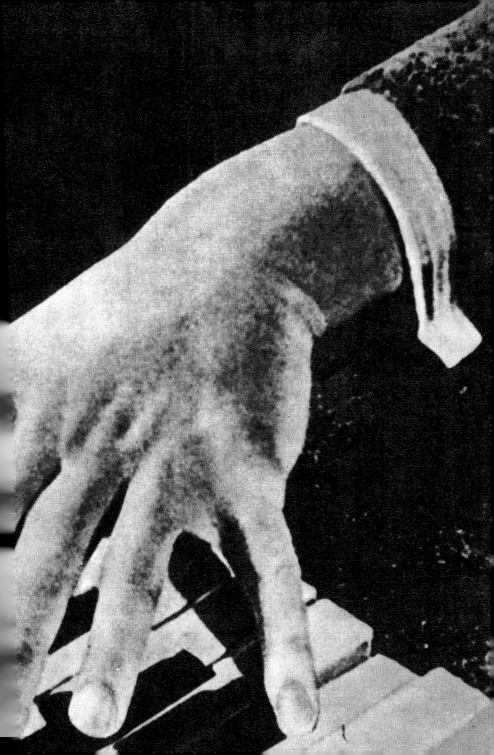

3

7

12

14

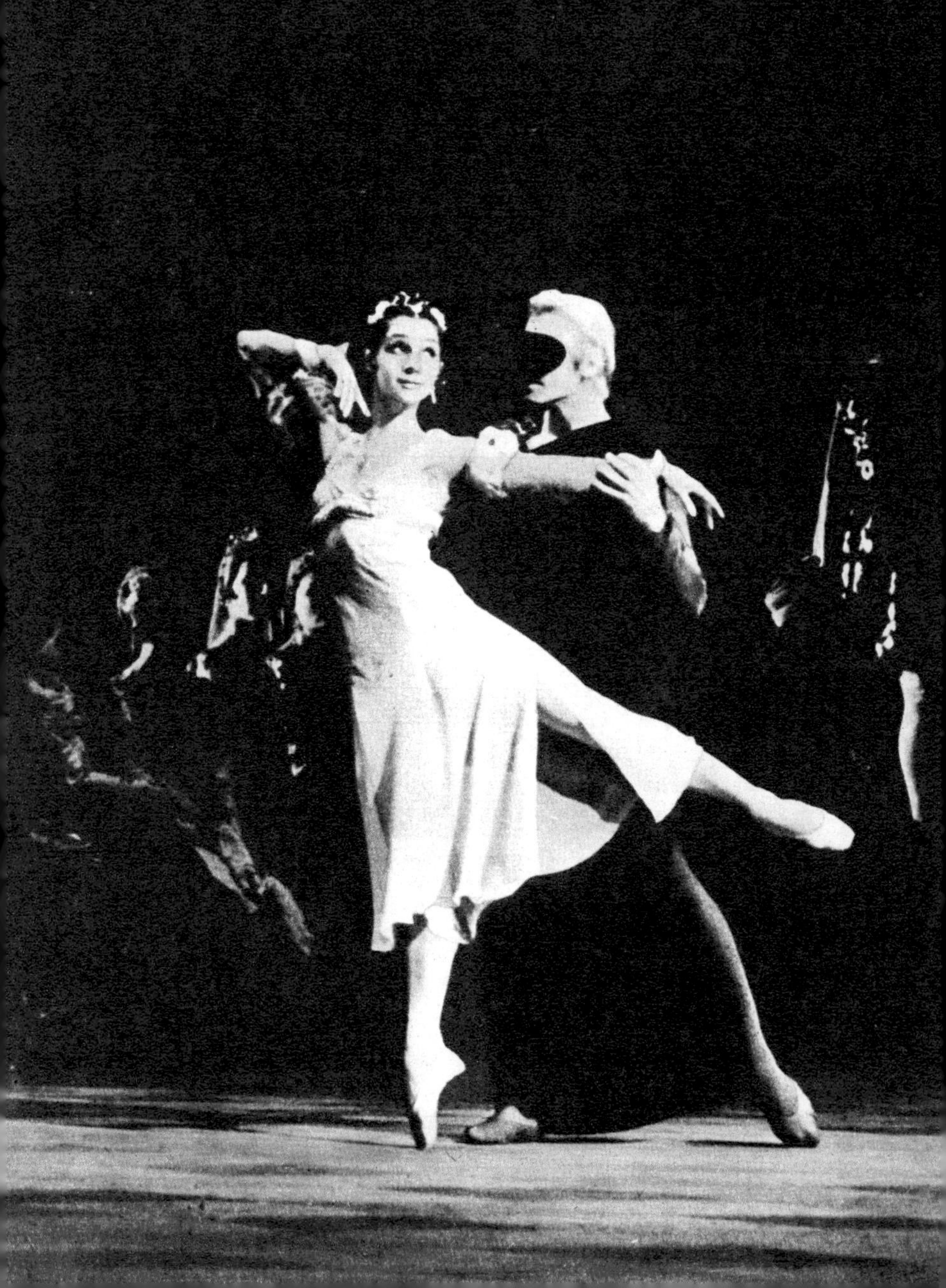

15

В дни великой отечественной войны нам стали особенно близки и дороги страницы романа Льва Толстого "Война и мир", повествующие о том, как в 1812 г. русский народ встал на защиту своей родины и изгнал неприятеля из России. Главными моими задачами, когда я писал оперу на этот сюжет, были: раскрыть внутренний мир основных персонажей романа, подчеркнуть сдвиги, что нисшедшие в их сознании в связи с опасностью, надвинувшейся на Россию, и показать народ — крестьян-ополченцев, русское войско, казаков, партизан — его страдания, гнев, мужество и победу над врагом.

С. Прокофьев

24 окт. 1944.

ГОСУДАРСТВЕННЫЙ ОРДЕНА ЛЕНИНА

АКАДЕМИЧЕСКИЙ

БОЛЬШОЙ ТЕАТР СССР

В ОЗНАМЕНОВАНИЕ 100-ЛЕТИЯ СО ДНЯ РОЖДЕНИЯ В. И. ЛЕНИНА

ПРЕМЬЕРА

ПРОКОФЬЕВ

Суббота **4**, понедельник **13** АПРЕЛЯ 1970 года

СЕМЕН КОТКО

Опера в 3 действиях

Либретто В. КАТАЕВА и С. ПРОКОФЬЕВА по повести В. КАТАЕВА „Я, СЫН ТРУДОВОГО НАРОДА"

22

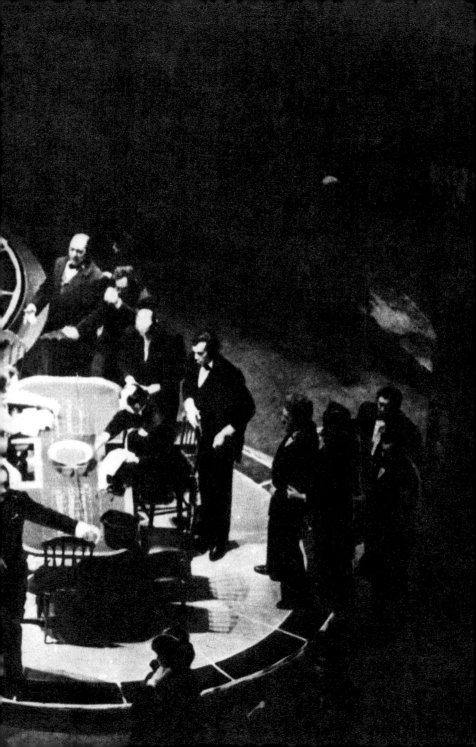

26

ЧЕТВЕРГ
19
МАЯ
1-й раз

ГОСУДАРСТВЕН. АКАДЕМИЧЕСК.

БОЛЬШОЙ ТЕАТР

СУББОТА
21
МАЯ
2-й раз

ПРЕМЬЕРА
в полной новой
постановке

ПРЕМЬЕРА
в полной новой
постановке

ЛЮБОВЬ

ОПЕРА

в 4 актах с 10 карт. с прологом.
Текст и музыка Сергея ПРОКОФЬЕВА (по Карло Гоцци).

ДЕЙСТВУЮЩИЕ ЛИЦА:

Артисты балета.

Артисты и артистки хора.

Артисты и артистки Комическ. Ансамбля.

Режиссер Комического Ансамбля ГАБТ

к ТРЕМ АПЕЛЬСИНАМ

Дирижер Н. С. ГОЛОВАНОВ

Постановка А. Д. ДИКОГО.

Хормейстер З-н др. У. О. АВРАНЕК

Художник И. М. РАБИНОВИЧ

Начало в 8 часов.

Предварительная продажа билетов производится в кассе Большого Театра ежедневно с 12 до 6 часов, суточная продажа с 12 до 4 час. вечера

Начало в 8 часов

ГОСУДАРСТВЕННЫЙ ОРДЕНА ЛЕНИНА АКАДЕМИЧЕСКИЙ
БОЛЬШОЙ ТЕАТР СОЮЗА ССР

ПАМЯТИ
С. С. ПРОКОФЬЕВА

к 10-летию со дня смерти

Март 1963 г.

**Оперы и балеты С. С. Прокофьева
НА СЦЕНЕ БОЛЬШОГО ТЕАТРА СОЮЗА ССР**

Вторник 5 марта **КАМЕННЫЙ ЦВЕТОК**	Четверг 14 марта **ВОЙНА и МИР**
Четверг 7 марта **РОМЕО и ДЖУЛЬЕТТА**	Вторник 19 марта **КАМЕННЫЙ ЦВЕТОК**
Суббота 9 марта **ПОВЕСТЬ О НАСТОЯЩЕМ ЧЕЛОВЕКЕ**	Среда 27 марта **РОМЕО и ДЖУЛЬЕТТА**
Среда 13 марта **ПОДПОРУЧИК КИЖЕ**	Суббота 30 марта **ПОДПОРУЧИК КИЖЕ**

НА СЦЕНЕ КРЕМЛЕВСКОГО ДВОРЦА СЪЕЗДОВ

Воскресенье 3 марта
ЗОЛУШКА

Среда 20 марта
КОНЦЕРТ ИЗ ПРОИЗВЕДЕНИЙ
С. С. ПРОКОФЬЕВА

Воскресенье 31 марта
ЗОЛУШКА

28

LIST OF ILLUSTRATION

Such thoughts came to my mind when I was becoming acquainted with the text of *Egyptian Nights* in the form it will take in Tairov's production at the Kamerny Theatre. This production extremely interested me from a musical standpoint, namely because in this case music can strengthen both the lyrical and dramatic impact. Above all, this music should not be intrusive and should not stand out as an independent element in the dramatic action. This kind of music can promote a more complete perception of the characters in the play, especially Cleopatra and Anthony, who are the most dramatic and fascinating personages in *Egyptian Nights*.

Izvestia, March 30, 1934

ON THE MUSIC FOR SHAKESPEARE'S *HAMLET*

My method of writing incidental music for a dramatic production is to get the producer to tell me what sort of music he wants for his production, then present my own ideas on the subject and fight it out with him until we finally come to some understanding.

In the case of *Hamlet* only the initial stage of this procedure was required because Sergei Radlov's wishes, set forth in a rather detailed letter written at my request, coincided with my own to such an extent that only a few details remained to be discussed before sitting down to write the music.

The following musical episodes were required: firstly, musical accompaniment for the shadow of Hamlet's father. There is no mysticism here, Shakespeare himself intended none; nor was there any need to convey the horror felt by the characters in the play or the spectators at the appearance of the ghost. The music here should convey the emotions of the wronged father appearing from the outer darkness to rouse his son to avenge his murder.

In contrast to this episode is the music of Claudius' entrance—a showy, "brilliant" march in keeping with the flashy pomp with which the usurper sought to surround himself. A few fanfares in the same style occur at different times in the same scenes.

With the "Mousetrap" scene, which I wrote in the style of a gavotte, the music passes from a mood of superficial gaiety to one of pent up tragedy. There are suggestions here, if semi-jocular, of the crime.

Then come the mad Ophelia's songs for which I partly used folk melodies of the Shakespearean period. In composing these songs I had to bear in mind that they were intended for a dramatic actress and not a professional singer. Although these are four separate songs they are woven by the dramatic action into a single pattern.

Passing over the somewhat ribald (as the text requires) song of the grave-digger, we come to the concluding scene of the tragedy—the death of Hamlet and the victory of Fortinbras. The heroes die, the villains too, but life triumphs, the life that Shakespeare loves and in which he believes. A triumphant march or rather an Adagio in march rhythm played softly in the beginning forms a background for the last words of the dying Hamlet and gradually rises to a triumphant C major on which the curtain falls.

Everyone knows that the orchestras of drama theatres are modest in size. Hence it took some accurate calculation of the gradual swelling of sound to achieve a natural apotheosis.

MUSIC FOR *ALEXANDER NEVSKY*

When Sergei Eisenstein approached me last May on behalf of the Mosfilm Studios with the suggestion that I write the music for the film *Alexander Nevsky* I accepted it with pleasure, for I have long been an admirer of his remarkable talent. My interest increased as the work advanced, for besides being a brilliant film director, Eisenstein proved to be a fine musician as well.

The action of the film takes place in the 13th century and is built up on two opposing elements: the Russians on the one hand, and the Teutonic knights on the other. The temptation to make use of the actual music of the period was naturally great. But a brief acquaintance with Catholic 13th-century choral singing was enough to show that this music has in the past seven centuries become far too remote and emotionally alien to us to be able to stimulate the imagination of the present-day film spectator. We therefore decided not to reproduce it as it sounded at the time of the Battle on the Ice seven centuries ago but to adapt it to the modern ear. The same applies to the Russian music of the period; that too had to be given a modern ring.

After the music had been composed the next problem was that of the recording. Notwithstanding the tremendous progress that had been made, and is still being made, in the field of sound recording, the latter was still far from perfect and even the best microphone distorted the sound. This gave us the idea of using the negative features of the microphone to produce some peculiar effects. For instance, we know that a strong wave of sound directed straight into the microphone will damage the tape and produce an unpleasant scratching noise when played back. But since the sound of the Teutonic bugles must have been unpleasant to the Russian ear I had the fanfares played directly into the microphone. The effect was extraordinarily dramatic. Microphone recordings may be used in many other ways as well. For instance, every orchestra has powerful instruments such as the trombone and weaker instruments like the bassoon. But if we place the bassoon right next to the microphone and the trombone 20 metres away from it, the result will be a barely audible trombone against the background of a mighty bassoon. This offers a wide field for a sort of "inverted" orchestration unthinkable in music for concert performance. Or take another example: we placed the brass in one studio and the choir in another and recorded them simultaneously. From each of the studios wires were run into the recording booth where by simply pressing a button the sound could be magnified or diminished as the action required. We also recorded on three microphones at once, a technique that demands much skill from the sound engineer in "mixing" the three different streams of sound. But our sound engineer, B. A. Volsky, was more than equal to the task.

The cinema is a young and very modern art that offers new and fascinating possibilities to the composer. These possibilities must be utilised. Composers ought to study and develop them, instead of merely writing the music and then leaving it to the mercy of the film people. Even the most skilled sound engineer cannot possibly handle the music as well as the composer himself. In working on *Alexander Nevsky* I was given every assistance both by the management of Mosfilm and by the sound recording staff. All of my ideas—and some of them were not at all successful—were instantly tried out. I have the most pleasant memories of our collaboration. But most remarkable of all was Eisenstein himself. We always invited him to be present during the final recording, and he never failed to contribute in some way to improving the quality of the recording by pointing out some detail that required highlighting, some dramatic effect that had to be emphasised. His respect for music was so great that at times he was prepared to cut or add to his sequences so as not to upset the balance of a musical episode.

Written on February 16, 1939, for the collection *Soviet Historical Film*, Moscow, March 1940

SEMYON KOTKO

To write an opera on a Soviet theme is by no means a simple task. One deals here with new people, new emotions, a new way of life and hence many of the forms and devices applicable to classical opera might prove unsuitable. For example, an aria sung by the chairman of a village Soviet could, with the slightest awkwardness on the part of the composer, be extremely puzzling to the listener. The recitative of a commissar making a telephone call may also seem strange.

I had long wanted to write a Soviet opera, but I hesitated to undertake the job until I had a clear idea of how to approach the task. Besides, it was not easy to find a plot. I did not want a stilted, static, or trivial plot or, on the contrary, a plot that pointed too obvious a moral. I wanted live flesh-and-blood human beings with human passions, love, hatred, joy and sorrow arising naturally from the new conditions.

This is what attracted me to Valentin Katayev's story, *I, Son of the Working People*. It combines so many contrasting elements: the love of young people, the hatred of the representatives of the old world, the heroism of struggle, mourning for the dead and the rich humour characteristic of the Ukrainian people. Katayev's people are very much alive, and that is the chief thing. They rejoice, they grieve, they laugh. This was the life I wanted to depict when I chose Katayev's story for my opera *Semyon Kotko*.

A person goes to a concert to listen to music. When he goes to an opera he wants not only to *hear* but to *see*. Hence the action must be dynamic, indeed that is why it is called action. Therefore, what must be scrupulously avoided are static moments on the stage, for however good the music might be in those scenes, the spectator will be bored because there is nothing for him to look at. In composing my opera I have tried not to let the action on the stage lapse for a single moment. But what about the arias? The aria has a legitimate place in opera; it enables the composer to develop a broad melody and gives the singer an opportunity to display his vocal talent. What can one do if for five minutes (and five minutes on the stage is an eternity) while the aria is being sung nothing happens except that the singer raises his arms now and again. From this standpoint I divide arias into two types: the Lensky type aria during which nothing happens, and that of the Tatyana's letter scene in the same opera. The latter is actually nothing more than a very long aria running for almost the entire scene. But in spite of the fact that there is very little physical movement during this scene, the drama is so tense that we cannot tear our eyes away from the stage and we do not notice the length of the aria. I want my opera to have the second type of the arias. That is, of course, far more difficult, and occasionally I have had to resort to melodious parts which, though not arias in the exact sense, offered no less opportunities for the singer.

The same applies to the choral parts. Here, too, I was afraid of breaks in the action when eighty or a hundred people sing at once and nothing happens. To avoid this, I tried adding a scene to the chorus to keep the action going.

I have avoided recitative as the least interesting element in opera. At the more emotional moments I have tried to make the recitative melodious, producing a sort of recitative melody. In the more "matter-of-fact" parts, on the other hand, I have used rhythmic speech. The tradition of speaking in opera is very old: Mozart's arias and ensembles are constantly interspersed with talking scenes. Nevertheless, I must admit that talking between singing is not always pleasant, and hence I preferred rhythmic speech, something in the nature of a chant. In each individual case I have endeavoured to make the transition from singing to speaking sound natural. And where I have succeeded the listener is not even aware of the transition, which is precisely what I set out to achieve.

I have paid special attention to melody in *Semyon Kotko*, for I believe melody to be one of the basic elements in any musical composition. Any melody is easy to memorise if its pattern is familiar. On the other hand, if the pattern is new, the melody will not impress itself on the ear of the listener until he has heard it several times. And more: an opera may have few tunes, but if each tune is repeated several times the listener will remember them. If there are too many tunes the listener will be unable to absorb them all at the first hearing and is apt to mistake abundance for poverty. For a long time it was generally believed that Wagner's *Gotterdammerung* was nothing but noise, but the trouble was that there were so many melodies that they crowded one another out. When *Eugene Onegin* was first performed the only arias the audience liked were Gremin's aria and Triquet's couplets.

Although it would obviously have been more advantageous from the standpoint of immediate success to have filled the opera with melodies of familiar pattern to be repeated on many occasions, I preferred to use a new approach and write new melodies of new pattern and as many as possible. This sort of music may be more difficult to understand at first, but after two or three hearings much will become clear. It is better for the listener to make new discoveries each time than to say, after hearing an opera for the second time, "Oh, I've heard all that before, there's no use listening to it any more."

New life, new subject matter call for new forms of expression, and the listener must not complain if he has to exert a little effort to grasp these forms.

Written for a planned collection devoted to the production of the opera at the Stanislavsky Theatre, 1940

BETROTHAL IN A NUNNERY "THE DUENNA"

In undertaking to write an opera on the subject of *The Duenna* I had first to decide which element to stress: the comic aspect of the story or the love angle. I chose the latter. I do not think I have been mistaken in emphasising the lyrical aspect of *The Duenna*: the love of two young, spirited, imaginative couples—Louisa and Antonio, and Clara and Ferdinand, the obstacles to their love, the happy betrothal, the poetic background of Seville where the action takes place, the tranquil evening landscape spreading before the eyes of the lovers, the nocturnal carnival, the old abandoned nunnery. At the same time I have been careful not to overlook any of the comic elements, for here Sheridan excels: the old Don Jerome, so blinded by rage that he drives his own daughter out of his house instead of the maid whose clothes she wears, thus unwittingly helping her to elope with her lover; the greedy Mendoza, so blinded by ducats that he allows himself to be duped and marries the old nurse-maid instead of the young enchantress Louisa; the impetuous Ferdinand who, maddened by jealousy, sees his Clara in every girl he meets in the company of a young man. These characters and the comical situations in which they are placed are offset by the lyrical scenes, especially when the comic *quid pro quo* is played with serious mien. Incidentally, the Moscow Kamerny Theatre which produced *The Duenna* after my opera had been written, laid all the emphasis on the comedy line stretching it in some places to the point of sheer buffoonery. The theatre deserves credit for having unearthed the original music of *The Duenna*, but, in my opinion, the exaggeration of the comedy angle was unjustified.

I wrote the libretto myself. Since I was adapting the story for opera I was able to take a few liberties. For example, at the end of the first scene, after a few lyrico-comical episodes I make use of the carnival to introduce a large ballet scene showing the town gradually retiring to rest. Elsewhere I make the action of one of the comic scenes unfold against the background of a trio played by Papa, Don Jerome, and his two friends; their performance is repeatedly interrupted by the action, and Don Jerome is so absorbed in playing his favourite minuet on his clarinet that he unwittingly gives his consent to his daughter's marriage to the undesirable Antonio, instead of the wealthy Mendoza.

The structure of Sheridan's play, with its abundance of couplets, enabled me to introduce many separate numbers—serenades, ariettas, duets, quartets and large ensembles—without interrupting the action. The texts of several numbers were written in the Sheridan manner by Myra Mendelson who later collaborated with me on the libretto of *War and Peace*. The opera has four acts and nine scenes. I called it *Betrothal in a Nunnery* since the word "Duenna" sounds awkward in Russian.

The opera was to have had its première in 1941, but the war intervened. Two years have passed since then, and on looking through the score recently I saw a number of places that I would like to change and found that some of the recitatives could be made more melodious. I hope to revise these sections within the next few weeks, after which the Moscow Bolshoi

Theatre will begin rehearsals with a view to completing the production by the opening of the autumn season. My opera *War and Peace* will be produced for the large stage of the Bolshoi, *The Duenna* for the smaller stage.

Written for the Sovinformbureau, March 26, 1943

ON *CINDERELLA*

What I wished to express above all in the music of *Cinderella* was the poetic love of Cinderella and the Prince, the birth and flowering of that love, the obstacles in its path and finally the dream fulfilled.

The fairy-tale offered a number of fascinating problems for me as a composer—the atmosphere of magic surrounding the Fairy Godmother, the twelve fantastic dwarfs that pop out of the clock as it strikes twelve, and dance *chechotka* (a kind of tap dance.—*Ed.*) reminding Cinderella that she must return home; the swift change of scene as the Prince journeys far and wide in search of Cinderella; the poetry of nature personified by the four fairies symbolising the four seasons—spring, summer, autumn and winter—and their companions. The producers of the ballet, however, wanted the fairy-tale to serve merely as a setting for the portrayal of flesh-and-blood human beings with human passions and failings. N. D. Volkov and I gave much thought to the dramatic aspect of the ballet. The music has three basic themes: first theme—Cinderella, the abused and ill-treated; second theme—Cinderella, chaste, pure, pensive; third, broad theme—Cinderella in love, radiant with happiness. I tried to convey the different characters through the music—the sweet, pensive Cinderella, her timid father, her ill-tempered stepmother, her selfish, capricious sisters, the passionate young Prince—in such a way that the spectators could not but share their joys and sorrows.

Apart from the dramatic structure I was anxious to make the ballet as "danceable" as possible, with a variety of dances that would flow from the pattern of the story, and give the dancers ample opportunity to display their art. I wrote *Cinderella* in the traditions of the old classical ballet, it has pas de deux, an adagious, gavotte, several waltzes, a pavane, passepied, bourree, mazurka and galop. Each character has his or her variation.

November 1945

ON THE FIFTH SYMPHONY

I wrote my Fifth Symphony in the summer of 1944 and I consider my work on this symphony very significant both because of the musical material put into it and because I returned to the symphonic form after a 16-year interval. The Fifth Symphony completes as it were a long period of my works. I conceived it as a symphony of the greatness of the human spirit.

From the introduction to the radio broadcast of a concert of Sergei Prokofiev's works, November 4, 1945

ON THE SIXTH SYMPHONY

...While working on the Sixth Symphony I strove to express in the music my admiration for the strength of the human spirit which so vividly manifests itself in our time, in our country.

Vechernyaya Moskva
October 30, 1947

BALLAD OF THE UNKNOWN BOY

While I was still in Tbilisi I read Pavel Antokolsky's poem "Ballad of the Unknown Boy" in the paper *Literatura i Iskusstvo* (Literature and the Arts). I decided to use this text for a cantata for dramatic tenor, dramatic soprano, choir, and orchestra. The cantata is based on an emotional story about the fate of a boy robbed of a happy childhood by the nazis, who killed his mother and sister. The boy's shaken soul matures and he acquires a readiness for a heroic feat. When the Germans are retreating from his native city he blows up an automobile carrying members of the nazi command with a grenade. The boy's name and fate remain unknown, but the glory of his courageous deed spreads over the battle and home fronts and serves as a call to advance. I wanted the cantata to be impetuous and dramatic, and the music to reflect the dramatic mood of the text. As I wrote it, I saw before me images of a broken childhood, of cruel enemy, inflexible bravery and an approaching bright victory.

From the article "Artist and War". Written on May 24, 1944, for Sovinformbureau

THE MASSES WANT GREAT MUSIC

The time is past when music was written for a handful of aesthetes. Today vast crowds of people have come face to face with serious music and are waiting with eager impatience. Composers: take heed of this if you repel these crowds they will turn away from you to jazz or vulgar music. But if you can hold them you will win an audience such as the world has never before seen. But this does not mean that you must pander to this audience. Pandering always has an element of insincerity about it and nothing good ever came of that. The masses want great music, great events, great love, lively dances. They understand far more than some composers think, and they want to deepen their understanding.

From a notebook. 1937

FROM REMINISCENCES OF MAXIM GORKY

I first met Gorky at the beginning of 1917 in Petrograd, just before the February revolution. This took place during a semi-private concert from the series organised by Dobychina, at which I played my *Sarcasms*. These had only just been composed and were then understood by few people.

Nevertheless, Gorky, to whom I was introduced after my performance, talked to me about these pieces very seriously and attentively, showing himself to be a person with an acute and profound feeling for music. It was quite natural that when I met him again many years later, I began to talk about music. I wanted to learn what he thought about the course it was following at the new stage of socialist construction.

He smiled and said good-naturedly:

"But after all you must know that."

I replied that in view of the vast scale of construction going on in the country, and the overall desire to build a cheerful and happy life, a cheerful and energetic music, too, was probably needed. Gorky added: "But we also need a sincere and tender music."

This remarkable humaneness of Gorky, his solicitous and humane attitude towards people never failed to surprise and touch me. In it lay his outstanding greatness as a writer.

Today I had the great honour to stand in the guard of honour by his coffin and I was struck by the calm and spiritual beauty of his face.

Text of a radio speech by Sergei Prokofiev on the day of A.M. Gorky's
funeral, June 19, 1936

MAURICE RAVEL

The telegraph has just brought the sad tidings of the death of Maurice Ravel.

The world has lost one of the greatest composers of the age. Not all musicians, I am sure, fully appreciate as yet the magnitude of his talent. While continuing to some extent the creative style of Debussy, Ravel contributed to music much that was highly individual and original.

For us Soviet musicians it is especially gratifying to know that, like Debussy, Ravel was not only keenly interested in Russian music but was influenced by it, and primarily by Moussorgsky and Rimsky-Korsakov. This influence can be traced in many of Ravel's compositions, in his *Daphnis* for example, and his superb symphonic transcription of Moussorgsky's *Pictures From an Exhibition* is striking evidence of Ravel's interest in Russian music, as is the very fact that he chose the subject of *Schéhérazade*, although he treats it in an entirely different aspect than Rimsky-Korsakov.

It is a great pity that owing to the erroneous conception of

43

his music as alien to our reality, Ravel's works have latterly been rarely performed here. I consider this attitude to Ravel to be groundless, to say the least. His *Bolero,* for instance, has the most direct effect on the listener: based on a theme in the style of folk music (as far as I know, the theme is not actually a Spanish melody but was composed in the spirit of Spanish folk music) it is a masterpiece of composition. With inimitable artistry Ravel clothes his theme in a thousand different grabs, leading it step by step to a powerful culmination. His development of folk song motifs, both French and Spanish, is of tremendous interest. His delightful string quartet might grace any chamber programme. And how beautiful is the soft lyricism of his *Pavane.*

Though some of Ravel's compositions may be marked by a certain lassitude and excessive refinement of style as compared with the lively and vigorous emotion we prefer, there is nevertheless much in these works that we might learn from, both as regards orchestration and harmony.

I first met Ravel in 1920 in Paris. It was at a musicale attended by Stravinsky, Ansermet and some other prominent musicians. A little man with sharp, distinctive features and a mane of hair beginning to turn grey entered the room. It was Ravel. Someone introduced me to him. When I expressed my pleasure at the opportunity of shaking hands with as distinguished a composer as himself and called him *maître* (a form of address commonly used in France in addressing noted artists) Ravel snatched away his hand as if I had been about to kiss it and exclaimed, "Oh, please do not call me *maître.*" He was an extremely modest person.

I do not doubt for a moment that Ravel was perfectly aware of his great talent, but he hated any sort of homage and did whatever he could to avoid all attempts to honour him.

One summer I lived in the south of France in a delightful little place called Ciboure on the shores of the Atlantic Ocean a few miles from the Spanish border town of Hendaye of which we have heard so much latterly in connection with the events in Spain. Ravel was born in these parts—Basque blood flowed in his veins, which, incidentally, explains why he was constantly returning to Spanish folk motifs. There is a street in Ciboure named after Ravel, a very narrow street running along the waterfront, lined with carts of fruit and fish pedlars and extremely inconvenient for driving, as I know from my own experience.

I remember attending one of the first performances of *Bolero* in the Paris Grand Opéra with Ravel conducting. We here know the *Bolero* as an independent symphonic work, but it was originally conceived as music for a ballet with a simple plot: a Spanish tavern, a huge round table lit up by a lamp suspended from the ceiling, and the entire action, the dancing, the scenes of love and jealousy taking place on and around the table.

Conducting was not one of Ravel's strong points, but he led the orchestra smoothly through the piece, wielding the baton with somewhat angular movements and almost surgical precision and skilfully restraining every attempt to accelerate the tempo. When the final chord crashed and the dancers on and around the table stiffened into tableau attitudes, the curtain for some reason did not drop. The dancers did not know what to do and had great difficulty in preserving their poses, but still the curtain did not go down. Suddenly Ravel stretched out his hand and pressed a button on his music stand.... The next moment the curtain descended—he had simply forgotten to press the button.

* * *

Ravel's death was not unexpected to his friends. He had long been suffering from a severe and apparently incurable brain disease. He spent the last years of his life in a state of semi-consciousness. Parisians loved him dearly, and when after a long interval they saw their favourite composer in the theatre at the performance of one of his works, the entire audience rose to their feet and accorded him a thunderous ovation. Ravel sat quite motionless in his loge until one of his companions whispered something in his ear, whereupon he rose submissively, bowed to the public, and resumed his seat in the same frozen attitude. He was hardly aware of his surroundings at this period, although sometimes there would be moments when he would be painfully conscious of his helpless condition.

There was a time shortly after the war when a group of young musicians in France—Honegger, Milhaud, Poulenc and several others—declared with fervour typical of their age that Ravel's music had outlived his time, that new composers and a

45

new musical idiom had appeared on the scene. The years passed, the new composers have taken their alloted place in French music, but Ravel still remains one of the leading French composers and one of the most outstanding musicians of our time.

Sovietskoye Iskusstvo,
January 4, 1938

CAN THERE BE AN END TO MELODY?

In a letter to the *Pioneer* magazine Senya Khaikin asks: "Will there come a time when all melodies, all harmonious combinations of sounds will come to an end? "

So much music is being composed, and has been for such a long time, that one might indeed think that it will soon be impossible to invent any new tunes and we shall have to repeat the old ones.

Now let us see whether the range of possible sound combinations is really so limited. We shall take chess by way of illustration, since, I am sure that most of the readers of the *Pioneer* are familiar with the game. I am very fond of it myself. Now, I once knew a chess player who got the idea of writing a book which would give the best answer to any chess problem. Let us see what came of it. White can open the game with any of his eight pawns, moving them up on one or two squares, or either of his two knights, each of which can make two moves. This makes a total of 20 moves to choose from. Black can reply with one of an equal number of moves. If you multiply 20 by 20 you get 400 variants by White's second move, and by Black's second move the number already amounts to 8,000. For the fourth move of the White there will be about 60 million variants, yet the game has barely started. And so the idea of writing the above book had to be given up.

In music we begin a tune with one or another note. For the second note we can choose any of those lying within the limits of the octave going up or the octave going down. Both octaves have 12 notes. If we add to this the note with which we have begun (for in a melody we can repeat one and the same note twice), we have already 25 variants for the second note of our tune, and 25 multiplied by 25 for the third, i.e., 625 variants.

Now imagine a short tune of say eight notes. How many

different variants does that offer us? I will tell you: 25 multiplied by 25 six times or 25^7. How much does that come to? Take a pencil and a slip of paper and work out the sum for yourself. The result, I believe, is something like 6,000 million possibilities. That does not mean that we have six thousand million tunes at our disposal. But there exist six thousand million combinations out of which the composer might choose those that would be melodious.

But that is not all. Notes have different lengths, and the rhythm changes the melody completely. Besides this, harmony, counterpoint, accompaniment also fundamentally change the character of the melody. Hence the six thousand million can be multiplied still more for all the possibilities to be exhausted.

The interesting thing is that the human ear is constantly changing. The music people enjoyed a few years ago does not appeal to us today; and on the contrary, melodies which were not considered melodies at all once, are now accepted, several centuries later, as beautiful and interesting.

I daresay many readers of the *Pioneer* have seen the film *Alexander Nevsky*. I wrote the music for that picture. Those who saw the film will remember that the Teutonic knights sing Catholic psalms as they launch an attack. Since the action takes place in the 13th century I wanted to know, above all, what sort of music the Catholics sang at that time. In the library of the Moscow Conservatoire I found a book in which Catholic church music of past centuries had been collected. And what did I find? The music was so completely alien to our ear that I had to give up the idea of using it in the film. No doubt the crusaders going into battle sang it with a sort of frenzy, yet to our ear it sounded cold and dull. I had to discard it and compose something better suited to our modern conception.

On the other hand, combinations of sounds once considered unmelodious turned out later to be beautiful melodies, as was the case with many great classical composers. When Beethoven composed his melodies they were so different from the music of his time that many of his contemporaries rejected them. "That deaf old man," they said, "cannot hear what he is composing." Yet Beethoven correctly divined the future, and today, a hundred years after his death, his melodies delight us. The same applies to Wagner, Liszt and many other great musicians. Consequently, combinations of notes formerly rejected as unmelodious may in future prove to be splendid music.

There is one other way of extending musical possibilities. The scale we now use did not always exist in the present form, it was Bach who introduced it some 200 years ago. Before his time the scale was somewhat different and had a narrower range of sounds.

Latterly musicians have often wondered whether it is not possible to extend the existing scale still further. In this respect the work of the Soviet scientist Ogolevets who proposes dividing the octave into 17 instead of 12 parts is of interest. He arrived at this idea after a long and careful study of our scale and some of the scales used by Oriental peoples. He was given special funds with which to construct a harmonium and later a piano with a 17-note octave. For this each black note was divided in two so that the performer could learn to play the new instrument with less difficulty.

It is still hard to say whether Ogolevets' invention will take root, but those who have played his instrument say that it gives combinations of sounds that are far more interesting than the 12-tone scale now in general use. If this instrument does come into general use it should not be thought that it will oust the existing piano, because far too much fine music has been written for the piano as we know it for anyone to wish to discard it. But both instruments can coexist, and then what a tremendous field for new melodies there would be.

So we need not be afraid that there will come a time when all melody will have been exhausted and we shall be obliged to repeat old tunes.

The future is full of such awesome possibilities. It makes one dizzy to think of them. For instance, there will come a time when the sun will cease to shine, when the earth will cool down and then, oh horrors! hosts of cold coffins that were once planets will whirl around the dark star that was once the sun....

Why should we worry about what will happen millions of years from now? Better let us learn to appreciate really good music. And what is good music? Not cheap little tunes which sound nice when you first hear them but which you soon get tired of, but melodies that have their roots in classical music and in folk songs. But why is classical and folk music considered good music? Because that music has stood the test

of time, it has lived for tens and even hundreds of years and
still gives us pleasure.

Pioneer, 1939
No. 7, pp. 80-83.

MUSICAL AMERICA

In spite of the assertions of some insufficiently informed
Europeans, Americans are very sincerely interested in music
and many of them entertain a feeling of genuine love for it.
In America, the desire to understand music and make it a part
of life is very great. The famous American motto—to have the
best of everything no matter what the cost—forces them to
spend vast sums of money to attract those who have succeeded in making a name for themselves in Europe. In this way all
the most talented performers gather in the USA. First-rate
orchestras are formed with musicians recruited from various
countries: France supplies the woodwinds, the Germans the
brass, etc. Orchestras such as the Boston Symphony Orchestra, the New York Philharmonic, or the Philadelphia Orchestra are, without doubt, the best in the world.

Concert life in the USA is a real holiday for the visiting
European, who can hear all the famous soloists and delight in
listening to outstanding ensembles.

As to the Americans themselves, they have learned to
appreciate and demand good performances, and I have noticed
that many European artists have to shape up or else they will
be immediately reproved for their shortcomings and imperfec-
tions.

As to composing music, the situation is quite different in
America. For while performers can be attracted from Europe,
you can't create a composer in this manner. And while there
are many composers among the artists who come to America,
its own, national American creativity has not yet blossomed
as could be wished.

Because of this the American music-lover has developed a
psychology which differs somewhat from ours. While we, for
the past hundred years, have had a continuous chain of great
composers who posed before the listener problems connected
with grasping their ideas, America lagged behind a little and

received only the composers already patented in Europe.

In the Soviet Union, France, and Central Europe, audiences grew to estimate properly the quality of music by new composers. I would say that the public even grew to like this occupation: people go with interest to performances of new works, debate them, praise or criticise them. True, they often criticise good works or loudly praise bad ones. However, the misunderstanding is sooner or later revealed and the "real" works triumph, though not always at once. But, after all, this is the pulse-beat of a genuine musical life.

In America, such practice hardly exists at all. Therefore it is difficult for a composer to force his way through. Music critics reason approximately like this: "It is not likely that more than one composer out of a hundred will live on for posterity. Therefore, if I don't understand innovations and write that they are bad, in 99 cases, out of 100 I will be right." The critics forget that their mission is precisely to discover and single out that "one" out of a hundred! For 20 years now I have occasionally given concerts in the USA and seen how Americans judge performers and performances more critically and accurately than they do the new idiom of a new composer. This does not mean that Americans do not have, in the long run, a love for and interest in composers. However both of these are slow in coming. Thus Brahms' music, devoid of outward effects and throbbing with rich inner life, is greatly respected there. This love for him testifies to the high level of American musical culture. But Americans came to love and understand him only many years after his death.

At the present time, in the USA there is a great striving to develop a truly American music. I would say that it is a yearning for a composer. And while this has not yet found its full realisation, a partial upsurge of American creativity can certainly be detected.

In this respect it is interesting to analyse what role jazz can play. On the one hand, jazz is a typical American product, but on the other, it seems to stand aside from truly great music.

Jazz was formed from many different elements. It has the rich syncopated rhythms of Negro origin. It has the melodic features typical of Anglo-American folk songs, i.e. part English and part English in an American interpretation. It has cabaret-dance features and sensuous howling of a lower origin, i.e. an element of cheap Gypsy-style singing.

Many serious musicians shun jazz while others evince interest in it. I think that it depends on which element you try to isolate from jazz: if it is a vulgar element, then jazz is importunate and repulsive; but if you try to choose all the best rhythmic, melodic, and instrumental sides can offer, then you can find great riches. In particular, many very interesting orchestral effects can be found in the best jazz arrangers. In addition, quite a few jazz players, for example trumpeters, trombonists, clarinettists, and drummers, have attained a technique their counterparts in the symphony orchestra couldn't dream of. It is interesting and useful not only for composers but also for performers to listen to them. Here, we often think that a jazz orchestra is necessarily something loud and bursting your ear-drums. It is exactly the opposite. The most famous American jazz ensembles are rich in nuances and show off spectacular piano effects.

It is in these best elements of jazz that contemporary American composers are trying to find the bedrock for their national music and are trying to screen out the vulgarity and preserve that which has unquestionable value.

The figure of the composer George Gershwin, who recently passed away at a relatively young age, is of interest in this respect.

Making at first a dazzling career as a composer of the light genre (jazz, songs, incidental music for films), he then tried to turn to serious music. His piano concerto and certain other works have been performed by symphony orchestras, and his opera—by major opera theatres.[1]

Gershwin possessed an undoubtedly great talent, but his past experience in light music was a rock around his neck in the sense of the development of his serious music. More precisely, he could not find the criterion for what he did in the field of symphonic music. Gershwin worked for so long on music of doubtful taste that even in his serious works, when he gave an example of talented creativity, he inadvertently slipped down to employ some little motif in bad style. Patriots of American music were ready to proclaim him their long-awaited star. Gershwin stood a good chance for this. One could have hoped that he would overcome this bad musical grounding, spread his wings, and fly high. Unfortunately, death claimed this interesting man much too soon. But his very appearance gives us grounds to assume that we can expect along this line other composers who will work out and create a new style of American music.

I would like to speak not only of Gershwin, but of a number of other American composers as well. About them, next time.

I began with Gershwin as the most typical American, at least from our European point of view.

Internatsionalnaya Literatura Nos. 7-8, 1939, pp. 289-290.

I ADHERE TO THE CONVICTION...

In America and Western Europe much is said about the mission of an artist and the freedom of his creativity. Indeed, can an artist stand aloof from life? Can he lock himself in an ephemeral "tower", circumscribe the circle of his creativity with subjective emotions, or should he be there where he is needed, where his word, his music, his chisel can help the people live a better and more interesting life?

Let us recall the creative paths of Beethoven and Shakespeare, Mozart and Tolstoy, Tchaikovsky and Dickens—those titans of the human intellect. Does not their greatness lie precisely in the fact that they, by their own will, by the call of duty and their souls, gave their mighty talents to the service of mankind? Are not their immortal works noted first and foremost for this trait?

When I was in the United States and in England I often heard people discuss the following questions: whom should music serve, what should a composer write about, and what should direct his creativity? I adhere to the conviction that a composer just as a poet, sculptor or painter is called upon to serve man and his people. He should beautify man's life and defend it. He is obligated, above all, to be a citizen in his art and to glorify man's life and lead man to a bright future. From my point of view, such is the firm code of art.

From the article "Music and Life" *Novosti*, No. 10, 1951.

FROM SERGEI PROKOFIEV'S CORRESPONDENCE
WITH NIKOLAI MYASKOVSKY

The seven letters of S. S. Prokofiev and N. Y. Myaskovsky published below are only a small part of their extensive correspondence lasting over 40 years. The letters of Prokofiev alone from 1907-1918, 1923-1930, and 1934-1950 number 312 (172 letters, 118 postcards, 5 telegrams, and 17 notes).

The exact period of the correspondence can be determined by the first two and the last two letters, which are included in this collection. The beginning (June 26-July 12, 1907) dates back to the time when both correspondents—students of A. K. Lyadov and N. A. Rimsky-Korsakov in the St. Petersburg Conservatoire—had just embarked on the path of independent composing. The elder, Myaskovsky, was 26, Prokofiev—16.

As Prokofiev relates in his autobiography *Early Years*, the grounds for their becoming close were their lively interest in new music and, in particular, Reger's visit (in December of 1906) when he conducted his Serenade in G major. Their acquaintance soon developed into friendship. "In summer Myaskovsky and I exchanged compositions and wrote letters to each other in which we discussed music at length. This correspondence gave me much more than Lyadov's dull lessons."

Already that one observation of Prokofiev reveals the importance that a correspondence could have for his scholastic biography and also shows the part his friendship with Myaskovsky played in it. Myaskovsky was the first who, still in the student years, encouraged Prokofiev in his creative darings, promoted his works on the major concert stage and with his penetrating, critical mind helped Prokofiev himself and many of the first listeners of his music to understand the true character of Prokofiev's creativity.

"My highly esteemed Nikolai Yakovlevich" (Dearest Kolyechka!) and "My well beloved Sergei Sergeyevich", "Seryozhenka"—such relationships, between these two great Soviet artists, permeated with mutual affection and respect, lasted to the ends of their lives.

The last letters (April 23-May 16, 1950) were written less than three months before the death of N. Y. Myaskovsky (August 8, 1950).

All the letters are published from the originals which are in the archives of S. S. Prokofiev and N. Y. Myaskovsky in the Central State Archives of Literature and Art in Moscow. They were first published by the compiler of this collection in the editions *S. S. Prokofiev. Materials. Documents. Reminiscences*, Moscow, 1956 and *N. Y. Myaskovsky. Articles. Letters. Reminiscences*, Moscow, 1960 (in Russian).

Sontsovka, June 26, 1907

My highly esteemed Nikolai Yakovlevich!
(Dearest Kolyechka! ....)

Together with this letter I am sending you two little dogs (small piano pieces.—*Ed.*) written for you. When you look them over, please pay serious attention to the tempi, for they play an important part. Then think of what to call them. Especially the second. It seems that the idea is clearly expressed in it, but I can't think up a name for it at all. Of course you will give me your most precise indications regarding various subtleties, in which you love to delve.

Well, how is your orchestral poem on a "very good" theme coming along? I have finished the first movement of the sonata I showed to you at the examination. It seems that I won't write the 2nd, 3rd, and 4th movements. Thus it will remain, à la Myaskovsky, in one movement—to good advantage, not dull, and beautiful. Recently, by chance, I wrote a sonatina in two movements. It was very interesting to write; I wrote it as simply as possible, and it came out merrily. Meanwhile, I am completing that Act IV of *Undine* which I gave you in May.

You shouldn't have left the examination so soon then. Kankarovich and I waited 5-10 minutes more and we were rewarded: we got into the director's office where Lyadov showed us the problems and corrections. Your fifths do stick out, but there were no other serious mistakes, just a little rough in places. Zakharov's had octaves; the others who went on to the fugue wrote the 5-voice one fluently. My 3-voice fugue turned out worse, though there weren't any glaring errors, and the stretto was even good. But, in general, only Asafyev passed according to all the rules, as in order to pass you had to get all 4's and no one else received them:

Asafyev	4	4
Myaskovsky	3	4
Zakharov	3	4
Prokofiev	4	3
Kankarovich	3	3
Saminsky		
Elkan	3	3
Chefranov		

They subsequently pulled five of us up to all 4's (even Kankarovich!....), but the other three apparently will have to be content with counterpoint. Well, so long—all the best. I expect dogs in reply.

You have, of course, forgotten my address: Yekaterinoslav Province, Bakhmutsky District, Postal Branch Andreyevka.

Respectfully yours,

S. Prokofiev

2

Oranienbaum, July 12, 1907.

Friend of my heart, Sergei Sergeyevich. I waited, but the right moment to reply properly to both your letter and especially, of course, the dogs that you sent didn't come. During all this time I haven't "created" anything that would have even the slightest chance of satisfying you, and have therefore decided to send you only this empty letter without anything to accompany it, thereby repaying you, of course, with the blackest ingratitude, but what can I do.... I was extremely pleased to receive your music; it has, along with your abominable scribblings (not for me, of course) in all sorts of horrible combinations (primarily in the 2nd), convincing enough moments, and the general structure, conquering passion, and what I particularly like in you, spikiness, if I may call it that, are so vivid in them that they undoubtedly make up for the deficiencies. I, of course, was at first angry that I only had to play a single note with each hand, and almost at opposite ends of the keyboard at that, but when I played them through in a tempo (of course, equal to half yours) sufficient enough to comprehend the general character, I was thoroughly pleased, especially with the first piece; the second has more inaccuracies, and they are somehow less concealed. As regards naming the second, I can't say anything. In general, I am not fond of all kinds of names and therefore was immediately satisfied with the piece as it was, without any name. *Carnival* suits the first; there is a lot of recklessness in it. Perhaps the 2nd is also from some kind of carnival figures—the beginning reminds me of Mimme with his sobbing. By the way, I think that it would be better to write the last *piu mosso* in the first piece with the left-hand octaves as eighths instead of quarters and the right hand should, accordingly, play broken chords in sixteenths, and leave it in the same tempo. The way you have it, one doesn't immediately grasp the tempo, whereas the real tempo is simply twice as fast, and your indication doesn't explain this. By your notes on these "little things" I concluded that they are mine, and therefore do not intend to return them. If you do not agree with my conclusion, then I will do as you say in your next letter. All my plans concerning an orchestral diversion were smashed by a long fit of laziness and inertness. I can't get further than the piano, or, occasionally, voice and piano. I occupy myself entirely with trifling things such as my 3rd piano sonata (in two movements), the first movement being a small 3-voice fugue (Lento). Besides this, from nothing better to do, I penned some 12 pianoforte snatches, some being indecently short (8 bars) and risky. I really cannot bring myself to send them. This week I wrote seven romances to words by Baratynsky but of a very ordinary character. For you they are not at all interesting. One of my most savoury distractions this summer are my harmony lessons with Mr. Kobylyansky, who was sent to me by Lyadov, probably to drive me to distraction In a few days I am going to Asafyev for consolation, and I expect from you a sonatina and a sonata (that which...).

Good-bye

Your N. Myaskovsky.

3

[Sontsovka],   August 4, 19[07].
   My joy, Nikolai Yakovlevich!
   I was terribly happy to receive your extremely interesting little dogs. I did not expect so many and so soon, and therefore am asking for more. As to these, well, I played them over, and here is my opinion on each of them (please, sit down and don't swear!). The first is attractive but nothing more. The ending is not good. At any rate you can write much better. I don't like the second one. I just don't like it and that's all. Besides, there is a lot of imitation of different composers, especially Rimsky-Korsakov, and this is just not like you. The third is a very nice waltz à la Chopin-Scriabin; it is the most innocent of all the little dogs, but, I repeat, very nice. I would recommend that in bar 5, in the bass, you use the fifth F sharp-C sharp so that the bass in the 4th bar fits in, since the C sharp of the melody in the 4th bar is very harsh and doesn't correspond with the rest. The

fourth (lullaby) is very good and I liked it from the very beginning; its forced ending spoils the impression; though it is in E minor there is so little of it in it that you did not even put the F sharp in the key signature. I don't like the fifth, though the theme itself (the first 4 bars) is good, but what makes you choose such inferior subjects for music! I could understand "He frets and fumes" and not "He sits on a chair and grumbles", I am surprised. Maybe from the point of view of *Il est mécontant* it is expressed picturesquely. The sixth, *Aux cnamps*, though simple, is very beautiful. Only it requires *allegretto*, not *molto lento*, for it is very drawn out. I don't like the seventh; I don't like that kind of harmonising; only the last 4 bars are good. The eighth is good at the beginning, the second half is a little strange and only the end of it is not bad. The march in Russian style is very good; when I play it I involuntarily think of the collateral theme of your C minor sonata. I especially like it after the repeat. The counterpoint in the march is à la Rimsky-Korsakov.... The 10th is very sweet up to the repeat. Further on you imitate the cries of birds and sparrows very successfully; but can there be anything musical in these cries? Agree with this. The 11th, the barcarolle, is very, very good. The alternating of the counterpoint with the melody, sometimes at the top, sometimes at the bottom, is beautiful and very unexpected. Bars 5, 6, and 7 are somewhat watery. I liked the 12th, the scherzo, even when I only looked at it and didn't play it yet. It is a very bright and original piece. I don't like the ending (or else I can't play it) and I would recommend you to add *senza replica* to the long epistle at the end for there is too much repetition. But my general impression of the lot is that there are many good things, though some were written too quickly and rashly. I consider the waltz, lullaby, *aux champs,* march, barcarolle, and scherzo the best, as good as your sonatas. Forgive me for such a frank and impudent judgement, and if you don't like it, burn it and forget about it. But for heaven's sake, I implore you to send me one of your new sonatas (better the one in four movements). I keep your Flofion (what does it mean?) under seven locks, and in the autumn will return it with gratitude along with the sonata which I hope you will send for me to look over. With this letter I am sending you my sonata and little dog until the autumn. In the sonata please pay attention to the constant alternation of two tempi. By the way, the tempi are very fast (consult your metronome); any slower and many pages will seem dull. I am not sending the sonatina as it is better suited for Asafyev. As regards the B minor little dog, I do not agree with naming it *Sorrow*. Have in mind that the tempo is indicated as *Furioso ma lento*, which means that the slower tempo subdues the impatient attacks of "Mimme's" theme. It is true that it resembles Mimme. I knew this, but I allowed it because of the great difference in purpose and character.

I also thought of making the *molto piu mosso* in *Carnival* twice as fast, as you suggested, but at the tempo in which I play what precedes it this is impossible. I have begun to correspond with Zakharov; now it is his turn, and he, lazy-bones, hasn't written for the whole last month.

So I am waiting for a sonata! Please think of a title for the E-flat minor little dog which I am sending with my sonata....

Yours S. Prokofiev

4

August 1909

Lieber Kolya,

I was extremely touched by your praise of my little sinfonietta. When you tactlessly but sincerely scolded my poor intermezzo, I became completely disillusioned with myself and, following your precept, wanted to quit writing any kind of "jolly" music and keep to only cumbersome music, of which you deemed it necessary to find me capable. And only because I know that your first opinion is always unfounded, I limited myself to only a few despairing days and then began to do things my own way again.

You are unfair as regards Tsatsa. And where did you find so much spite to even stop being your own self and turn to indecent wise-cracks!

You correctly noticed that there is no climax in the first movement. But does it lose anything because of this? It seems to me that thanks to its character and size it is possibly like a strip of lace—smooth, without bumps or peaks.

The descending fifths should flow very nicely *in the orchestra*. I don't think that this section is empty. The beginning of the secondary subject is a little dry, but by no means colourless. You will become accustomed to it yet.

Thank you for the Brahms. You shouldn't have sent it. Oh yes, why did you send five rubles when it only cost four? Won't you be so kind as to tell me what rate of interest you used!

Recently I dug out my second sonata (F minor). The sonata is very sweet. I will rework it and show it to Lyada in the fall.

Your themes continue to please me. When I come to St. Petersburg I will be sure to transcribe the first movement for four hands. I want to give you something in thanks for so obligingly and, mainly, so willingly transcribing my poor *yemolka*. [E-moll piece.—*Ed.*]

And what about your *Silence*? Are you really going to ... keep silent?

Good-bye. I am leaving tomorrow for Yessentuki for about ten days. My dear mother is having her rheumatism treated there.

Your

Prokofiev

Has Zakharia written you anything?

5

To Sergei Sergeyevich Prokofiev

Petrograd
Izmailovsky Regiment, First Company, Bldg. 4, Apt. 4
Jan. 31, 1916

Well, dearest Seryozha, it seems that the passions raging thanks to your beautiful Ala have not yet calmed? Drop me a line and tell me how everything is. As far as I was able to find out at the concert, the more unprejudiced people were very satisfied. As for me, I am only sorry that I couldn't be at the rehearsals, where maybe all your captivatingly stunning images would have impressed themselves upon my brain all the more vividly. Now when I recall certain striking moments I often can't remember in which piece they figured. However the general impression I got was tremendous: vivid and striking in thought, strong and distinct in expression, now and then extremely refined, harmonically murky yet tangible, and very fresh, captivatingly laconic, poetic, full of imagery, and finally, in my view, simply, beautifully, and originally orchestrated. In one word—it is splendid, significant, and *self-sufficingly valuable*. I don't know for sure, but it seems to me that it is one of your best compositions. Well, all the best. My hearty regards.

Your

Drop me a line.   N. Myaskovsky

6

(Moscow, Nikolina Gora),
April 23, 1950.

Dear Seryozhechka, congratulations on your 59th birthday! I embrace you heartily and hope to see you soon at Nikolina Gora in the best of health.

Forgive me for the parcel, it might not suit your taste; but for some reason I took a fancy to it at once. We were all delighted with your *Bonfire*.

Warm regards to Myra Alexandrovna.

With all my heart

N. Myaskovsky

Enraptured with Cinderella!

7

(Moscow, Nikolina Gora),
May 16, 1950

Dear Nikolai Yakovlevich,

I embrace you with all my heart. I think of you all the time. Come to Nikolina Gora as soon as possible.

Your
S.P.

3

NEW PUBLICATIONS

Vladimir Blok

PROKOFIEV IS JUST BEGINNING

A book long-awaited by many, S. Prokofiev's *Autobiography*, has come off the press.

It has already appeared twice in an abridged form specially prepared by the composer for the magazine *Sovietskaya Muzyka*. But of the full version only part I—"Childhood"— has been published twice (also in somewhat abbreviated form). Part II of the full version—"The Conservatoire"—is now presented to the reader for the first time.

How did Prokofiev's *Autobiography* come to be written? In a short preface, which the composer has entitled "A Preface of Apology," he writes:

"At the age of twenty-one, after reading Rimsky-Korsakov's *Chronicle* and a large biography of Tchaikovsky and feeling myself to be a composer in whom people were beginning to take an interest, I decided that one day I would write my autobiography. I had once heard someone say:

"'It should be compulsory for all famous people to write their autobiography.

"'Well, I already have some material,' I thought, 'all I need to do now is become famous.'

"...But by the age of forty the bragging of youth had gone, my views on life had become wiser, and I asked myself: is it really worth writing so much and so lengthily about myself?

"...Two arguments won the day: I had certain achievements to my credit, and therefore my autobiography might be of use to someone. Secondly: I had met many famous people, and my accounts of them might be interesting."

Alongside these aspects which determine for us the importance of Prokofiev's *Autobiography*, it contains a full and vivid picture of the breadth of the artist's impressions as a child and young man, his precise character studies, his inscrutable humour (which reminds one of Glinka's autobiographical *Notes*), and a lively, original literary style.

The autobiographies of famous composers usually throw little light on their childhood. Prokofiev's *Autobiography* does exactly the opposite. The description of his childhood is not only fascinating, but most detailed: the hundred and eighty pages of Part I grip one's attention throughout.

Ilya Ehrenburg once said very aptly of Prokofiev: "He felt the heartbeat of time." This lively sense of and ability to record the times first manifested themselves not only in the early compositions of the very young Seryozha Prokofiev, but also in the keen, enquiring attitude to the world around him which he showed from childhood. The extracts from the diaries of the young Prokofiev, his letters, and the correspondence, diaries and reminiscences of relatives and friends which the author frequently inserts into his narrative, are interesting "records of the times".

The natural "watershed" between the two parts is the move to St. Petersburg and entrance to the Conservatoire. Part II of the *Autobiography* is considerably longer than Part I, although it remained unfinished. New impressions and meetings, new names and acquaintances.... A man and artist, who combined both past and present in his life and work, Prokofiev knew many people. After Glière, who gave the boy his first lessons in composition in the Ukrainian village of Sontsovka, and Taneyev, who got to know his works first in Moscow, then, in St. Petersburg, come Rimsky-Korsakov, Glazunov, and Lyadov. They appear on the pages of the *Autobiography* in an unexpected light, without the conventional gloss. Beside these celebrated names we find other musicians who have left their mark on the history of Russian art. Composers such as the erudite and charming Cherepnin and the reserved, kind-hearted Witol, and such pianists as the modest Vinkler and the famous Yesipova.

Almost all the above-mentioned personalities were Prokofiev's teachers (at that time Glazunov was director of the St. Petersburg Conservatoire). Striving to find himself in music, the young composer even in his student years was not an obedient little "goody-goody" and took nothing for granted: and a small piece of music would often give rise to a great dispute in class.

The maturing talent of young Prokofiev was already recognised by his strict teachers at the St. Petersburg Conservatoire. "Capable, diligent"—was the laconic comment by Rimsky-Korsakov at the end of the instrumentation course. And Glazunov wrote as follows about Prokofiev the pianist: "Brilliant technique, splendid tone, marks for technical examination—5/5, public performance—5/5."

New truths in art were being discovered not only in the strict atmosphere of the Conservatoire classes, however. The musical life of St. Petersburg was rich and varied. On the pages of the *Autobiography* we find the memorable figures of Karatygin, Nuvel and Nurok—the founders of the Modern Music Evenings, fellow-students Zakharov and Schmidthof and, finally, the young Myaskovsky with whom Prokofiev struck up a long-lasting friendship.

* * *

According to official statistics, Prokofiev is the most frequently performed composer of the twentieth century. Yet nevertheless his archive (unfortunately split up in a number of music depositories) still contains much music which has never been presented to the public. The same applies to an even greater extent to literary and epistolary "Prokofieviana": for example, only a fraction of Prokofiev's correspondence with Myaskovsky has been published. Access to other writings by Prokofiev would also bring much of interest to professionals and music lovers alike.... So, the literary Prokofiev is, indeed, just beginning!

Muzykalnaya Zhizn,
No. 4, 1974

Sergei Prokofiev

EXTRACTS FROM *AUTOBIOGRAPHY*

From Chapter 9 (1904)

...Permission to attend rehearsals of symphony concerts by the Russian Musical Society added a touch of liveliness to musical life. The concerts were held on Saturdays, and the final rehearsals on Friday mornings. All Conservatoire students who paid for their tuition, that is, who possessed a student book, were admitted to •final rehearsals on presentation of this book. The theory students, myself included, also had the right to attend Thursday rehearsals. Parallel to the concerts of the Russian Musical Society, which kept to a conservative programme, there were the Siloti concerts. Siloti, a pupil of Liszt, a good pianist, but a poor conductor, and a rich man who spent much time abroad, arranged excellently organised symphony concerts often with new foreign pieces and artists little known in Russia. His concerts were more popular with the public than those of the Russian Musical Society.

...Rehearsals began at nine o'clock, so one had to get up early, at half past seven, when it was still dark. One dry autumn morning I was walking to a rehearsal, my heels clattering loudly, on the pavement. A colonel came out of a side street, jingling his spurs, and walked behind me. Being a military man and hearing my measured tread, he began to walk in step with me and for a while the tap-tap of my heels merged with the jungle-fingle of his spurs. I noticed this and liked it at first, but then I wanted to walk in syncopation. I paused for half a pace, then began walking normally, my foot touching the ground in between the jingling of his spurs. Tap-jingle-tap-jingle-tap-jingle. The colonel, who was probably immersed in his own thoughts, suddenly noticed that he was out of step and corrected himself.

The tapping again coincided with the jingle. Two steps later I changed to syncopation again. The colonel again corrected himself, but I was already wise to his game and started a new syncopation just as he was correcting his pace. The fact that he could not get in step was obviously irritating him: his spurs jingled more agitatedly, I heard several corrections with some stamping of the foot, then the spurs sounded more faintly, somewhere at the side. I squinted in that direction and saw the colonel cross the street diagonally and walk away on the other side.

Apart from symphonic rehearsals, I went to the opera several times and heard *Carmen, The Queen of Spades, Pan Voevoda* and *Boris Godunov.* I wrote in a rather independent tone to my father about *The Queen of Spades* that "The opera is a good one, but the singing, acting and sets are disgusting". *Pan Voevoda* was Rimsky-Korsakov's latest opera, which had just been put on by a private opera company. It did not make any special impression, but the symphonic nocturne played with an empty stage showing a night landscape is memorable....

From Chapter 37 (1905)

This autumn I began writing down the names of works which I had heard played by an orchestra and giving them marks, like books one has read. The list begins with the overture to Borodin's *Prince Igor,* which I awarded a bad mark. This is surprising, but I can still remember how much I disliked the overture. Beethoven's *Egmont* overture, which I also disliked, got a satisfactory mark, in spite of a second hearing. What I did like was: the suite from Rimsky-Korsakov's *Mlada,* Glazunov's *Lyrical Poem,* Tchaikovsky's *Variations on a Rococo Theme,* Lyadov's *Russian Songs for Orchestra,* and Taneyev's symphony, the latter possibly out of respect for the author.

Prokofiev's mother to his father in Sontsovka. St. Petersburg, October 23, [November 5,] 1905.

"Yesterday the three of us went to a Siloti concert. We saw all the celebrities: Rimsky-Korsakov, Glazunov, Lyadov, Vinkler[2], only at a distance, of course, or on the stage. Rimsky-Korsakov received a great ovation, the whole hall thundered and he was called out three times; he was very moved and even reeled slightly (after the performance of the suite from *Mlada*)."

At the next Siloti concert they played Taneyev's Symphony which I listened to most attentively. This explains the good marks which it received, for such a complex work might easily have evoked an unfavourable reaction. At the same concert I was most impressed by Borodin's romance "For the shores of my far-off homeland", orchestrated by Glazunov; it has been one of my favourite romances ever since....

From Chapter 39 (1905–1906)

During December 1905 and January 1906 I heard and approved Beethoven's Third and Eighth Symphonies, Schumann's Second, Glazunov's Sixth, Rachmaninov's Second Concerto, Tchaikovsky's *Romeo and Juliet*, Dukas' *The Sorcerer's Apprentice*, and a Bach's suite. My attitude towards Mozart remained cool as before, but I listened with interest, following the score, to his Symphony in G minor, which Glière had gone through with me once.

One of the most interesting concerts was on January 14 (27), by Siloti, when some rather large extracts from Wagner's *Die Meistersinger von Nürnberg* were played. At that time *Die Meistersinger von Nürnberg* was not put on by the St. Petersburg Opera, so a good concert performance with singers and orchestra was of considerable interest. I met Grosman, my last year's harmony class mate, at the concert. Neat and well-groomed as ever, in a good-fitting student uniform, he was holding the score of *Die Meistersinger von Nürnberg,* so I joined him to follow it during the performance. I found *Die Meistersinger* interesting, although I cannot say that I immediately perceived all the entrancing beauty of this opera which I came to love so dearly later.

From Chapter 81 (1907)

...I heard Wagner's *Siegfried Idyll* and was enraptured by this entrancing music. I was equally delighted by Rimsky-Korsakov's piano concerto, which was being rehearsed in the Conservatoire by the students: Lemba[3] played and Malko[4] conducted. I have worshipped both works ever since. But the quality of the concerto's performance gave rise to several criticisms from me, which were ignored because Lemba and Malko were final-year students, that is to say, somehow superior from the point of view of Conservatoire achievements, while I was still somewhere around the middle of the Conservatoire scale, and it was not for me to judge whether they had performed well or badly. I wrote in my diary: "I would probably make a good music critic and a dirty dog, to boot!"

There was also a concert of Glazunov's works to raise funds for the student canteen at the Conservatoire. I found the Seventh Symphony somewhat flat: written, but not composed. Yet Rimsky-Korsakov was extremely appreciative, he sat in the front row with the score at rehearsals, uttering laudatory remarks. I must say that after playing it together with Mvaskovsky I liked it better, particularly the first movement. Glazunov was conducting. In spite of his tremendous size and bulky figure, he adores conducting, although he is not exactly brilliant at it. He looks particularly amusing when he conducts at quick fourths, making little signs of the cross under his nose at the orchestra. But Glazunov enjoys great prestige with the orchestra, so the musicians are very attentive and try to play well

Taneyev gave a chamber concert in the Smaller Hall. The programme included string ensembles with piano, the part of which he played himself. He asked me to turn over the pages for him, to which I proudly consented. Before the concert Taneyev gave me a long, careful explanation of how to turn pages.

"When there are about two bars to go, stand up and take hold of the upper corner of the page. At the end of the last bar turn it over quickly and straighten the page immediately, but in such a way that your hand does not obscure the upper bars from the player."

Another piece of music which I got to know but completely underrated was Richard Strauss' opera *Salome*. Myaskovsky handed it to me with a smile, saying that it was the most modern of contemporary works. But I could not understand its meaning and found no pleasure in its tricks. So I returned it back to Myaskovsky. The encounter was not a fruitful one.

We are now approaching an event, albeit a minor one, which represents a small step forward in my musical life. A poster appeared on the wall of the Conservatoire announcing that on

71

December 17 (30), 1907, there would be a meeting of budding composers to take a look at their works and that those which were deemed worthy would subsequently be performed in public. Conservatoire students of composition were invited. The organiser was Ranushevich, who had graduated from the theory of composition class the year before. I had heard little about Ranushevich, apart from the fact that she was a lady getting on in years; but the promise to perform "worthy works" was tempting, and so I went. There were about fifteen people present. I played *The Reproach, The Fairy-Tale* and *The Phantom*. I believe that *Badinage* also belonged to this group of pieces and was later published as Op. No. 3[5], but I did not risk playing it: too daring, not respectable enough. My pieces, as I recorded at the time, produced some "lively discussion". Other composers also played, but their works were bad. A week later another meeting was held. Instead of increasing, the number of participants dropped. I was asked to repeat the pieces I had played before. This time they were praised without any particular reservations. But by now I was disappointed with these "budding composers": they could not do anything themselves and no one came to their meetings. What sort of circle was this! Ranushevich said to me:

"You know, people are saying that Prokofiev can't stand two right notes in succession. Because his piano at home is out of tune, and he's got used to it."

With this the venture lapsed. But it did have some consequences for me, although of a different nature. More of that below.

Now something from the "post box" to round off 1907. My most regular exchange of letters in the second half of 1907 was with Morolev[6] because he and I carried on four games of chess by post and exchanged at least four letters a month. The real business, so to say, was chess, and the chess moves were accompanied by discussions of music and the chatter of sixteen-year-old boys.

It is interesting that I was very keen on popularising Beethoven and Wagner.

"You must buy the second volume of Beethoven symphonies for two hands," I wrote to Morolev. "Even a beginner must know them. Start with the Seventh (here I made several notes). The first two movements are marvellous and sound splendid on the piano. The third is good as well, but difficult to play on the piano, because you cannot get the purely orchestral effects. Incidentally, pay attention to the trio in the third movement: almost all the way through it you have the note A which is given to the trumpets in the orchestra and occasionally produces a most original effect. The finale is weaker... After the Seventh, take the Sixth. The Ninth is the most famous, but it is very difficult if you have not heard it played by an orchestra."

This passion for Beethoven symphonies is somewhat unexpected, but it does show that I have always been fond of classical music.

"I should really like you to know more about Wagner: you would take a completely different view of things," I wrote in another letter.

I was particularly insistent about *The Ring of the Nibelungs*[7] which was my great passion at the time.

"*The Rhinegold* costs only two rubles, and the other—two rubles seventy kopecks each, and the amount of music they contain! " I wrote. "If you are still interested in piano concertos, buy Rachmaninov's Second: it's very beautiful."

In fact, this was the period when I discovered a new type of music: piano concertos. In the Smaller Hall at the Conservatoire there were constant performances by students: if any of the students had learnt a piece and played it well, he would be asked to perform it at a student evening, which was attended by the whole Conservatoire. At the same time, by attending these concerts, students familiarised themselves with the classical repertoire. I turned my attention to a form of composition of which I knew rather little before, namely, piano concertos. Suddenly I discovered that they contained a wealth of the most beautiful music and were technically most interesting. I listened and commented constantly on their merits. Zakharov[8] even said on one occasion:

"It's remarkable. Seryozha is always talking about the quality of the music and forgetting to mention the performance."

I was particularly fond of the concertos by Beethoven, Liszt, and Rimsky-Korsakov, Tchaikovsky's First, Saint-Saëns' Second and Fourth (Cherepnin[9] pointed out to me that Saint-Saëns was particularly good at combining piano and orchestra), Rachmaninov and others. I was less enthusiastic about those of Chopin, Schumann, Brahms and Scriabin: Chopin's concertos did not seem to me to be concertos at all, but pieces for the piano alone, to which an orchestra had been attached. I adored the theme in E minor, but here one could do very well without the orchestral accompaniment: Schumann's concerto was nice musically, but of little interest technically; Brahms drifted past my ears, etc. I described my liking for Rachmaninov and Beethoven in my letters to Morolev, whom I advised to buy the concertos and study them.

Serious discussion of music in these letters was often accompanied by childish jokes: one of the letters is written on a circular sheet with the lines running a spiral, like grooves on a gramophone record, up to the centre where the reader is invited to "crawl into the hole" (which was actually there in the middle of the sheet), and on the other side you have to read backwards along the spiral from the centre to the edge. This joke produced a number of indignant comments from Morolev in his reply.

One of the more serious things I told Morolev was that at the Conservatoire I was engaged in studying scales of double thirds (learning all their applications was like mathematics). Actually this is very important: it means that I am preparing to transfer to the senior course, the only really serious part of studying the piano at the St. Petersburg Conservatoire. When you have passed technique and have then been transferred from the junior to the senior course, you spend the rest of the time concentrating mainly on the artistic aspect.

From my correspondence with Myaskovsky, which was far less profuse than with Morolev (since we lived in the same town), I still have some postcards. On one I wrote: "My dear friend, I knew that beforehand and thoroughly dislike you." Then there is a pencilled note in Myaskovsky's handwriting: "Perhaps I should have come and did not." On another I inform him in a postscript (dated December 28-January 10): "Have written *Snow* and *Autumnal Sketch*." Myaskovsky and I had agreed that we would both write a piano piece depicting falling snow. Myaskovsky depicted "horrid snow, stinging and with a blizzard", as he put it. I, however, portrayed a gentle snow falling in large flakes.

The piece was pleasant and gentle, in spite of the parallel seconds and parallel chords. However, I did not include it later in Opus 3, which contains the pieces of that period, for it seemed to me that my *Snow* lacked thematic material and was more of an "experiment" than a piece. The manuscript got lost and part of the music was reconstructed from memory. Memory is a peculiar thing: pieces composed forty years ago can be reconstructed with comparative ease, but the ones written five or ten years ago are just as easily forgotten. Myaskovsky kept his piece and after being slightly revised it was published by him much later in the collection *Reminiscences*, Opus 29, as No. 6[10].

Snow aroused the interest of others as well as Myaskovsky, mainly because it was curious: parallel seconds yet it sounded gentle. Lyadov soon got to hear about it.

"What do you think you're doing," he asked in his usual querulous fashion, "writing a piece in which the parts move in seconds, seconds, seconds, all the time?"

He was waving two fingers which kept opening and closing to illustrate the seconds.

"Yes, I thought it could be done quite harmoniously," I replied, somewhat confused.

Lyadov was not listening, however. Evidently he did not require an answer: he had turned to another student and begun talking to him.

The second piece mentioned on the postcard to Myaskovsky was called *Autumnal Sketch*. Myaskovsky gave it this name, if I am not mistaken. I cannot remember at all what it was like, and the manuscript has also disappeared. The symphonic picture *Autumnal Sketch*, which appeared three years later has nothing in common with it except the name. Evidently I liked the title, but found the music of the first version lacking. I returned twice to this theme[11].

Ludvig Karklinš

"MY MUSIC WILL ALWAYS BE RUSSIAN...."

(About an Interview in Riga)

...According to accounts of concert life in the past, Riga first became acquainted with the work of Sergei Prokofiev in 1923 during a guest tour by the prominent Russian pianist Nikolai Orlov. Music critics made special mention of the great wit, in respect of both melody and harmony, with which *Fugitive Visions* was conceived, and the overwhelming effect which the inspiration, originality and freshness of Prokofiev's Third Sonata had on the audience.

In the following season the town was visited by the Warsaw Philharmonic Symphony Orchestra. The orchestra's conductor Grzegorz Fitelberg, already well-known as an active propagandist of Slavonic music, played three modern works on this occasion: S. Noskosvky's symphonic variations *From the Life of the People,* F. Busoni's suite from the opera based on Carlo Gozzi's play *Turandot,* and Prokofiev's *Classical Symphony.* The central place was, naturally, occupied by the symphony, which became the chief topic of discussion in musical circles.

Conservative critics (Ekab Graubin, for example) were dissatisfied. They considered that the "monotonous rhythms", "structurally diffuse melodies", "impure harmonies" and unusual orchestration had nothing in common with classicism, and nor did the forms of the various movements. They were challenged by the progressive Latvian composer and musicologist Jan Zalit: "*The Classical Symphony* by the Russian modernist Prokofiev is a work to which some will listen with pleasure and others with dislike, even anger. I belong to the former. Let neither Professor Witol, nor that loyal custodian of his pure traditions Graubin, look askance at me. I too respect pure, mature classical forms. But I do not think it a sin if a more carefree and more temperamental artist permits himself to improvise on their firm foundation. Particularly if he does so as effortlessly as Prokofiev. Let us forgive him with a light heart for all these 'blemishes' of slightly modernistic harmonies, for his peculiar modulations and the typically Russian angular and irrepressible temperament. Let us imagine: it is only improvisation in the classical spirit! Nor is there any lack of humour in the symphony's four movements. They say Haydn composed at his best when he put on his gala suit. This is significant. It would seem that Prokofiev, in his turn, feels happier within the framework of classical form".

In 1924 Prokofiev's music was again heard in Riga. The Polish pianist Zbigniew Drzewiecki and the symphony orchestra of the National Opera conducted by Teodor Reiter played his First Piano Concerto. This was also too radical for Jan Zalit, whose general aesthetic evaluation of this work was noteworthy: "Prokofiev is as gusty and fresh as a spring wind, but also as turbid as April waters."

Resounding success came to Prokofiev's work in the autumn of 1926 when the celebrated conductor Emil Cooper visited Riga. At one of his symphony concerts (in which A. Casella took part, incidentally) Rigans were introduced to music from the opera *Love for Three Oranges*. Even the above-mentioned Ekab Graubin wrote: "I liked his *Love for Three Oranges* very much indeed. It is original music with a most colourful orchestration. It contains strength, passion and joy to which no one can remain indifferent."

The public was delighted, and Prokofiev's name became increasingly popular in musical circles.

In the winter of 1927 the composer made his first visit to Latvia, where some acquaintances of his from the St. Petersburg period were living and working—his former fellow-students the pianist P. Schubert and the singer K. Petrauskas, and also Prokofiev's teacher Witol, who had become rector of the Riga Conservatoire. On the day of the concert Rigans found in the evening newspaper a long and interesting interview with Prokofiev, which is now probably known to but a few.

"I have been away from Russia for nine years. I spent most of this time living in America and only became a 'subject' of Europe in the last few years. I gave concerts and composed a great deal. Opera music attracts me most of all: I became fascinated by the scenic arts at the Conservatoire and know the stage very well. In my compositions I have sought for new paths, but my music is and will always be Russian. Now I am returning again to my native land to avoid becoming a stranger among my own people from long absence. At present I am working on a new opera *The Flaming Angel*, which is to be put on in Berlin with Bruno Walter in March.

"*The Love for Three Oranges* is an opera with a lively, interesting subject. It is a great success in America, as well as in Europe and Russia. I recently signed a contract with the Moscow Bolshoi Theatre which is planning to put it on. The opera is now being presented in Leningrad, at the former Mariinsky Theatre, remarkably well, I am told, and most successfully. The opera has an interesting history: when I was living in America the Chicago Opera Theatre commissioned me to write it. This was the first time in America that a composer had been commissioned to write an opera. The Berlin production of the *Oranges* produced an impression of insincerity. The musical side was on an excellent level, the finest performers took part, but all the same.... I was told: 'We cannot produce action at a quick "Italian" tempo. We have "Germanised" it slightly'.... But this 'Germanisation' resulted in the capricious Prince bearing a remarkable resemblance to the tragic Siegfried.

"It must be said that America today has all the best in world opera. Dollars are attracting the most talented artists, musicians and composers to the States. Thanks to this the Americans' musical taste has improved considerably. Opera is doing well in Italy also. Interestingly enough, there singers find it more difficult to perform in the smaller towns than in Rome and Milan. Provincial opera repertoires are often repeated, so the public, which is comparatively musical, knows almost every note by heart, and if an artist makes a mistake it catches him out at once.

"Diaghilev recently made a remark to the effect that opera would die and ballet would take its place. Yet there can be no doubt that the opera is progressing. To my mind, interest in it is like a wave which keeps rising and falling. In Mozart's day the public demanded something gay, lively and joyful, so *Figaro* and *Don Juan* appeared, then came Wagner, Gounod, etc. Now there is a new wave—the demand for more life. Opera itself will never disappear.

"At the concert this evening I shall perform two of my sonatas: the Third and the Fifth, which are written 'in the spirit of the present day'. In addition to other compositions of my own I shall also play works by Myaskovsky, who is now remarkably popular in both Russian and foreign musical circles. My wife Lyna Lyubera, who studied singing in New York and sang for several years in Italian opera companies, will perform a number of my romances, and also romances and songs by other prominent composers (Stravinsky, for example)."

At his first concert, apart from the Third and Fifth sonatas, Prokofiev introduced Rigans to several of his smaller works—the Dance, Op. 32, the March and Scherzo from the opera *Love for Three Oranges*, the Toccata, Op. 11, and that lyrical jewel—the second piece of the cycle *Old Granny's Tales*, Op. 31.

The most interesting review of the concert appeared in the newspaper *Segodnya vecherom*. The composer and critic Vidvud Jurevič described Prokofiev as a magnificent pianist with a subtle, refined interpretation: no technical effects, not the slightest effort to highlight anything. Just let the work speak for itself.

The Rigan audiences, used to virtuoso pianists, were amazed at the simplicity and naturalness of Prokofiev's playing, in which technical skill was subordinated to the revealing of content, and all difficulties were overcome effortlessly, almost jokingly.

The Rigans' acquaintance with Prokofiev's music continued in subsequent years. The conductor L. Matachich included his works in his concert programme in 1931, as did A. Coates in 1932. In 1933 the celebrated composer again visited Latvia. This time his programme included the Second and Third sonatas, the twelve pieces from the cycle *Fugitive Visions*, and the Scherzo and Etude from Op. 52.

In a review of this concert Jan Zalit ranks Prokofiev with the great names of modern music, Stravinsky and Honegger. The reviewer regarded the spirit of Prokofiev's work as particularly close to the great Moussorgsky. He stressed the freshness, profound veracity and originality of the music, and the absence of external glitter. He also rated Prokofiev most highly as a pianist.

Zalit's references in this review to the Prokofiev of the St. Petersburg student days are of particular interest. "While still at the Conservatoire he stood out from his other colleagues for his original taste and creative skylarking, which was, of course, not to the liking of the professors. I still remember a most uncomplimentary remark by an eminent Conservatoire teacher about one of Prokofiev's stylistically most radical works. 'Your music makes me think of savages leaping about in a wild dance, as they burn their heels.' But Prokofiev remained unruffled. He went his own way, ignoring such utterances."

S. Prokofiev's concerts in Riga in the 1920s and 1930s were not only delightful encounters with an outstanding talent. His novel art had a profound influence on whole generations of Latvian composers: suffice it to mention here the First Piano Sonata of Janis Ivanov (1930—1931), then only beginning his career.

And, finally, the Riga visits by the great Russian musician played an important political role, promoting the drawing together of cultures destined by history to develop hand in hand.

Sovietskaya Muzyka,
No. 4, 1970

Vladimir Blok

"MOST OF ALL I WAS INTERESTED
IN *EUGENE ONEGIN*"

Prokofiev was very fond of the theatre. And not only the musical theatre. As a child in the village of Sontsovka he and his playmates put on shows, and the future composer wrote plays for these house entertainments. Later his love for the theatre found expression in the imagery of much of his instrumental music—chamber and symphonic. It manifested itself even more vividly in music for the dramatic theatre, in which Prokofiev became interested in his "adult" work. Thus there emerged the music for Shakespeare's *Hamlet*, and for productions of the Kamerny Theatre directed by Alexander Tairov—*Egyptian Nights* (based on works by Shakespeare, Pushkin and Shaw), Pushkin's *Boris Godunov*, and the stage adaptation of *Eugene Onegin* by the dramatist S. Krzhizhanovsky.

Of all these works only *Hamlet* was "lucky"—since then Prokofiev's brilliant music has accompanied many productions both at home and abroad. After the Kamerny Theatre production *Egyptian Nights* did not appear anywhere—the composer himself called this attempt to combine different types of classical drama in one production a "curious venture". The Pushkin productions were, unfortunately, never put on.

The manuscripts for the music of the Pushkin productions are carefully preserved in the Central State Archives of Literature and the Arts, which contains the bulk of Prokofiev's manuscripts. This music has never been publicly performed, with the exception of a few excerpts included by the conductor Gennady Rozhdestvensky in his *Pushkiniana* Suite.

Prokofiev rated the importance of music in the dramatic theatre rather modestly. "Music in a dramatic production," he wrote, "should appear at points where it reinforces the impression, and not where the dramatic action can manage without it. Moreover, music should never drown the spoken word which it accompanies." Yet, in spite of the specific limitations imposed by the stage, Prokofiev has created much of lasting artistic value here too. As in the music of Bizet's *L'Arlésienne*, Grieg's *Peer Gynt*, and Tchaikovsky's *The Snow Maiden*, we find here too images of rare beauty and originality. And just as with Grieg, Bizet or Tchaikovsky, much of Prokofiev's theatre music acquires an independent artistic importance.

Speaking of the Pushkin theme in his works, Prokofiev wrote: "...Most of all I was interested in *Eugene Onegin*... Personally I make it my aim to delve as deeply as possible into the true spirit of Pushkin."

With his love of and subtle feeling for Pushkin's age of poetry and music, Prokofiev has recorded its features on many occasions. The lyrical pages of *War and Peace* and the *Pushkin Waltzes,* the music for the film *Lermontov* and the screen version of *The Queen of Spades* which was never filmed.

Sometimes, to quote Sergei Sergeyevich himself, "Glinka's smile flashes"—bright and gentle—in this music.

Such is this published fragment from the music for *Eugene Onegin.* It is to be hoped that this tiny masterpiece by Prokofiev will bring delight to many, many people, both audiences and performers alike. This music, worthy of adorning the programme of miniatures for concerts by professional artists, is also well within the range of the amateur pianist. As in his large, epic canvases, here too, within the limits of the delightful miniature, we find embodied that which D. Shostakovich in describing Prokofiev's music, called "directness of feeling, fertilised by the wisdom of a great master".

Sovietskaya Kultura,
April 24, 1971

Andante con tristezza ♩ = 72

Izrail Nestyev

NEW DISCOVERIES ABOUT
THE GREAT MASTER

Eighty years have passed since the birth of Sergei Sergeyevich Prokofiev. It is now eighteen years since he departed from us. But his music lives on with an exceptional and ever growing intensity. Former prejudices which hindered a proper appreciation of the highly original works by this Russian master are disappearing. These works are taking their place with increasing confidence alongside the classics. For proof of this, it is enough to look at the programmes of our radio, piano and symphony concerts—almost every day they contain some music by Prokofiev. Fortunate is the destiny of the artist whose work brings joy to people every day, adorning their lives and inspiring faith in a happy future.

Soviet musicology has expended a great deal of labour on Prokofiev's heritage. Two decades have produced a mass of publications devoted to the composer: books, theses, brochures, articles, and final diploma essays by university students. No less than twenty-five Candidate of Science theses alone have been written (or are in the process of being written). And the first doctoral thesis on this subject has recently been successfully defended (M. Tarakanov—*The Style of Prokofiev's Symphonies*). The lion's share of this research belongs to the theoreticians who have succeeded in making a profound and comprehensive study of the modal-harmonic structure, melody, rhythm and dramaturgic features of Prokofiev's music. There are quite a few studies where researchers examine the various genres of the great composer's work—opera, symphony, ballet, and piano music. Their study of the specific features of Prokofiev's musical style has enabled gifted scholars to trace certain general processes of the development of modern harmony, to provide new theoretical explanations of the fertile modal innovations in 20th-century music. There has occasionally been some exaggeration here, for attempts have been made to find in Prokofiev's harmony a kind of *universal standard of contemporariness*, whereas by avoiding destructive tendencies in modal thinking it has to a large extent been the antithesis of avant-garde extremism. (This has been most convincingly shown by such leading Soviet theoretical musicologists as L. Mazel and Y. Tyulin.)

But, as often happens, rapid progress in one direction has been accompanied by a deplorable lack of advance in another. While achieving a great deal in the analysis of Prokofiev's musical idiom, our musicology has done almost nothing by way of studying his archives, his scores, manuscripts and letters. After the publication of the well-known collection *Materials, Documents, Reminiscences* edited by S. Shlifstein (1956) and the collection *Articles and Materials* (1962) we have had too few noteworthy publications of this kind.

Yet Soviet archives contain a vast amount of valuable material which remains unstudied by our historiographers. (It is a good thing that Sergei Sergeyevich was such an assiduous, far-sighted person that he preserved a large number of letters and documents for posterity—including copies and drafts, notebooks, synopses, recordings, hundreds of newspaper cuttings, etc.)

Prokofiev's most valuable correspondence with Myaskovsky, about which Dmitry Kabalevsky has written, still awaits publication. It is to be regretted that these important documents, which embrace almost half a century of Russian musical life, are still not available to scholars. The safes of the Central State Archives of Literature and the Arts and the State Central Museum of Musical Culture contain Prokofiev's letters to B. Asafyev, V. Derzhanovsky, I. Stravinsky, B. Yavorsky and E. Damskaya. Many of them are of outstanding interest, revealing unknown facts about the composer's biography and throwing new light on details of his creative process. It need hardly be said that here our study of musical sources is obviously lagging behind the tempo of Russian research in the years immediately before and after the Revolution. Let us recall, for example, the correspondence between Tchaikovsky and Taneyev published in 1916 (a year after Taneyev's death!), the three-volume *Life of P.I. Tchaikovsky* which contains many important letters by the composer (1901—1903), and the numerous editions of the epistolary legacy of Balakirev, Rimsky-Korsakov, Stassov, Moussorgsky, Lyadov and Borodin. Yet the materials of our eminent contemporaries—Prokofiev, Asafyev and Myaskovsky—are of no less aesthetic and social importance. Can one reconcile oneself to the fact that B. Asafyev's talented book of memoires *Thoughts and Reflections*, which contains most valuable observations on the musical life of the years immediately preceding the Revolution, including reminiscences about Prokofiev, has not yet seen the light of day?

It is equally regrettable that Prokofiev's own unique book of memoires which covers his childhood years and the period of study at the St. Petersburg Conservatoire (up to 1909), has not yet been published in full.

The Central State Archives of Literature and the Arts—a splendid institution which has done so much for our research—contains invaluable music manuscripts, including Prokofiev's notebooks in which he sketched themes and musical ideas. With their help one can trace the train of the musical thought of the greatest melodist of our time, the complex fates of musical ideas which underwent various changes. So far hardly anyone has touched this material. Much of it is, unfortunately, not available to scholars. (Although it contains nothing "secret", for those who might have objected to the publication of certain harsh or offensive remarks have long passed away). And so books, articles and studies are being written by authors who are not properly armed with the facts, because they are deprived of the possibility of using the archives.

The vast collection of foreign reviews and articles in Prokofiev's archive is practically untouched. These include many penetrating critical observations from the pen of erudite Western writers (particularly French ones—Marnold, Roland-Manuel, Roussel, Auric, Prunières, Florent Schmitt all wrote about Prokofiev); here too are many important interviews by the composer, containing his sharp and principled views on modern art.

Our musicologists also have yet to study the material in foreign archives or publications. The archive of the London music publishers Boosey and Hawkes contains the manuscript of Prokofiev's first opera *Maddalena* which has never been heard. There can be no doubt that these works, which once earned the high praise of his contemporaries—N. Myaskovsky,

86

K. Sarajev, K. Marjanov—would be of interest not only to scholars, but also to our theatres and concert organisations. The conductor Gennady Rozhdestvensky once told of his attempts to obtain a photocopy of the *Maddalena* manuscript, which had ended in a complete fiasco. Yet we have long-standing cultural ties with the progressive British intelligentsia, and I do not doubt that a little effort on the part of the public would have procured a copy of this most valuable manuscript. English scholars have access to the material contained in the Boosey and Hawkes archive, and a young musicologist A. MacAlister from Scotland recently wrote a thesis on Prokofiev's operas on the basis of this material.

There are also manuscripts connected with Prokofiev's activities in other archives, not all of which are probably accessible. I would mention, first and foremost, the archives of S. Diaghilev, S. Koussevitzky, I. Stravinsky, P. Souvtchinsky, the violinists Joseph Szigeti and R. Soëtans, and certain ballet-masters and conductors. Many foreign publications devoted to Prokofiev have not received due appraisal in our press, for example, the special issues of the English magazine *Tempo*, the West German chronicle *Musik der Zeit*, the Polish collection *O twórczosci S. Prokofiewa*, the French collection *Musique russe*, Vol. II (articles by F. Poulenc and A. Golea), the Italian collection *L'aprodo musicale* (1961, No. 13), etc. In recent years a great many monographs about Prokofiev of varying length and scholarship have come out abroad. Most of them have been written with an unquestionable knowledge of the subject and profound respect for the composer's memory—I would mention the French studies by K. Samuel and R. Hofman, the German ones (GDR)—H. A. Brockhaus, F. Streller, the Polish ones— T. Zielinsky, Z. Sliwinski, the books by I. Wajda (Slovakia) and I. Khlebarov (Bulgaria), and so on. Serious theoretical works are in course of preparation in the USA, FRG and Britain.

But, unfortunately, one also finds extremely dubious authors who are trying to meet the growing public interest in Prokofiev's work with cheap criticism or flagrant anti-Soviet writing. Thus, in the USA, a queer, dilettantish book by L. and E. Henson was followed by a voluminous "study" by the émigré V. Serov, which can only arouse distaste and indignation. His opus appeared under the "expressive" title of *Prokofiev. A Soviet Tragedy*. Without bothering to analyse the music, the author constructs his narrative in the traditions of crude political slander. His interest as a researcher is directed mainly at all manner of family and matrimonial events and similar morsels. With an enviable zeal Serov procures such unique documents as a copy of the birth-certificate of Prokofiev's first wife and a copy of his marriage certificate. The family tree of the first wife is traced right back to the great grandparents on her father's and mother's side. In his attempts to catch the fancy of the American reader, the author actually distorts the facts. We are told, for example, that Prokofiev's second wife was the niece of a high-ranking Soviet official in the 1940s and that with her help the communist authorities sought to take the famous composer "in hand". All these vulgar concoctions, which are insulting to Prokofiev's memory and have nothing to do with true scholarship, have been put out by a respectable publishers in a large *de luxe* edition. Unfortunately none of our press organs have put this shameless author, whose work has been encouraged by definite trends in American reactionary circles, in his place.

Our historiographers are greatly indebted to Prokofiev's memory. They have yet to examine, comment on and publish a vast number of documents, study music manuscripts, and properly assess books, articles and reminiscences which have appeared in foreign countries. And, of course, a study of Prokofiev's legacy should not be limited to abstract, academic questions. The degree to which individual works are performed and gain public recognition frequently depends on the accuracy of the critic's judgement. Unfortunately, wrong evaluations published by us in the past still hinder the active popularisation of perfectly deserving works. This is the case, for example, with the opera *The Flaming Angel* which has the firm reputation of being a "mystical", "morbid" work connected with the worst influences of decadence. The life of this opera on foreign stages, in particular its brilliant production in the GDR at the Berlin Staatsoper, decisively refutes this unfortunate misapprehension. *The Flaming Angel* is actually an anti-clerical work which boldly denounces all obscurantism, superstition and mysticism; it contains the finest features of Prokofiev's bold realism, and its music is rich in melody and highly dramatic. It is no wonder that N. Myaskovsky noted with admiration that in *The Flaming Angel* Prokofiev appeared "in his full stature as a musician and artist", who has matured "to full genius". Has the time not come—forty or more years after this splendid opera was completed—to show it to Russian audiences if only in a concert performance? The opera *The Gambler* and certain ballet scores—the *Tale of the Buffoon, The Prodigal Son, The Age of Steel* and *On the Dnieper* are also awaiting new scenic interpretations. These ballets were put on in Czechoslovakia at the Prokofiev Festival in 1963. But we can still only get to know them from gramophone records or, at the best, from infrequent orchestral performances.

Our critics face the task of thoroughly and scientifically refuting the one-sided judgements of the past and helping the collectives of music theatres (and the large Soviet audience) to master more extensively Prokofiev's operatic and ballet works.

* * *

In the course of preparing my fundamentally revised monograph on Prokofiev for the press, I came across many interesting documents which I had not known previously. A study of this new material revealed processes which had hitherto been hidden, and forced me to reappraise one-sided and erroneous conclusions of ealier years. A new light is thrown on the composer's relations with the founders of the Evenings of Modern Music (A. Nurok and V. Nuvel), with S. Diaghilev and S. Koussevitzky. A passing reference (in a letter to Asafyev) about meetings and talks with Chaliapine (in the autumn of 1917) enables us to raise more broadly the question of the ways in which Prokofiev's operatic aesthetics developed. More complex are his relations with the work of Scriabin, Debussy and Stravinsky, with the poetry of the acmeists and "cubo-futurists". We learn more about some of the composer's influential consultants and advisers (V. Meyerhold, B. Demchinsky and P. Souvtchinsky) and of his many extremely characteristic musical plans which remained unrealised. But there is no need to go into all the details here, for the reader will be able to study the new material when the book comes out. I shall simply permit myself to quote from a few documents of particular interest, to my mind, which will probably attract the attention not only of scholars, but of all those who love and appreciate Prokofiev's art.

...Thirty years ago with much trepidation I showed Sergei Sergeyevich the first, very modest version of my monograph written for his fiftieth birthday. It was in 1941, and the outbreak of war had prevented publication of this naive book, which Prokofiev agreed to read. The type of the unfortunate monograph was soon dismantled for reasons connected with the war. But I retained eleven pages of comments by Prokofiev, of which I could not make use until many years later. With his customary precision and exactingness, the composer read through the proofs, noting down a few dozen minor inaccuracies in the titles of opuses and the spelling of towns and foreign words. But the most important and valuable thing were Prokofiev's clear and sharp critical comments, which, to my mind, still retain their aesthetic and historico-biographical significance.

Firstly, Sergei Sergeyevich flatly disputed my statement that the period he had spent abroad was "the least significant one". *"I shall always dispute this,"* he commented, *"without it what followed would have been on a lower level".*

"This was new and strange," I had written about the piano pieces composed in the late 1920s and the early 1930s in Paris. *"And a good thing too, that means a widening of range,"* replied my opponent. Further on he added: *"I benefited from my period abroad for my work in the Soviet period .... It was only by passing through the 'philosophical period' that I was able to develop properly in the following one."*

My one-sided remarks about the activity of S. Diaghilev and S. Koussevitzky, who gave Prokofiev active support in his period abroad, provoked his profound disagreement. I had said that Diaghilev's aesthetic position concealed "indifference to man". Sergei Sergeyevich countered: *"Diaghilev and indifference to man! But what about 'The Prodigal Son' which he rated above all my other works? "*And further on about Koussevitzky: *"The word 'businessman' does not fit Koussevitzky, because he did not receive any financial gain from his publishing activities...."*

My book expressed the thought that Prokofiev underrated the traditions of classical opera. This provoked the perplexed question: *"Why is a rejection of the canons of old opera an obstacle to the creation of Soviet opera? It would seem to be quite the reverse!"* Nor did he agree with the criticism of his mass songs: *"Who writes mass songs on a higher level? They must be compared with other composers' works in the same genre."*

I shall also quote his apt remarks on individual compositions and musical productions.

About the music for *Tale of the Buffoon:* *"Be kinder about* the 'Buffoon'... *Folk tales are often wicked, you cannot blame me for that. And in view of its musical qualities, the 'Buffoon' should be recommended to the reader."*

About public indifference to the Cello Concerto, Op. 58: *"Be more careful with the Cello Concerto: it is very close to the Second Violin Concerto. The indifference is mere stupidity."*

About the production of *Romeo and Juliet* at the Bolshoi Theatre: *"I do not agree with the high opinion of Lavrovsky (he often contradicts the music) and Williams (a well-groomed tidy artist)."*

About my description of the characters in *Semyon Kotko,* in particular the sailor Tsaryov: *"You should point out that Mikola and Tsaryov are not only roguish (this adjective is quite unsuitable for Tsaryov), but also positive charecters."*

And a very minor, but indicative touch: The composer suggested that M. Gorky's comment, which I had quoted in a footnote, on somewhat "autobiographic nature" of *The Ugly Duckling,* be transferred to the main text, to which I readily consented. This "trifle" showed once again his tremendous respect for the great writer's memory.

For all his strictness and exactingness, Sergei Sergeyevich approved of my works in general, and kept inquiring in his letters in 1942, after he was evacuated, when the book was coming out. In my revision of the monograph I have made use of the valuable advice and comments of my first reviewer with great piety and gratitude.

Two documents are reproduced below which were written by Prokofiev and relate to different periods of his creative life. The first is a long-forgotten article about I. Stravinsky, published in 1919 in the USA in Russian. This article shows how close Stravinsky's work in the period of *The Rite of Spring* and *The Wedding* was to Prokofiev. However critical some of his comments on Stravinsky's work were in letters to friends, Prokofiev undoubtedly made a careful study of all the compositions of his famous compatriot and learned a great deal from his experience. In the 1920s, when Stravinsky turned to neoclassicism, Prokofiev's attitude toward him cooled. But even then, when he flatly rejected his tendencies of stylisation, Sergei Sergeyevich wrote: "I hesitate to criticise him, for Stravinsky has often deceived us, and what seemed ugly at first glance turned out to be interesting later" (from a letter to Asafyev of August 9, 1926). In his turn, Stravinsky had great respect for the work of his younger contemporary, which can be seen, for example, from a very warm comment in the book *Chronicle of My Life.* In an interview in 1928 when asked who was the most outstanding composer in Soviet Russia Stravinsky replied: "I don't know anyone there except Prokofiev ... I have the greatest admiration for him."

The second document, which I found in the composer's archive in the Central State Archive of Literature and the Arts, is a manuscript written in an abbreviated form which Prokofiev often used—without vowels. It is a synopsis of a speech at a meeting of the Composers' Union in Moscow on April 9, 1937. This was the period of widespread discussion on formalism which followed the publication in the central newspapers of critical articles on Shostakovich's works. There was also a great deal of argument at that time about I. Dzerzhinsky's operas *And Quiet Flows the Don* and *Virgin Soil Upturned* produced by the Bolshoi Theatre. In his synopsis Sergei Sergeyevich outlined a clear aesthetic programme, condemning the false interpretation of the term "formalism", disdain of real skill, and pandering to undeveloped tastes. The overdirect analogies made by Prokofiev between the modern technique of musical composition and new industrial technology (see the references to cars Ford, GAZ, ZIM, M-1) is probably open to dispute. But in general, Prokofiev's remarks, profound in thought and vividly polemical in form, still retain their relevance, dealing with the vital problems of musical creativity and the aesthetic education of the masses. Reproduced here is the manuscript of the synopsis with some minor abbreviations (and a little literary retouching to restore some words which were left out).

1. About Igor Stravinsky

On December 6, 1919, the New York newspaper *Russkoye Slovo* announced a forthcoming concert by the Greek singer Vera Yanokopulos. As well as some classical romances by Chopin, Grieg, Debussy and Fauré, and also Russian composers—Rimsky-Korsakov and Moussorgsky (in Russian), the singer included Stravinsky's *Pribautki* (Ditties) in the programme—to the accompaniment of an ensemble of soloists from the New York Philharmonic Orchestra. (The concert took place in the Aeolian Hall on December 10. Prokofiev wrote to I. Stravinsky on the same day: "Yanokopulos sang splendidly... I sat next to Fokine, and we shouted 'bravo' as loudly as we could.") "The part played by Stravinsky in Russian music is so great," *Russkoye Slovo* wrote, "that the following comment by the Russian composer Sergei Prokofiev has been dedicated to him and, thus, to Madame Yanokopulos' forthcoming concert:

"Igor Stravinsky's father was a famous bass and one of the finest singers of his time. In the Novo-Devichy convent in Petrograd, you will find a beautiful marble figure bending over the grave of this singer next to the monument to Rimsky-Korsakov. Stravinsky's brother, who died during Brusilov's offensive, was also an artist in the Imperial Opera[12].

"Igor Stravinsky was a most promising pupil of Rimsky-Korsakov's when Diaghilev, without long deliberation, commissioned the ballet *The Firebird* from him, which was duly written and put on in Paris immediately. The success of this ballet, the brilliant orchestration, the use of Russian folk themes, and the death of Rimsky-Korsakov prompted circles who were close to the latter to regard Stravinsky as Rimsky-Korsakov's heir.

"Stravinsky's second ballet *Petrouchka* brought him worldwide fame. But this ballet revealed such innovation and audacity that the people who have just proclaimed him as Rimsky-Korsakov's successor recoiled in horror, whispering that the new generation called for new ideas and new sounds. But they were not to halt Stravinsky's ever-growing success!

"The next ballet, *The Rite of Spring*, was a more profound work than *Petrouchka*, both in material and exposition, but even more progressive in its audacity. This time not only Rimsky-Korsakov's ageing friends protested, but the whole of Paris, so avid for modern art, was in an uproar—the music was so weird and incomprehensible. The music world can hardly have known a more scandalous evening that the one when *The Rite of Spring* had its première in Paris. During the performance the auditorium, packed with a most select audience of musical gourmands, rang so loudly with whistles and groans that the ballet barely reached final curtain. But in the following season a crowd of newly-converted pilgrims carried Stravinsky on their shoulders in the selfsame Paris.

"The opera which followed *The Rite of Spring—The Nightingale*, based on Andersen's fairy-tale, was not a favourite with the author, because he did not believe in the opera form and thought that the future belonged to the ballet. Whether the opera form will die, as Stravinsky thinks, or the ballet, is a matter of dispute: but our author had already discovered a new [form] and written, if one might use the expression, a 'vocal ballet'—*The Wedding*, which had not yet been put on anywhere because of the war. In *The Wedding* there is a ballet on the stage, and a choir and instruments in the orchestra—all the motifs of Russian songs and humorous folk sayings or ditties.

"*Pribautki* which are shortly to be performed on the American stage, are in the same style. They are small songs based on folk sayings which are remarkable for their absurdity and delightful for their old-fashionedness. They are accompanied by a tiny orchestra of eight instruments and resound with all the fancifulness and brilliance of which this bold composer is capable."

2. Summary of a speech ... at a meeting of activists of the Union of Composers on April 9, 1937

"A great deal has been said here about the poor order within the Union of Composers, about the mistakes of the management, about the political immaturity of certain composers, about everyday difficulties, and the difficulties of performing compositions.

"But little has been said about creative questions, creative purposefulness.

"I shall attempt to fill this breach [in our discussion]. [For] what would we be worth if we started to compose badly.

"The tasks of Soviet composers fall into two divisions:

1) symphonic, chamber and operatic music (what is called "great music")

and 2) music for the masses.

"('Great music' for me is a collective term. I do not wish to infer by it that music for the masses is 'minor music'....)

"So, to deal first with division 1.

"Many people here regard me as a Westerniser in the bad sense.

"Yes, I have spent much time in the West, but this does not mean I have become a "Westerniser".

"After all, our engineers are not Westernisers, nor is a Ford imported into the Soviet Union, or workers in heavy industry [who make] new machines.

"[I should like to talk] about the usefulness of self-criticism among us. The usefulness of the view from the outside.

"I should like to make use of this 'view from the outside'.

"Are people abroad interested in our music? Do they play it? Yes. Whom do they play?

"1. Myaskovsky, Shostakovich [deleted: Shostakovich—First Symphony, Piano Concerto. Myaskovsky—depth of thought, but....]

"2. Mosolov, Shaporin, Shebalin, Khrennikov, Dzerzhinsky.

"3. Chamber music—Khachaturyan, Gavriil Popov.

"The interest is not limited to these names. They are interested in theoretical ideas of Ogolevets. In Russian music of the past: The Big Five, Scriabin, Stravinsky.

"They are looking for something new in Soviet composers. In so doing they are often disappointed: the USSR is the new world, but the composers are chewing over old things.

"Is there discrepancy between the processes of development of the USSR and—composers?

"One might think why should we care about the opinion of the West? If the Soviet Union had listened to other people's opinions, it would probably not exist any longer. Yet it would be wrong to ignore that which could help us advance.

"Yes, the question of whether Soviet composers have a language of their own is a serious one.

"Historical note: Schumann, Chopin and Liszt, Moussorgsky, Tchaikovsky and Scriabin had a language of their own, an impeccable technique of their own. In speaking of a Soviet composers' own language I do not mean simply technique, but a Soviet style.

"Much has been said and evidently it must be said again and again that: the struggle against formalism is not a struggle against the perfection and improvement of technique.

"GAZ, M-1, ZIS—this is not formalism.

"Lazy-minded or uncultured comrades were overjoyed: It is us! We are writing without any clever philosophising....

"This attitude tends to lower the standard of our musical culture.

"If one compares the arrangement of delightful folk songs in *Boris Godunov* and in Dzerzhinsky's opera, one is amazed at the way we have started throwing around the precious folk song instead of developing it carefully and lovingly.

"So, comrades, concern for

1) proper arrangement and development of the folk song,
2) development of our own language,
3) improvement of technique

is our direct duty ⟨ ... ⟩

"It is said of certain young composers 'the symphony is written in the best classical traditions....' Careful, they are only learners! ...

"We are striving ahead in all spheres of the Soviet economy. Politically we are not only contemporary, but the country of the future.

1) Collective farms are an idea of the future embodied in the present day,
2) industry.

"Why then do· our comrade musicians imagine that they alone can feed on yesterday's bread and rotten beef? Is there not the danger here of being thrown overboard?

"Second division—music for the masses.

"Soviet power has done a great thing in opening the portals of music for the masses.

"But they must be directed in order to flower musically.

"What is the cultural level of the masses for whom we are composing music?

"A very important and delicate question. The simple-minded solve it thus: they play down to the masses, and all playing down in art means insincerity and causes harm.

"Many people know little about music, although they are highly developed politically, and also technically, in their own field.

"Answer: the masses have a considerable level of general culture, but the area of musical culture has been neglected. Although many have a potentially high taste, cultivated on the folk song and Russian classical music.

"It is criminal to give the masses cheap music!

"What am I driving at? What is the answer?

"The answer is a difficult one, and depends largely on the intuition and tact of composers. Our work is firing at moving targets.

1) We must not try to get away with cheap music, because the masses are allegedly not cultured enough. This causes harm!

2) Music for the masses should be written with the same creative effort as a symphony.

3) It is better to write a little bit harder than a little bit easier.

"In conclusion I would ask comrades not to regard what has been said as a set of recipes. I simply wished to express the ideas which occurred to me as the result of many sleepless nights."

P.S. The critical reader may get the impression that the author of the synopsis is advocating a view of musical-technical innovation as an end in itself. In order to allay these fears we reproduce the final passage from an unpublished New Year's article by Prokofiev, written on December 23, 1938, for the newspaper *Izvestia*:

"Innovation can be fruitful only when it is based on technical mastery, otherwise it risks becoming replaced by unfruitful, I would say 'obscure' striving for originality. I should like to propose a New Year's toast to innovation, and not obscure striving for originality, to mastery and to the flowering of our art."

Sovietskaya Muzyka,
No. 4, 1971

4

STUDIES

Larissa Danko

S. PROKOFIEV IN HIS WORK ON *THE DUENNA*

(The writing of the libretto)

Throughout his creative life Prokofiev was constantly occupied with the genre of the musical stage: he had an excellent knowledge of the theatre, which never ceased to fascinate him, and he was always full of musical projects for it.

Prokofiev read a great deal and took a lively interest in literature. In reading new works he usually made notes in the text and margins: these were outlines for scenarios and comments on the possibility of giving the literary subject a musical embodiment.

The nature of these notes can be seen from a copy of Bryusov's *The Flaming Angel* in the composer's archive. The future libretto is outlined in a concise exposition of the individual chapters in the margins. The dialogues and descriptions which reveal most vividly the development of the main plot, the characters' emotions, and features of their appearance and behaviour are marked in the text. Musical themes are occasionally jotted down. He used the same method with other works which served him as the basis for a libretto, in particular, Sheridan's play *The Duenna*, about which more is said in detail below.

Prokofiev defined the process of the "musical interpretation" of a literary work in the creation of music for stage and screen as follows: "*When I am asked to write music for a dramatic production or a film, I hardly ever consent at once; even if I know the text of the play I take five or ten days to 'see' it, i.e., to see the characterisation of the personages, the illustration of their emotions, the illustration of the events. During this perusal the main themes usually suggest themselves.*"

In his search for operatic subjects the composer turned mainly to works—stories and novels—which gave scope for a free arrangement of the scenario (F. Dostoyevsky's *The Gambler*, Bryusov's *The Flaming Angel*, V. Katayev's *I, Son of the Working People*, L. Tolstoy's *War and Peace* and B. Polevoi's *Story of a Real Man*). On their basis he consistently followed his principles of composition for a musical production, striving for lively action, vivid theatricality, and sharply contrasting events. Prokofiev's method of turning a narrative work into dramatic action is most revealing. While observing the general laws of operatic drama, which consist of concentrated action, expanded lyrical content, and a greater generalisation of characters, Prokofiev also developed *his own* creative manner, revealing *his* attitude to the specific nature of operatic forms.

The Duenna occupies a special place among Prokofiev's opera librettos. This time the composer made use of a dramatic play—a lively, effective play full of unexpected contrasts, which was similar in its mode of exposition to an opera scenario because it contained a considerable number of musical numbers—songs, duets and trios. Nevertheless in his work on this opera Prokofiev displayed a great deal of creative initiative, invention and feeling for the stage, adding to, condensing and rearranging the text of the original. Consequently a study of his work on the libretto of this delightful lyrico-comic opera, which is today firmly established in theatre repertoires at home and abroad, is of special interest.

* * *

The popularity of Sheridan's *The Duenna* was unprecedented in the history of the English theatre. No other play could rival it in the number of performances during its first season (1775). For seventy-five evenings in succession *The Duenna* met with a rapturous reception from audiences at the Drury Lane theatre.

Sheridan had chosen for his work the genre of the ballad opera, first established by John Gay's *The Beggars' Opera* (1724) and developed further in the work of Fielding. It was a satirical musical comedy, the couplets of which were sung to well-known tunes.

The music for this production of *The Duenna* was written by a contemporary of Sheridan's, Thomas Linley, the author of popular songs which were known all over the country.

The unusual success of *The Duenna* was due to the fact that in it Sheridan overcame the conventionality and one-sidedness of the ballad opera as a parody genre and extended its range of artistic expression. Sheridan introduced into *The Duenna* features which were characteristic of English comedy as a whole: a complex plot on several levels, a most lively action, and convincing, full-blooded main characters. The play is full of dynamic events, apt, laconic phrases, and brilliantly witty dialogue. Its content, which deals mainly with the morals and the manners of the day, is most indicative of English satirical comedy of the 1770s and corresponds to the rules which had been set for satirical dramatists: "Comedy should aim not at showing the virtues of the middle class, but at exposing its stupidity and vices."

The target of many comedies of this period was the *nouveau riche*, the perverted morals and egoism of the privileged classes. Examples of this in Sheridan's play are the characters Mendoza and Jerome, who are typical of their age and express the main trend of the times—when "big speculators purchased noble titles, and the old aristocracy easily combined family pride with sheer bourgeois money-grubbing."

The playwright is equally merciless in his ridicule of the main "virtue" of the English ruling classes—hypocrisy, which masks ignorance and the desire for wealth, the cupidity behind all activities. The hypocritical type of the bourgeois Puritan is exposed by Sheridan in the figures of the "holy fathers" who behave with unmatched impudence and cynicism within the monastery walls. For censorship considerations the famous writer transferred the action of his play to Spain. But this enforced "masquerade" does not conceal the biting satire on English 18th-century morals and manners.

Certain lyrical episodes in the play are also of a sharply polemical nature. In the scene of Mendoza's proposal to the Duenna, Sheridan, with his love of paradox and the grotesque, makes the ancient Margarita describe her marriage in the way in which young girls from the best families dreamed of it. The character of Carlos is a challenge to the love-lorn, "constantly sighing" heroes of sentimental comedy. The affected feelings of Ferdinand and Clara, their tiresome seriousness, are ridiculed by the author. They are contrasted with the second pair of young lovers—Louisa and Antonio, who are full of energy, vigour, and firmly defend their right to happiness. Their presence on the stage creates an atmosphere of bright, joyous lyricism which is an unfading element in Sheridan's play. Everything in it is motivated by love, life blazes forth in the struggle for love, youthful emotions seethe as befits true "Spanish feelings", everything is imbued with a turbulent dynamism, yet also with the special poetry of youth. And this is not hindered by either the prose of the language or the comic, sometimes grotesque nature of the various situations.

Prokofiev read *The Duenna* as one of Sheridan's most lyrical plays. It is this lyrical content which the composer sought above all to bring out in his opera too.

"*When I began work on the opera of 'The Duenna',*" Prokofiev wrote, "*I was faced with a choice of two methods. The first was to emphasise the comic aspect in my music; the second to emphasise the lyricism. I chose the latter. I thought I could not go wrong if I paid special attention to the lyricism of 'The Duenna': the love of the two young, joyful, romantic couples Louisa and Antonio, and Clara and Ferdinand; the obstacles in the way of this love; the happy betrothal.*" The composer's imagination added the background against which the love intrigue develops: "*the poetry of Seville ... a quiet evening spread out before the lovers' eyes; a night carnival dying away; an old, deserted nunnery.*"

Nor could Prokofiev help being attracted by the comic, satirical poignancy of the subject. Humour, infectious laughter, and biting irony were constant features of his work which condemned meanness and empty routine, cruelty and stupidity, greed and selfishness. "*I did not reject any of the comic elements so brilliant in Sheridan,*" Prokofiev wrote: "*old Don Jerome, so blinded with rage that, instead of the nurse who has incurred his wrath, he drives his own daughter out of the house, dressed up in her nurse's clothes, and thus himself helps to put into effect her plan to run away with her beloved; the greedy Mendoza, so blinded by ducats that he lets himself be tricked, and, instead of the enchanting young Louisa, marries her old nanny; the ardent Ferdinand so jealous that he thinks any girl walking in the company of a young man is Clara deceiving him. These characters and the comic situations in which they find themselves are all the more vivid against the background of the lyrical scenes, especially if the comic quid-pro-quos are acted with a straight face.*"

Prokofiev frequently criticised external comedy in dramatic productions of *The Duenna.* In connection with the proposed production of the opera in 1943 at the second stage of the Bolshoi Theatre he wrote: *"Incidentally, the Moscow Kamerny Theatre, which put on 'The Duenna' after my opera had been completed, really overemphasised the comic line, turning it into a burlesque in some places. The theatre must be credited with having acquired the original music, but this exaggeration of the comic element was not justified to my mind."* In the composer's view it was not the physical ugliness of Mendoza or the Duenna that should produce laughter, but the absurd situations in which they found themselves. Prokofiev also pointed this out to the producers of the opera, protesting at the grotesque make-up of Mendoza and the Duenna.

The remoteness of the subject in terms of time made it possible for Prokofiev to throw a new light on a number of problems posed in the play of this fine 18th-century writer and to make a slight adjustment of emphasis on the ideological content as seen by our contemporary.

The comic, satirical aspect of the plot retained its relevance more than the polemical aspect of the lyrical characters. However, the portrayal of social phenomena of the past demanded a new approach. In this connection the following remarks by the well-known translator of classical works M. Lozinsky are most relevant: "If Sheridan's dialogue is not to sound strange to us, it must be conveyed by the devices of the literary language of our day ... If the *shades of the real Russian speech* are correctly imposed on the *stylistic pattern of the original* [My italics.–L.D.] they will recreate both the spirit of the age and the atmosphere of the environment which Sheridan depicted. And then that bygone age will come to life before us and shine like the present day."

These words are a remarkably fitting description of the creative method of Prokofiev the librettist and composer. He was one of the first in our country to take Sheridan's *Duenna* and make it accessible to modern audiences. In writing a libretto based on the English original, Prokofiev also performed the function of a translator. His translation of *The Duenna* was made at a time when only manuscript texts were available in our theatres. The play was not published in M. Lozinsky's translation until considerably later.

The archive materials on the libretto of *The Duenna* enable us to reconstruct the process of the composer's work. They consist of sketches for the plan of the scenario, fragments of the libretto, passages from the play translated in the margins of a typewritten copy of the English text of *The Duenna* and, finally, the composer's manuscript of the libretto completed on May 27, 1940, and the general plan of the opera which preceded the writing of the score.

* * *

The first stage in the work on *The Duenna* was to draw up a plan of the scenario based on Sheridan's comedy. The preliminary plan of the opera was as follows:

II—*Louisa and the Duenna*
III—*as scene 5* (meaning scene 5 of Sheridan's play).
IV—*as the beginning of Act II* (added in pencil: "*Mendoza with Don Jerome and the Duenna*").
V—*as scene 4, Act II to the end* (in pencil: "*Antonio meets Louisa at Mendoza's house*").
VI—*Jerome reads the letters*.
VII—*Mendoza meets Ferdinand* (this scene was subsequently omitted).
VIII—*A nunnery*.
IX—*Monks*.
X—*At Jerome's house*.

From this plan the following correspondence of scenes emerges:

Libretto	Play	
Scene II corresponds to	scenes III and IV of	Act 1
III	scene V	Act 1
IV	scenes I, II and III	Act 2
V	scene IV	Act 2
VI	scene I	Act 3
VII	scene II	Act 3
VIII	scene III	Act 3
IX	scenes V, VI	Act 3
X	scene VII	Act 3

Prokofiev frequently returned to the original plan of the opera, as can be seen from the notes in different ink and pencil.

Thus, having rearranged scenes from Sheridan's play into scenes for the opera, he then explained their content (see scenes III, IV, and V). A number of additions and explanations concerning the musical drama of the acts were then inserted in the plan of the scenario. The composer wrote by scene III: *"A Market. Fish. Fish! The best fish of Mendoza's barge fromGuadalbullon.... Mendoza and Carlos (Mendoza is happy, trade is doing well). Carlos is fastidious and affected."* Another comment was made there at a different time: *"Mendoza meets Louisa. Returns at the end: Fish! Fish!"* Thus even at the initial stage of planning the libretto there are references to the setting of the action, an outline of its content and of the general structure of the act, and a short but expressive description of the moods of the dramatis personae.

Prokofiev's method of writing the scenario plan is typical of him. He records briefly and precisely the elements which are most important for a given scene. His notes on various scenes show that he had a clear idea of the scenic embodiment of the play. In striving to give the acts a clear and dynamic structure, he also tried to expand the importance of the musical numbers. Thus, the directions for scene five are essential for its musical drama: *"eavesdropping to the theme of abduction"*; scene seven—*"choir 'Mendoza is off to get married' at the beginning, the end and in the middle"*; and scene ten—*"aria with playing on glasses?"*. In this very first outline of the scenario we find the idea for the original musical treatment of scene six—one of the most interesting in terms of treatment. There is the following faint note in pencil: *"duet Fl+trba+servant on..."* (illegible).

As well as the above-mentioned plan for the scenario of the whole opera there are separate sheets giving the libretto for a number of episodes from the play. These are obviously preliminary sketches of the scenes which fired Prokofiev's imagination most of all (I, II, and IX—scene VIII in the final version).

In the margins of the typewritten copy of the English text of *The Duenna* Prokofiev made a translation of scenes which interested him, in the form in which they were included in the libretto. The texts in verse were polished by M. Mendelson, and most of them rearranged in metric schemes provided by the composer.

107

* * *

The act to be changed most was the first, expositional one. The first three scenes written by Prokofiev introduced the events which in Sheridan's play are understood as having happened before the curtain rises. In the opera they take one straight into the plot and add a vital emotional "charge" to the action. In showing the deal between Jerome and Mendoza, Prokofiev combines the beginning of the plot with the exposition of the main characters.

From the first phrase of the libretto Prokofiev seeks for an original "key" to the creation of a vivid, dynamic opera.

This phrase is Jerome's words: *"But that is a chimera! Quite incredible!"* They both describe the events taking place on the stage and create a definite atmosphere for the action. Jerome's exclamation produces a similar attitude to the character of Mendoza and his plans. By opening the scene in the middle of the conversation, as it were, Prokofiev makes it extremely lively.

Mendoza is given a concrete occupation: he is a fish-seller. This makes it possible to use some everyday elements in the musical drama of the opera. Thus, in the first scene Jerome and Mendoza sing a song about fish. It expresses their mutual interest and gives musical reinforcement to the agreement they have reached. In this sense the theme of the song is repeated several times in the opera.

In the second scene considerable attention is paid to the inner state of the characters. Prokofiev describes this as follows: *"Mendoza walks up and down in rapture and excitement. Jerome regards him critically. A few caustic remarks. He consoles himself"* (pencilled addition: *"a quiet husband, there are too many young rascals hanging round his daughter"*.)

The emotional background or "undercurrent" of the events requires musical generalisation in orchestral themes. And the role of the instrumental element increases considerably in the second scene. For example the theme connected with Mendoza's proud, sprightly gait becomes one of its main leitmotivs (No. 15).

At the same time the development of the external action continues: *"Mendoza has not yet seen the daughter. Jerome describes her like a piece of goods. He is interrupted by Mendoza's exclamations: oh, ah, oo! Mendoza describes the fish interrupted by Jerome's exclamations: oh, ah, oo!"* (insert: *"Mendoza: Carlos! (Runs in)—at your service, Señor.—No, Pedro! —points to a fish, gives it to Jerome. Second time: Pedro! —at your service, Señor.—No, Carlos! They go out"*). This scene, composed entirely by the librettist, fits in perfectly with the music. The similarity in the reconstruction of the two descriptions—about the daughter and about the fish—constitutes its inner unity. The musically generalised images are in the middle of the scene. By supplementing both arioso descriptions with the "impassioned" sighs of the listener, Prokofiev retains the comic atmosphere. The appearance of the servants adds scenic mobility to the action and enlivens its intimate nature.

The third scene is the gradual fall, abatement, of the first stage of the development of the plot. The meeting of the two friends ends comically in the amusing episode of the lobster bite. The emotional charge which was provided by Jerome's opening words is dispersed in the slow tempo. But there is no full, "complete" cadence. Just when it seems as if the action should stop, be exhausted, Ferdinand and Lopez appear. Their remarks add some more touches to the picture of Mendoza, and at the same time a new level of action arises—the lyrical one. A dramatic effect which is known in music as the "intruding cadence" is produced: two different phenomena are combined simultaneously, the end of one coinciding with the beginning of the other. The exposition of the comic characters ends as the exposition of the lyrical ones begins.

The sense of the sudden, and therefore active, dynamic intrusion of the emotional sphere is produced by Ferdinand's pathetic aria which is not prepared by the plot or the situation. It begins with the words: "Oh, Clara, Clara, how pitilessly you have stolen my peace," borrowed from the dialogue of Ferdinand and Lopez in scene two of Sheridan's play. The draft libretto for this scene contains the following note by Prokofiev: *"fewer colourful recitatives, combine in numbers."* The need for musical generalisation of the lyrical state of the hero suggested the introduction of a well-rounded number. However, Prokofiev rejects the text of the aria which Sheridan gave to this character, and creates a new musical-dramatic form in keeping with his own operatic ideals. Not only is the character of Ferdinand revealed more vividly and originally in the dialogue with Lopez, but the remarks of the servant, who comments on the sufferings of his young master, form an interesting counterpoint which reinforces the dynamism of the lyrical arioso. In such forms Prokofiev borrows from the Mozart tradition of arias and ensembles, "interlaid with conversation scenes". Prokofiev combines these two elements, the recitative scenes appearing *within* the aria.

Unlike the drama of action of comic characters, whose features are unfolded gradually, Prokofiev makes use of the drama of *mood* to show his lyrical characters, which demands more generalised expression, sweeping brushwork. These characters are by nature more static, their emotional "portrait" remains almost unchanged throughout the opera from the moment they appear on the stage. However, in addition to the common dramatic basis of the lyrical characters, Prokofiev applies different devices of musical characterisation. Ferdinand's rapturous pathetic aria (No. 31) and Antonio's serenade (No. 40) provide a sharp contrast to the romance-arioso and song elements, making the characters more vividly individual.

In using a genre number, the serenade, to convey the musical portrait of Antonio, the composer skilfully dynamises its form and achieves a continuous development of the action. The serenade is interrupted by the sudden appearance of the masks, then turns into a duet between Louisa and Antonio, and is later drowned by the angry exclamations of the awakened Jerome. All these devices were borrowed from the corresponding scene in Sheridan's play, but Prokofiev did not content himself with them alone. He plays up scenically and musically that which is contained in Jerome's threats. The scenario reads: "*Serenade. Musket. Catch him! Fire! Round-up! Antonio runs away.*" The last words, which were added by the librettist, give a picture of the pandemonium at Jerome's house.

Prokofiev produced several versions for the end of scene one. The first was as follows: "*perhaps it ends with Jerome's song (there is no worse misfortune). But now everything will be over. Mendoza... A quiet son-in-law ... fish ...*

> *ducats ... fish*
> *fish ... ducats*
> *ducats ... fish*
> *fish ... fish*
> *Curtain.*"

The following entry was made in different ink: "*Or Jerome sings "there is no worse plague than" against the background of a ballet of masks which pester him. Jerome breaks off the song*

with the words *"leave me alone"*. There is the pencilled addi-
tion: *"Oh, stop your tricks,*
    Quite out of place."
And yet another note in pencil: *"or it ends with a night ballet.
Masks? Masks interrupted Antonio before as well?"* At the
bottom of the page in small writing: *"it ends poetically with
Celli soli on the stage and V-ni with V-le soli."*

Later this afterthought was developed as follows: *"The masks
disperse. The strains of a cello are heard in the distance, in the
wings. It is quite dark. New masks appear. They are visible
almost only in silhouette and dance silently."* The score creates
the effect of a gradually disappearing carnival. The sound
of the solo instruments fades away slowly, dissolving
into the velvet quietness of the night (No. 107).

The idea of a night carnival was obviously connected with
Sheridan's stage direction in scene one: "Enter Don Antonio
with masks and musicians" [My italics—L.D.]. Prokofiev develops this episode. The masks which accompanied Antonio are
turned into participants in a night ballet. The extended
portrayal of the setting of the action supplements the exposition of the main characters. The fascinating, colourful picture
of Seville at night enhances the poetry and lyricism of the
subject. The carnival scenes and Antonio's serenade are some of
the most important Spanish touches in the opera and give it an
interesting national flavour. They seem to revive popular
theatrical traditions, in particular Italian masked comedy which
was usually put on at carnival time.

In Prokofiev's libretto this scene rounds off the exposition of
the characters. Most typical of the composer with his fear of
"scenic immobility" are the remarks that *"masks interrupted* Antonio before as well" or "Jerome *sings* ... against
the background of a ballet of masks which *pester* him"
[My italics—L.D.]. Thus the ballet in masks is an organic
part of the development of the action and not a separate
divertissement.

All three versions of the end of the scene were included in
the libretto in the following order: Jerome sings an aria against
the background of a ballet in masks (scene 5), then follows
Jerome's monologue: "find her a husband quickly, marry her
off to Mendoza" (scene 7) and everything ends gradually with
the subsiding night carnival (scene 8).

The *second scene* to a certain extent supplements the first, expositional one. It gives a detailed picture of Louisa and the Duenna. The changes introduced in the libretto mainly concern devices for introducing this or that situation. For the most part Prokofiev develops the principles followed in his work on Act I: the characters are more sharply contrasted (the conspiracy between Louisa and the Duenna), events which were understood as taking place behind the scenes in the original are shown on stage in the opera (the scene with Antonio's letter). But one also finds a new tendency of great importance for the opera: the striving for a more emotional portrayal of individual episodes. To this end the narrative is transferred from one character to another who is directly involved in the given situation. This is the case in scene 1. Prokofiev makes it Louisa who tells the Duenna about Jerome's intention to marry his daughter to the old fish-seller Mendoza. Her account shows clearly her dislike of Mendoza and her reluctance to submit to her father's will (No. 113).

Louisa's feelings for Antonio are revealed in an arioso composed, as it were, of short, abrupt thoughts "to herself". Here too Prokofiev rejects Sheridan's verse and bases the musical image of Louisa on her dialogue with the Duenna. This dramatic device, noted above in Ferdinand's aria, enables the composer to depict the character more clearly and convey all the shades of Louisa's mood and delightful spontaneity.

The character of the Duenna is deliberately made coarser in the libretto, enhancing the contrast between the naive remarks of the young girl and the down-to-earth views of the servant. The Duenna's comments on Louisa's timid admissions produce the two levels of action characteristic of this opera.

The second episode of scene two is most interesting example of the way in which Prokofiev makes the textual material increasingly more dynamic. It is revealing to compare Jerome's monologue in Sheridan's play with the libretto of the opera.

In the play Jerome's speeches to his children are of an edifying nature. In the libretto, however, he is full of indignation and anger. "*Splendid, Señor, splendid: you sing serenades at night, at the same time as other windbags are serenading under my window. They howl, howl, like a dozen dogs or cats, and stop me from sleeping. Of course, you will marry Mendoza, Louisa.*'

The repetition in the following passage of the libretto of the same turns of phrase and the insistent question "what else?" intensifies the emotional "explosiveness" of the scene. Jerome's irritation has reached its limit. His remark: "No objections" provokes a new stream of arguments from Ferdinand, creating a tenser atmosphere than in the play.

The opera gives a lengthy portrayal of the argument between Jerome and the Duenna, which developed from Ferdinand's remark: "What is all that commotion? It is my father battling with the Duenna." In the opera the "battle" takes place right on the stage and the music conveys the yells of the participants (No. 149). Jerome's parody in reading the letter strengthens the comic element.

* * *

Scene three of the opera is based on two meetings: of Louisa and Clara, and Louisa and Mendoza. In working on the libretto of this act Prokofiev tried to find a unifying element which would ensure the organic integrity of the action, its balanced architectonics. Mendoza's occupation suggested an interesting scene from everyday life: the market place and the selling of fish. Against this background the character of Mendoza stands out in greater relief.

Gorky once said that it is not the business of the dramatist "to highlight the mood of a character by a description of nature, of the setting." This law does not apply to the opera. It is sometimes expedient to use musical devices to create the setting for the action, thereby encouraging the audience to respond in a certain way to the feelings of a character (the dawn in the scene of Tatiana's letter, thunderstorms in operas, etc.). In the case in question the choir of women fish-sellers creates the environment most typical for Mendoza (No. 173).

The social portrait of Mendoza is made more profound in his talk with Carlos which takes place against the background of the choir. In Sheridan's play the corresponding scene is limited to an exchange of remarks on Mendoza's appearance. Prokofiev adds to the text, sharpening the contrasting views and characters of the main protagonists.

Carlos: "Ah, dear Mendoza, what are they selling? Fish! If only it were weapons, gems or rings! ..."

Mendoza: "You see fish, I see ducats."

Carlos' high "ideals" merely highlight the primitive nature of Mendoza, who desires wealth at all costs.

Prokofiev originally wanted to replace the quixotic Carlos by a very old nurse who fusses around Mendoza, addressing him with the words "Oh, my little one." Having rejected this idea, Prokofiev returned to the historically authentic type of the "noble" dependant on the vain fishmonger. The contrast of these two characters produces a number of comic situations which serve the main plot well.

The changes made in the scene of the meeting between the two fleeing women are also of interest. While retaining their dialogue almost entirely, Prokofiev adds a short duet-tongue-twister:

You ran away?
And you ran away?
And I ran away,
And I ran away,
She ran away,
Yes, yes, yes, she ran away.
We ran away,
We both ran away,
We both,
We both,
Both,
(together) Both.

This duet enhances the comedy of the situation laconically and vividly by the frequent repetition of the word "ran".

The most vivid elements of the musical generalisation are connected with the exposition of two new characters—Clara and Carlos. Their arias are the self-contained forms which create the key points of the musical drama. It is no accident that they are placed symmetrically in the act: Clara's aria constitutes the third scene and Carlos' the sixth. They seem to combine all the individual melodic elements of the preceding scenes. Clara's aria exists in Sheridan's play too. M. Mendelson's free translation of it, made at the composer's request, acquired rondo-like features. This form was suited to the poetic content of the girl's story, in which her feelings are accentuated by the background of Seville at night.

Carlos' canzonet combines elements from his aria in scene 5 of Act I in the play—about his selfless devotion to Louisa—and scene 4 of Act II—about his faithless beloved. The nobility of his feelings is given expression in the form of an old romance.

The finale of the act, which was added by Prokofiev in place of the final trio, is extremely successful. The dialogue between Louisa and Carlos takes place against the background of the choir of women fish-sellers. True to his principles of making the opera form more dynamic, Prokofiev simultaneously combines both levels of the action. Louisa and Carlos differ in their attitude to the voices of the fish-sellers. With her typical archness Louisa tries to expose Carlos, who has just revealed his chivalrous soul to her. Carlos pretends not to notice the baseness of their surroundings and does his best to distract Louisa.

* * *

Scene four of the opera also contains a number of important changes dictated by the specific nature of musical drama. Prokofiev conveys only the main idea behind the lengthy dialogue between Jerome and Mendoza on Clara's flight: ridicule of the unfortunate father who has allowed his daughter to run away. The subsequent events in the opera are also portrayed with greater dynamism. In Sheridan's play it is Jerome, not wishing to see his obstinate daughter, who leaves Mendoza alone with the Duenna disguised as Louisa. To make the action livelier Prokofiev brings on a servant girl who announces several times that Louisa will only come to her suitor after her father has departed. Jerome's description of Louisa's charms provides an excellent background for Mendoza's growing restlessness. The waiting becomes more and more tense. A kind of prolonged emotional build-up is created, which is followed by a breakdown instead of a culmination. The events develop with lightning speed. The librettist selects the following main psychological points from scene 2, the meeting of Mendoza and the Duenna:

1) mutual embarrassment, fear of being the first to reveal oneself,

2) Mendoza's horror at the Duenna's appearance,

3) the Duenna takes the initiative and wins over Mendoza.

The condensed translation of the scene which was included in the libretto follows this outline. Naturally in condensing the dialogue Prokofiev had to make it as vivid and expressive as possible. In this respect the words of the emboldened Mendoza to the Duenna were most effective: "*Oh, let me gaze upon thy dimple.*" Inflamed by Jerome's description: he is struck dumb at the sight of his betrothed's face. Taking advantage of Mendoza's confusion, the Duenna quickly assumes the offensive. Her melodic arioso about her betrothed's comely appearance constitutes a turning point in the action. Mendoza begins to listen to her flattering words. The situation is enhanced by the Duenna's song: "When around a silly young girl." Prokofiev, who avoided the inclusion of Sheridan's verse in the opera, made a note on the play at this point: "*sings, perhaps?*" and further on "*then Mendoza finally makes a proposal just after 'I cannot help it, I must steal her away' *" (the whole text of the play after the song up to these words is crossed out). In the final version of the libretto the song is followed immediately by Mendoza's words: "*Let us go and fall at your father's feet.*" During the Duenna's song Mendoza reaches his final decision which he is ready to act upon.

The end of the scene—the abduction plan—was added by Prokofiev to develop the "romantic" element and the portrayal of the comic characters in a lyrical light.

In the draft libretto Prokofiev summarises the changes in the play: "*1) short, 2) Carlos does not appear, 3) the Duenna goes off, 4) Jerome enters and on p. 12 (Jerome appears with champagne).*"

To concentrate the action Prokofiev omits the episode with Carlos' song of praise. He did not want to divert attention from the development of the plot—the Duenna-Mendoza-Jerome—which is central to this act. For the same reason Ferdinand is not brought on to the stage at the end. The act ends as follows in the libretto:

"*Jerome: Charming, yes, yes, yes (opens the bottle noisily). Short song. Curtain.*" Below there is a note: "*Perhaps Ferdinand enters during the song.*" But this idea was not realised. The song of Jerome and Mendoza, which is borrowed from the text of the play, their "brindisi", as it were, completes the fourth scene, giving musical generalisation to a new stage in their relationship (No. 266).

* * *

In *scene five* of the opera the lyrical element is made much stronger than in the play. This is assisted even by the apparently insignificant rearrangement of sentences in Louisa's part. In the play the action begins with the girl's complaint about the strange circumstances of her flight, which is followed by her song about time passing so slowly now that she is parted from her beloved. Prokofiev combines these two poetic images in Louisa's arioso, which begins: *"Ah, time will not move, it seems to be hanging in space."* This phrase immediately creates a certain mood which is enhanced by the quiet evening and Antonio's restless waiting (No. 270).

In the same scene Prokofiev omits Carlos' song about his faithless beloved, the words of which have been already used in part in the canzonet of Act III. The song is replaced by an arioso about the quick passing of time. Thus we have in poetic form the contrast between youth and old age with their different attitudes towards life around them.

The comic episode of the eavesdropping is most effective in this scene. Prokofiev expanded it to develop the theme of the young people's love in the music. This treatment of the scene suggested itself right at the initial stage of his plan for the opera. Prokofiev's note in the draft scenario: *"eavesdropping to the theme of abduction"* is quoted above. By combining two levels of the action, that which is seen and that which takes place off-stage, Prokofiev fills it with conflicting emotions, making interesting use of polyphony.

The active nature of the situation is also supported by the conflicting emotions of Mendoza and Carlos. Whereas in Sheridan's play they share the same curiosity, in the opera libretto Carlos expresses indignation at Mendoza's "tactless" behaviour.

The insertion of the final ensemble is of great importance for enhancing the lyrical mood of the whole act. The corresponding male trio in the play expressed their mutual trust and friendship. Prokofiev introduces a "double" duet: Louisa and Antonio, and Mendoza and Carlos, thereby differentiating between the feelings of his characters. The young couple are happy in their love and full of bright hopes and dreams. Carlos laments the passing of youth. Mendoza looks forward to the abduction of his "beauty". In contrast to the dynamism of the preceding acts, a kind of bewitchment prevails here, a stability of mood shared by all the members of the ensemble (No. 304).

The fluid, plastic melody seems to soar over the even chords of the accompaniment. The bright, harmonic sound of the singing voices brings to mind the classical ensembles of Glinka,

Rimsky-Korsakov and Tchaikovsky. This is one of the lyrical points in the action which appeared in Prokofiev's operas as a result of the strengthening of the lyrical element in his later work. The culmination of the characters' exalted feelings is one of the opera's most poetic episodes.

* * *

Scene six, described in the scenario *"Jerome reads the letters",* presented considerable difficulties for the creation of the large-scale operatic form. Prokofiev showed great inventiveness in depicting the development of the plot against the background of a scene from everyday life: *"Don Jerome is playing music with two friends,"* the composer explains, *"this music-making is constantly interrupted by the course of the action, and Don Jerome, while playing his favourite minuet on the clarinet, gives his blessing to his daughter's marriage to Antonio, of whom he disapproves, instead of to the rich Mendoza, without realising what is happening."* The minuet, which is heard over and over again in the act, gives it an authentic everyday touch and enlivens the action. Making skilful use of the expressive potential of the music, Prokofiev sharpens the comic nature of the events on the stage (No. 311).

The draft libretto contains the following note in the margin of the typewritten copy of *The Duenna: "Jerome on the cl, a friend on the trumpet, a servant on a large drum. Pauses, mistakes. Finally Jerome himself makes a mistake."* Then follows the text of the scene. It contains precise directions as to when the trio plays and gives the rhythmic pattern of the drum.

It also contains such notes as *"g.c. (grand cassa) makes P a delicate, rhythmical roll"....* At the same time as this scene was translated into Russian, its "score" was also written.

The comic effect of the trio is achieved by the unusual combination of professional ensembles of the clarinet, the cornet-à-pistons and the drum. The "pauses and mistakes" also enhance the comic element. They indicate not only the players' lack of skill, but also Jerome's confusion after hearing the news of Louisa's flight.

The rondo-like structure of the scene, in which the music of minuet serves as a peculiar refrain, makes it architectonically well-balanced and lends it specific operatic scope.

The following scene—"*Mendoza meets Ferdinand*"—was subsequently omitted. Prokofiev wanted to continue the principle of giving the dialogue scenes a musico-genre framework. The scenario plan contains the note: "*Choir 'Mendoza is off to get married' at the beginning and at the end*", with a pencilled addition: "*and in the middle*". In the margin of the typewritten copy of Sheridan's comedy we find the words for the choir and their arrangement in the text of the libretto. The choir was to comment on the events taking place, to philosophise, as it were, on behalf of the author.

Ferdinand's threats of "Think quickly" are followed by individual remarks by members of the choir.

The idea of introducing a choir into the text belongs to Prokofiev and was undoubtedly connected with his search for a musical generalisation of the scene in question.

Prokofiev rejected this scene, however, in the final version of the libretto. Involving minor characters, it would have diverted attention from the development of the main plot by occupying too large a place in the opera.

* * *

Prokofiev regarded *scene seven* as the most lyrical one. It concerns the fate of the young lovers: Louisa and Antonio and Clara and Ferdinand. Making very few changes in Sheridan's text, Prokofiev expands some of the situations by introducing rounded musical numbers of a lyrical nature. These are the duet between Louisa and Antonio and Clara's aria and arioso.

Clara's words added by the librettist at the beginning of scene one are worthy of note: "*And here am I, a nun, roaming in this large, silent, overgrown garden. I hail, thee, dumb cloister, a prison for the saintly, a grave for love.*"

The setting of the action, a deserted nunnery, is described in a few brief but expressive touches. Against this background the emotions of the young lovers become more vivid and significant, their passion contrasting strongly with the joyless, monotonous life of the nuns.

The musical generalisation of the happiness and joy of Louisa and Antonio is conveyed in their love duet. Prokofiev inserts it in place of Antonio's couplet song in the play. The words of the duet, which was rewritten, develop the following idea in Sheridan's text: "Here they come, happy in the love which they have confessed to each other."

The phrase "I am doomed to solitude", borrowed from the play, serves as the basis for Clara's scene on her own. The librettist reveals her state of mind in a three-part aria, an interesting poetic culmination of the character: *"Ne'er thought I that it would be my fate to end my days here, in this quiet cloister, amid silent nuns. But if I have lost Ferdinand, if he really does not love me, why live upon this earth, what is the world and worldly joys to me? In this dungeon of the saintly, in this grave for love I shall bury forever my hopes and dreams all that life promised me"* (No. 370).

The appearance of Ferdinand dispels Clara's melancholy. The new gamma of her emotions—now rapturous and joyful—is conveyed in the arioso: *"My Ferdinand, are you so jealous? My dear, my beloved! I am angry no longer, I am all yours, I am everywhere wherever you are. And perhaps it will not be Louisa alone whom a wedding unites with her beloved."* This text replaced the song in which Clara bade farewell to the nunnery which had sheltered her for a while. Prokofiev makes it possible for the heroine to reveal the full force of her emotions. At the same time he has found a more interesting framework for the opera. The nuns appear in the background. Their mournful singing throws the passions of the young lovers into even greater relief.

* * *

Scene eight of the opera contains a biting satire on the hypocrisy and sanctimoniousness of the priesthood. Prokofiev frequently returned to this act with ideas for its embodiment on the musical stage. The archives contain several sketches for it. One of the first drafts consisted of an account of the contents and notes on the musical treatment: *"After Bacchic songs the monks come out to the suppliants, singing psalms."* Prokofiev gave detailed thought to the contrasting of these two elements. On the second sheet of the draft we read: *"2 starts singing 'the sun' (Brother Elustaph, tenor). P(ablo)—Quiet, brother! —The others strike up a song of abstinence, 2 continues as before, breaking off with 'what are they singing? ', play up.*" The same idea is developed in the margins of the typewritten copy: "*When they change from the song to the psalm one drunken monk does not realise, until he is led off (moment for counterpoint).*" There was no similar situation in Sheridan's play, it was suggested by Prokofiev's feeling for the stage. The musical contrast between the song and the psalm creates a sharp distinction between the monks' real character and their hypocritical pretence. The text of the Bacchic song is borrowed from the play. It is used in the libretto as a refrain which provides a framework for the dialogue scenes. By condensing the latter, Prokofiev makes the individual exchanges remarkably sharp and lively.

In the episode of the arrival of the suppliants Prokofiev omits the minor figure of the door-keeper and concentrates attention on the song of fasting and abstinence which the monks are droning. Only the irrepressible Elustaph continues to sing about the gaily revolving world. The melodic ostinato, one of the composer's favourite devices, imparts a special "devoutness" to the merry monk. The counterpoint of these two elements—hypocritic pretence and drunken ecstasy—makes this a vivid, brilliantly witty scene.

The singing of the psalms is heard by Mendoza and Antonio who have arrived at the monastery and throws them into confusion. The drafts contain the note: "Antonio and Mendoza are most confused, and do not know what to do." And below as a footnote:

"Monk. *My son ...*
Antonio. *My father ...* } *bis, bis*
Antonio. *I don't know how to begin*

This episode is absent in the play. In the opera it enhances the comedy of the situation, taking place against the background of the song of abstinence.

Mendoza is the one who decides how to deal with the situation, although in Sheridan's play it is Antonio who takes the initiative. His replacement in the libretto by Mendoza is obviously explained by the desire to use the theme of the "enterprising" Mendoza (No. 421). In one of the first drafts this scene contains the pencilled note: "*the cunning lad*". These words correspond to the above-mentioned theme.

The scene of the betrothal is more poetic in the opera than in the play. Witbout adding to the text, Prokofiev includes in this scene the main themes of the lyrical characters. The required emotional effect is achieved here with purely musical devices.

* * *

A lively kaleidoscope of characters and events appears in scene nine. It contains the denouement, the apotheosis of happy, joyful feelings.

Prokofiev strives for an organic connection between the finale and the preceding acts, a kind of synthesis of the opera's main musical themes. This is felt in the very first scene.

Two elements introduced into the libretto are of interest: Jerome's dismay and confusion caused by the absence of his children, and the reference to his "favourite minuet". Both these additions make possible the musical associations which form the dramatic basis of the finale. The music of the minuet anticipates the appearance of the betrothed couples, recalling, as it were, the confusion during Jerome's amateur music-making. Musical themes from the preceding acts take the place of lengthy dialogues. In the opera there is no need to explain in detail how the Duenna became Mendoza's wife or Louisa was betrothed to her lover. By reproducing the relevant musical images, the composer reminds us of how everything took place. It is no accident that all the themes used in the finale are marked in his manuscript copy of the libretto. Thus, in the episode when the Duenna appears there is a note: "*like the Duenna's exit in scene four*" (her first appearance disguised as Louisa); the Duenna's words "my dear husband, you carried me away from home yourself" are accompanied by the explanation: "*to her song*" (from the scene of the "abduction" in scene four). At the moment when Louisa and Antonio, Clara and Ferdinand appear before the perplexed Jerome, the orchestra strikes up their main themes.

The rapid succession of events is frequently interrupted by the appearance of a servant who announces the arrival of the guests. This original refrain in the stage action adds to the sense of festive commotion which prevails in Jerome's house. The servant's announcements come at regular intervals in the succession of scenes and episodes. This is illustrated clearly in Prokofiev's plan:

Jerome cannot understand what has happened

Lopez' first announcement and the conversation about Ferdi-
nand
Mendoza 1) alone
2) the Duenna
3) the Duenna embraces Jerome
(minuet off-stage)
4) Lopez and servants
Minuet; enter Louisa and Antonio
Lopez' second announcement
Scene 1) Louisa—Jerome
2) Jerome—Mendoza
3) Mendoza—the Duenna
Lopez' third announcement
Antonio and Louisa: the cunning lad
Ferdinand and Clara
Mendoza—the Duenna: 1) Mendoza—the Duenna
2) The very cunning lad
3) Mendoza goes off in a fury
Jerome gives his blessing: 1) I don't understand anything (minuet)
2) Father, bless us
3) Ponders, gives his blessing
Guests rush in
Joy of the lovers
Aria with glasses
Choir and ballet

This turbulent stream of life does not stop for a minute. The universal joy and merriment find expression in the choir which corresponds to the final couplets of the play (No. 478). Don Jerome sings an aria accompanied by playing on glasses. This is another example of Prokofiev's brilliant inventiveness: the special ring of these unusual instruments enhances the festive quality of the finale even more.

* * *

Thus, most of the changes inserted in the text of the libretto are connected with the specific musical features of the operatic genre, and, above all, with the features of Prokofiev's operatic dramaturgy. The composer's striving for vivid dynamism, fast-moving action, is felt in all the acts. It shows itself, particularly, in the way in which indirect action is turned into direct action:

123

events which are described by the characters in the play are shown directly in the opera. Thus, the composer gives original treatment to the exposition of the characters of Jerome and Mendoza, the scene of the quarrel between Jerome and the Duenna, and a number of less important episodes. The dynamic progression of the events demanded a more active presentation of the text, greater sharpness of individual exchanges and dialogues. In this connection, the abbreviations and changes made in the scene of the quarrel between Jerome, Louisa and Ferdinand, the scene in which Mendoza proposes to the Duenna, and the dialogue scenes in the monastery are most illuminating. The aphoristic nature and apt expressions of Prokofiev's libretto are equalled by the vivid characterisation of his musical images.

The method of combining different levels of action is widespread in Prokofiev's operatic works. It helps to give a comprehensive picture of life and also enlivens the musico-scenic forms. There is a most interesting combination of comic and lyrical elements in the eavesdropping scene in scene five. It appears in a less developed form in the scene with Ferdinand and Lopez, Louisa and the Duenna.

No less important for Prokofiev's drama is the principle of heightening contrasts. This is found in the contrasting of the characters of Mendoza and Jerome, Antonio and Ferdinand, Louisa and the Duenna, and Mendoza and Carlos. The strict differentiation between the individual qualities of these characters in the text of the libretto makes their musical portraits more expressive. Thus, in Antonio and Ferdinand we have the song and arioso elements respectively, and in Mendoza and Carlos the short recitative and the old romance.

The expansion of the genre element in the opera is striking. Prokofiev was always attracted by the concrete, the sharply characteristic. But to my mind in the scene of the night carnival and the scene of the market place we find, above all, the influence of the full-blooded everyday episodes from the ballet *Romeo and Juliet*. The "Shakespearean" element enriches the content of the opera, giving it new features of authentic, everyday life. The poetic images of the play become more vivid, its emotional content richer, and Mendoza and the other characters are shown in greater relief. Genre-generalising elements acquire more significance in the musical dramaturgy of the opera. Both the choir of fish-sellers and the minuet play a kind of cementing role in the development of the plot, uniting the individual episodes into large operatic forms.

The principle of selecting the verse texts and creating new forms of arias and ariosos is most revealing in the libretto. Prokofiev wrote: *"The structure of Sheridan's play, which contained many small songs, enabled me to make a whole series of complete, rounded numbers in it, without stopping the course of the action,—serenades, ariettas, duets, quartets and large ensembles."* However, of the twenty-seven verse texts in the play Prokofiev borrowed only six. He made use of those verses of Sheridan's which expressed the most essential features of the character in question. Of Antonio's various songs Prokofiev chose one—the serenade, turning it into a musical portrait of the hero. The libretto also retained some songs which highlighted a particular situation, for example, the Duenna's song, the brindisi of Jerome and Mendoza, the choir of monks, and the final choir. In all other cases self-contained, rounded numbers were composed *based on* Sheridan, their subject motivs being given a new form. Thus, we have Ferdinand's arioso, Carlos' canzonet, and Clara's aria in scene seven. Prokofiev changed the structure of the self-contained numbers to suit the musical plan of the opera. For everything that Prokofiev did bears the mark of his original creative personality, his great, unique talent.

Vladimir Blok

PROKOFIEV'S MUSIC FOR CHILDREN

Children's Music and A Summer Day

Prokofiev wrote his first music for children in one of his favourite genres, that of piano miniatures. This was published as a collection of twelve easy pieces called *Children's Music*. Recalling his work on this cycle, the composer wrote: "In the summer of 1935, while working on *Romeo and Juliet* I also composed easy piano pieces for children which awakened my old love for sonatineness, developed, so it seemed to me, to the most 'childlike' form here. By the autumn I had a whole dozen of these pieces, which I later published under the general title of *Children's Music*."

For a clearer understanding of what the composer meant by the word sonatineness invented by him, let us cite some other statements of his: "Sonatinas always attracted me: I liked the idea of writing a very simple piece of music in such a superior form as the sonata." And this is what he wrote about his new sonatina from the cycle of Op. 59: "I managed to make this one-movement sonatina clearer and more sonatina-like than the two preceding ones." Obviously, what Prokofiev meant by sonatineness was a particularly clear exposition of musical thoughts, a relative simplicity, and, as a rule, a transparency of the piano-music texture.

Writing *Children's Music* was quite a challenge. Piano music for children has its rich and rather old traditions, and so it was not a simple thing to bring novelty into the genre. Prokofiev, it must be said, coped with the task he set himself brilliantly. He catched sensitively the intonations and images most appealing to children in the very breath of contemporary life, and herein, perhaps, lies the secret of this cycle's popularity which has lasted now for several generations.

126

The pieces included in the collection are grouped according to subject matter. There are the watercolour pieces *Morning, Evening, Rain and Rainbow*; the scenes of children's games *(March, Catchers)*; dance pieces *Waltz, Tarantella*, and the psychologically subtle renderings of children's emotions such as *Fairy-Tale* and *Remorse*.

It is an interesting point that all the twelve pieces have a clearly expressed three-part structure. This form, allowing for both contrast and reiteration in rendering the principal thoughts, contained in the work, made it easier for the young listeners and performers to appreciate the music intended for them.

The first two pieces in the cycle called *Morning* and *Stroll* have the same colouring and the same pastorale sweetness. *Morning* is bright with brief flashes of chords (that are like patches of sunlight), while the melody of *Stroll* has a measured, gentle flow.

The touchingly simple, plaintive melody of *Fairy-Tale* is remindful of a Russian *zhaleika* pipe tune expressively offset by the "supporting" polyphonic texture of the music. The melody brings back to mind Prokofiev's early piano pieces, such as *Old Granny's Tales* and *Fugitive Visions*, and an episode from the finale of the Second Piano Concerto. A development of Lyadov's attachment to the Russian legend or lay, is also undoubtedly traceable here.

Next comes the *Tarantella*. The music of the first and last parts is distinguished for the tautness of the rhythm and the impetuosity peculiar to the temperamental Italian dance.

The charming melody of the middle episode, full of gentle humour and smiles, presents a striking contrast, and yet all the time the pulse of the vigorous movement beats as steadily and energetically.

There is not a single authentic Italian melody in "Tarantella", and the national colour of the music has been recreated by Prokofiev with amazing artistic understanding.

Remorse—the fifth piece in the collection—is, for the most part, a psychological musical narrative, revealing the inner world of a child. An expressive declamation can be traced in the flowing melody.

The lovely *Waltz* with its captivatingly plastic melodic line was later used by Prokofiev in his ballet *The Tale of the Stone Flower* for the *Waltz of Diamonds*.

The second theme of *Waltz* is like a small ballet solo. The music is graceful, a bit capricious, and construed as an expressive monologue.

After this come *A Procession of Grasshoppers, Rain and Rainbow* and *Catchers*, forming a small triad within the *Children's Music*. Energetic bugle intonations prevail in the first piece—a miniature scherzo with the features of a march.

Rain and Rainbow is perceived as a small intermezzo and makes an interesting example of Prokofiev's colouristic sound recording.

The free flowing and sweeping melody (which really has something of the rainbow in it) calls to mind the lyrical pages of Prokofiev's *A Winter Bonfire* suite, written later.

Catchers seems to echo *Tarantella* in the character of the music, in the melodic pattern, and also in the texture of the composition. But the music of *Catchers* is still more volante: there is much humour, mischief, unexpected melodic turns and accents in it. In this respect *Catchers* also echoes *A Procession of Grasshoppers*.

In world and Russian classical music there are quite a few doll-and-toy marches (suffice it to recall Tchaikovsky's marches from his first symphonic suite and *The Nutcracker*). While developing these traditions, Prokofiev did not, of course, forfeit any traits of his own inimitable style. What is more, "Dollishness" is not a dominating feature of his music. In *March* the toy colouring (especially in the middle part) is ingeniously combined with a clever interpretation of a dashing song sung by soldiers on the march.

The cycle ends with two melodious pieces, of which *Evening* resembles a small poetic nocturne painted with delicate watercolours. Eventually, this piece was also used in *Tale of the Stone Flower* to become one of the musical characteristics of the heroine, Katerina.

The piece *The Moon Goes Over the Meadows* has an affinity to Russian round-dance songs in the purity of its melodic pattern and the serenity of its rhythms. "I wrote this piece not on a folk theme, but on a theme of my own," said Prokofiev. "At the time I was staying at Polenovo in a cottage with a balcony facing the Oka, and in the evenings I watched the new moon above the fields and meadows."

128

Studying the suite as a whole, we see that many parts of the cycle echo one another as it were in their imaginal content. Thus, the music of *Evening* with its soft, watercolour hues is close to *Morning* while both *Fairy-Tale* and *The Moon Goes Over the Meadows* very gently and tactfully guide the young listener into the magic world of Russian fairy-tales and folk songs. This echoing of the first and last parts of the cycle (the two first and the two last pieces) frames the work, as it were, with a double border. This compositional device is used not only in music, but in literature too—the author's foreword in a short story, the narrator's opening and concluding words in a *bylina* the prologue and epilogue in a play. In Prokofiev's suite this technique is connected with the content of the narrative which, in *Children's Music* is a generalised content, typifying the cycle as a whole. *Children's Music* can be regarded as a series of musical pictures illustrating a child's day, from morning till night.

As we have seen, the miniatures contained in the middle of the suite have a similar connecting bridge to link them. Such a consistently developed interconnection is not often encountered in music intended for children. And in young listeners and performers this particular feature of the suite cultivates a generalised artistic perception.

* * *

Children's Music did not immediately become a fixture in the concert or teaching repertoire. In large measure this was due to the conservatism of many teachers who were frightened off by the unusual intonations and the novelty of Prokofiev's harmonic idiom (in its day, the music of a genius like Moussorgsky was also not immediately accepted by some musicians who were inhibited by the canons of "classroom" harmony which they had diligently mastered). Other teachers disapproved of the violation of classroom piano-playing standards, or rather the established notion of it. (Opinions were voiced that *Tarantella* was too difficult, and *Catchers* was not suitable for the piano at all). The critics were not unanimous in their opinions either. While A. Isakov wrote that Prokofiev's pieces would "unquestionably enrich children's piano literature", K. Kuznetsov characterised this novel and original music as "drawing-room music".

But time confirmed the opinion of critics like A. Isakov. After all, it is the novelty of this music's melodic and harmonic language that in its very nature synchronises as it were with the artlessness and freshness of a child's perception of the world. The notions of what music is "convenient" and what is "awkward" to play are changing irreversibly with time. Teaching methods and practice have greatly advanced. Nowadays most of the pieces in Prokofiev's suite are played not by child prodigies but by ordinary boys and girls, and they are fond of the music and love rendering it.

Five years after publication of *Children's Music* Prokofiev arranged seven of the twelve pieces in it for a symphony orchestra of a very modest size. This arrangement received a new title. The composer was to say later: "The first part is called *Morning* and the part before last—*Evening*, while the suite as a whole is called *A Summer Day*." The new suite included *Morning, Catchers, Waltz, Remorse, March, Evening* and *The Moon Goes Over the Meadows*.

Orchestral colours lent a new freshness to this wonderful poetic music. But still it is much less popular than its original piano version. What can the reason be?

For one thing, a solo instrument version—even when the orchestration is superlative—very often takes less time to reach a large number of performers (it was thus with the piano score of the ballet *Romeo and Juliet* which captivated the hearts of listeners long before the ballet was staged). However, the point is not only in the difference of the techniques used.

For another thing, the orchestral variant of Prokofiev's cycle was clearly the poorer imaginally. Reducing the number of parts to seven, the composer made them more contrasting (with fewer parts the importance of each one in the cycle was enhanced). But in doing this, he dropped some parts which were no less impressive in their imagery than the ones which he kept in.

One can hardly agree with the opinion voiced by I. Nestyev in his book *Prokofiev* that the orchestration made the music "somewhat heavy". Rather the contrary—the score is very transparent and light, and in places the orchestra sounds most poetic. Yet, the orchestral colours might have been even more vivid and original. In this score one does feel too clearly that which L. Gakkel calls "the influence of piano-composing techniques on the manner of Prokofiev's orchestration." This influence, though not a constant one, is indeed one of the typical traits of Prokofiev's orchestral style. (The "reverse" influence on his piano composing style, especially in his later works, has been hardly investigated, but it is unquestionable nonetheless.) However, most of his orchestral compositions show only a general influence of his piano style, in a greater or lesser degree, and do not have any definite "piano score" predecessors.

It may be that being so accustomed to the piano rendering of *Children's Music* was something of a hindrance to Prokofiev in giving the familiar images a full-blooded orchestral expression.

Of course, in Prokofiev's orchestral music there are no few scores with a classically clear-cut pattern, sufficiently laconic and at the same time sparkling with colours. Such are, for example, his First ("Classical") and Fourth symphonies, his *Sinfonietta,* the symphonic suite based on the music for the film *Lieutenant Kizhe,* his *Pushkin Waltzes,* and the music for the plays *Eugene Onegin,* and *Boris Godunov.* Almost simultaneously with *Children's Music* Prokofiev produced a symphonic work addressed to children in which the finest qualities of his orchestral style were revealed in all their vividness and eloquence. This work was *Peter and the Wolf.* It stands on a par with the most outstanding compositions of the mature Prokofiev, and is considered one of the best symphonic works ever written for children.

In his autobiographical notes Prokofiev devotes a bit more space to *Peter and the Wolf* than he does to his *Children's Music*. He writes: "There was a big demand for children's music and in the spring of 1936 I started a symphonic tale for children entitled *Peter and the Wolf* Op. 67, to a text of my own. Every character has its own motif played each time by the same instrument: the duck was played by the oboe, the grandfather, by the bassoon, etc. Before each performance the instruments were shown to the children and the themes played for them; during the performance the children heard these themes repeated several times and learned to recognise the timbres of the different instruments. In this lay the educational purpose of the fairy-tale. The text was read during the pauses in the music which was disproportionately longer than the text,—for me the story was important only as a means of inducing the children to listen to the music. I composed the music quickly, approximately within one week, and another week was spent on the orchestration."

This fairy-tale has an interesting history. It came to the concert stage from the Central Children's Theatre for which it was, in fact, written. Apart from plays, the theatre also arranged concerts for children. At this point it is best to give the floor to Natalia Ilyinichna Satz.

"I've been thinking for a long time that new symphonies ought to be written for children. I wanted to start cultivating musical tastes in children from the first years of school, a love for and an understanding of music. To be sure, little children are more open to visual than auditory impressions, but still we could and had to find new methods of promoting our concert work on lines that would appeal to them. Our experience indicated various courses to follow. We had a cycle of concerts which enjoyed popularity and were called: 'Acquaintance with Musical Instruments'. I was also thinking that even the youngest children readily listened to songs—words combined with music.... What if, apart from the introduction, we had a text to accompany the music, supposing we had symphonic fairy-tales which would help children to make their first acquaintance with the musical instruments which comprise a symphony orchestra?

"I decided to get Prokofiev interested in this idea, and to see him as the author of the first such symphonic fairy-tale. I rang him up and asked if I could come over to talk about a most important matter. He heard me out very attentively, and then said: 'I like the concreteness with which you set forth your ideas.' Evidently, I did get him interested.... He called me up a few days later and said that he should like to see me as he had some thoughts to share about a symphony for children. He came to my place, and we sat talking till late, until the last tram, making up all sorts of plots—he with the help of music, and I with words. We came to the conclusion that images had to be found that would be easily associated with the sound of different instruments. The first one which occurred to me was the flute—a little bird. I said so and immediately regretted it, fearing Sergei Sergeyevich's reaction to the banality of my suggestion. But what he said was:

" 'A flute-bird we'll certainly have. It's quite all right for us to use the children's primitive concepts as well. The most important thing is for us to find a common language with them.'

"We decided that in a symphonic fairy-tale for the youngest listeners the images should be striking and utterly unlike one another in character.

" 'I think it's a good idea to have different animals and birds playing a part in the symphony, but there definitely must be at least one human being,' I said.

"Sergei Sergeyevich nodded in agreement, and said:

" 'If we cast one instrument for the "role" of each animal or bird, we'll have to have something like a string quartet to play the human being because, of course, there'll be more facets to his character.' Carried away, he continued: 'Yes, yes, we've got to begin with concrete, impressive and, above all else, contrasting images. A wolf—a bird, good—evil, big—small. Striking characters, pronounced and different musical timbres, and every character with a leitmotif of his own.'

"We wanted the plot to be thrilling and packed with events, otherwise children would not be able to concentrate and sit still for even the twenty or twenty-five minutes into which we meant to fit the whole fairy-tale.

"Four days later, Prokofiev brought the piano score of *Peter and the Wolf*. There was a gathering of children in the room next door, and I asked Sergei Sergeyevich to come there and play his newly-born composition. The children listened to it with unflagging attention. And at their request he had to play the concluding march three times."

At first it was planned to have the text in verse, and the theatre asked the poetess N. Sakonskaya to write it. Prokofiev, however, was not satisfied with the verses she produced. "There are too many rhymed words," he said. "In a work such as this the relations between words and music have to be very delicate, and words have to know their place. Words should help the listener to understand the music, but they can also divert him from it." That is why the composer decided to write the text himself. He coped with the task magnificently, producing a story that was exciting and witty. He was not a novice in writing, of course, as he had written the librettos (in co-authorship in some instances) for practically all his operas and ballets. The impressions of his own childhood were reflected (subconsciously perhaps) in the plot. In this connection, an excerpt from Prokofiev's autobiographical notes deserves to be cited:

"On New Year's Eve, my parents suddenly became mysterious, locked themselves up in the sitting room, saying that guests had come, and when they opened the door there were animal masks pinned to the backs of the armchairs—a bear, a parrot, a monkey.... And Mother said: 'This might give you some new ideas for your shows.'

"Some ideas did come to me after a time, and that summer I wrote four plays in which the toy animals given me were the main characters. The first of these plays was called *People*....The animals hold a conference in a deep, dark forest because a threat hangs over their lives—people have been sighted not far away. What should they do? Some propose putting up a resistance, some suggest hiding in the thickets. The donkey is stupid and arrogant, the pug-dog is pugnacious and hot-tempered, the monkey dodges the issue, and the parrot chatters without pause.... Passions run high, quarrels break out and while they are busy bickering the hunters appear. Shots ring out and the animals perish."

We can actually trace a connection between the two plots—between the little play written by Prokofiev when he was a young boy and his *Peter and the Wolf* (true, it isn't people now who threaten the lives of the animals, but the bad wolf who frightens Peter's grandfather, the cat and the duck). As a boy Prokofiev was at home in the world of children's ideas and notions, and as a mature artist he still preserved his access to this world and therefore the genuineness of his images.

There is no need to tell the plot of *Peter and the Wolf* which is sufficiently well known, and so we shall dwell on the music—its imagery, expressiveness, and structure.

The leitmotifs of the characters are very contrasting, but this, of course, does not simply mean the use of contrasting instruments (or groups of instruments). The contrast shows, above all, in the character of the musical themes and in the peculiarities of intonation.

Here is the theme of Peter with which the story begins. The bright and good-natured character of the melody calls to mind the pieces called *Morning* and *Stroll* from *Children's Music*. Played with a light touch by a string quartet to a measured, flowing accompaniment, the melody is like a softly wistled little song.

The "whistling" impression is even more tangible in the theme of the little bird, that is like a gay, miniature "etching". The chirping, flitting melody of the flute produces an ingenious effect in the top register which enhances the emotional expressiveness of the perky, joyous and carefree music.

Next comes another witty characterisation, and another great contrast. This is the musical characterisation of the waddling duck, comic in her self-importance. The melodic pattern of the theme is so plastic and expressive that the music itself seems to "waddle" clumsily along. The impression is enhanced by the specific timbre of the oboe playing in the low register.

In the theme of the cat, the feline softness of the melodic line accords with the seemingly artless, intentionally muted playing of the clarinet in the low register.

After the three "animal" melodies, the theme of the grandfather splendidly conveys the emotionality of human speech, and in the motifs repeated over and over again we hear the grumblings of an old man, parodied with kindly humour, whose scoldings are boring in their monotony.

The theme of the wolf is really "frightening" for children. But the wolf, besides being frightening, is also hungry, and his pitiful wailing is rendered with much humour.

The theme of the hunters is also written with a sense of humour. Firing all the time, they arrive when everything is over but the shouting, and the wolf has already been caught. In this episode the composer has displayed his very subtle feeling of genre. The theme of the hunters is perceived as a humorous parody of a dashing soldiers' march for brass band.

Allegro moderato ♩=116

For all the imaginativeness and vividness of the initial statement of the themes characterising the different characters, the expressiveness and musical dramaturgy of the fairy-tale are not confined to this exposition of the themes. The development of the images is most important, and the *transformation* of the musical themes also plays a very special role. This refers in particular to the theme of Peter, the "pivotal" melody.

In the first and as yet not very substantial transformation of the theme ("Peter attached no importance whatever to his grandfather's words, and said that Young Pioneers were not afraid of wolves") the melody does not change in outline, but it already sounds against a background of a more energetic, "throbbing" accompaniment. In another episode ("In the meantime, the Young Pioneer Peter who remained behind the locked gate and saw everything, was not a bit frightened") the theme assumes scope; the composer emphasises its melodic breadth, its songfulness, and the inner concentration of the musical thought. The theme developed in this manner seems to disclose the workings of main character's mind.

The transformations of the themes of the grandfather and the wolf are very amusing. In the first of these ("...Grandfather took Peter by the hand, brought him home, and locked the gate securely") the composer emphasises the tedious repetitiousness of the grumpy intonations. As for the theme of the wolf, in the concluding part where it has a march rhythm for an accompaniment it unexpectedly acquires the tragicomic character of a funeral procession:

137

Prokofiev also finds other interesting ways for developing the dramaturgy of this fascinating composition. A musical theme, for example, acquires an entirely new quality when a melody which we have been associating with one of the characters is used to describe someone else. There are two instances of this, and both will be found in the musical characterisation of the gay little bird. One, when it picks up Peter's theme, imitating him ("Peter said to the bird: 'Fly down and circle around the wolf's nose, only mind he doesn't gobble you up.' ")

Two, when it takes off the hunters ("Look at us and Peter! Look whom we caught! ")

The polyphonic combinations of the themes-characterisation are no less important in the development of the musical image

138

than the transformation of the themes and instances of shared melodies. In the polyphonic episodes the themes either collide (as in the argument between the duck and the little bird), or are placed in expressive juxtaposition (the grandfather and the cat in the concluding procession).

As we have seen, there is representative portrayal in the initial statements of the themes (of the little bird, the duck, the cat), and also in the episodes where the thematic patterns undergo a transformation (the cat scrambling up a tree, the duck waddling away, the little bird teasing the wolf). In other episodes representation is not connected with the changes in the main thematic patterns and plays a more independent part. Such, for example, is the episode where Peter, who has climbed a tree, drops down a rope with a noose at the end to catch the wolf; here, the melody seems to "dangle" like the rope in a continuous tremolo.

Only a composer endowed with a prolific sense of humour, a remarkable melodic plasticity, and an ability to feel the psychological reaction of the youngest listeners could have created such all but visible images.

After the first performances of *Peter and the Wolf* some critics spoke of an excessive sound-portraiture in this work. Georgy Polyanovsky wrote: "The principle of leitmotifs employed by the composer to characterise Peter, his grandfather, the duck, the cat, the little bird and the wolf by means of different instruments, is based on sound imitation.... In this way children easily recognise the characters in this musical fairy-tale and get an elementary idea of the timbre of this or that instrument in the orchestra. That is good. What is bad is that there are no genuinely artistic images in this fairy-tale."

More than thirty years have passed since the première of

Peter and the Wolf. And now that this wonderful fairy-tale has really conquered the world, such extreme of criticism has been nullified by life itself. There is hardly any need today to prove that the images in *Peter and the Wolf* are remarkably vivid and artistic. Needless to say, sound-portraiture is not an aim in itself here, nor is it a self-sufficient quality of the music. It is simply a means of giving the most graphic representation of the emotional essence of the music. We agree with what Natalia Satz says in her book *Children Come to the Theatre*: "Although the quacking of a duck and the howling of a wolf did sound in the music, this was not portraiture, which composers often resort to in writing music for cartoons, for instance, but a means of expressiveness which made the characters three-dimensional."

To be sure *Peter and the Wolf* was above all intended for children (and very little children), but the texture of its character development is not simple at all. Nor can we call the intonational idiom of this music the acme of simplicity. Still, because the music is melodically vivid, distinct in genre and clear-cut in pattern, it is well assimilated by children.

In this work Prokofiev often employs intonations and rhythms of the basic musical genres—the song, the dance, and the march, which, as Dmitry Kabalevsky calls them, are the three whales on which music rests. The song prevails in the first statement of Peter's theme, the dance—in the cat's, and the march in the hunters' theme. The transformations in the themes we have already spoken about sometimes also involve the genre—thus, the song quality of Peter's theme takes on the rhythm of a march in the concluding episode of the procession and is "scanned" with a ceremonial flourish.

The general structure of the symphonic fairy-tale is largely determined by the correlation of the text and the music. Almost everywhere the composer prefers to have the words and the music sound in turns and not simultaneously (among the rare exceptions there are the episodes of the duck arguing with the little bird, and the wolf chasing the duck). Children who grasp things well by ear would find the tale easier to assimilate this way. And Prokofiev must have been guided by this consideration. As we know from the recollections of N. Satz, referred to previously, and the statements of Prokofiev himself, his firm opinion was that in a work such as *Peter and the Wolf* the literary text had to play a supporting role.

The obvious novelty of Prokofiev's interpretation of the rela-

140

tion between word and music is that he carried this relation over from the customary sphere of vocal compositions to a symphonic work. The very "method" of having the literary text read out loud is novel, and has never been encountered in programme symphonic music before. Of course, Prokofiev's innovations produced such brilliant results because they were introduced with a competent knowledge of the mentality of children at that given age and of the associative character of their musical perception. Such a parallel development of images and dramatic action made the wonderful music of the tale all the more vivid and understandable. And, naturally enough, it was the children, uninhibited by any biases or mental inertia who gave the tale its most rousing reception.

Those critics who failed to appreciate the innovative handling of the dramaturgy could well envy the artistic sensitiveness of the children. One of them, A. Isakov, wrote about the literary text that "this introductory talk is superfluous, and by imposing some literary association upon the child at a given moment and deciphering every beat of the music for him leaves him no chance to perceive the music creatively and independently. There is no need to say how tendentious this attempt is and how unwarranted artistically."

Time has settled this argument too, and there is no need today to disprove such criticisms. As N. Satz says in her book: "It was not the music that had to illustrate the tale, but the tale had to teach children how to listen to music.... How well the composer succeeded in combining the concrete images and the fairy-tale plot with the continuous development of the musical idea!"

Important though it is, the alternation of the text and music is, naturally, not the only distinctive feature in the structure and dramaturgy of *Peter and the Wolf. Varying* and *reiterating* the themes are other, purely musical principles used here. Prokofiev employs variation enhancing the vividness of the imagery and occasionally also giving the initial theme a genre reinterpretation.

Variations are typical of practically all the themes, but mainly of that of Peter.

On the other hand, the very regularity with which Peter's theme in variations, alternating with other themes, recurs resembles the structural principle of the rondo. In some rondos there is, besides the "absolute" contrast between the refrain and the episodes, a derivative contrast engendered by a substantial transformation of the refrain when it repeats itself. The striking transformations of Peter's theme are a splendid example of such a contrast.

The transformations of Peter's theme and the importance they acquire in the cycle call back to mind the theme of *Stroll* which plays a similar role in Moussorgsky's *Pictures From an Exhibition*. But while in *Pictures From an Exhibition*, apart from them having elements of variations and a rondo-likeness, there is also a definite suite-like quality in the way the rather large parts are alternated, in the case of *Peter and the Wolf* it would, we believe, be a mistake to attribute such suite-like quality. The musical narrative here is too much of an integral whole and develops too dynamically for this comparison to apply. Offhand one might say that the fairy-tale is rather episodic because of the breaks in the music filled in by the textual interludes. But these breaks are of essential importance considering the psychology of the audience's age.

After all, the limitations of a child's artistic and auditive experience will not, as a rule, "allow him to focus his attention on a fast developing musical thought" (to quote V. Zak from his article "Prokofiev From the Beginning"). However, in the present case we should not equate the *structural* and *dramaturgical* continuity of development.

Of vast importance here is the coda which sums up, as it were all the wealth of the fairy-tale's imagery. The ceremonial procession in the finale (a marvellous dramaturgical find!) is constructed in such a way that all the characters pass before the audience once again.

This musical fairy-tale may be defined as a one-movement programme symphonic poem where the wonderful music and the amusing text blend into a perfect whole.

As usual, Prokofiev addressed this work to a definite audience and when composing it bore in mind the abilities and peculiarities of the musicians who were to perform it. L. Polovinkin, a composer who was at the time the musical director of the Central Children's Theatre in Moscow, said shortly before Prokofiev wrote his symphonic tale: "For our theatre we always try to have music with vivid, impressive imagery, a dramatic plot, a definite melodic and rhythmic pattern, a wealth of constructive elements, and last but not least—*colourful* and *expedient* orchestration." Clearly, *Peter and the Wolf* answers all these requirements perfectly.

The orchestration of this work appears simple, and in most of the episodes it has the lucidity of watercolours. But this seeming simplicity has taken the skill of a big master to achieve. In the score of *Peter and the Wolf* the vividness and clearness of the colours combine with the clear-cut dramaturgy of the music rendered by the orchestra's means of expression. And while the literary text, as Prokofiev himself said, was merely a "pretext" for developing the music, the music was definitely not merely a "pretext" for "enabling the children to learn to distinguish the timbres of different instruments by hearing the themes played over and over again." Actually, a demonstration of the timbres of the different instruments and their expressive potentialities help to bring out the beauty and the rich imagery of the music.

Perhaps Saint-Saëns' *Le carnaval des animaux* was the only symphonic composition before Prokofiev's *Peter and the Wolf* as packed with images which young children would find so concretely associable and understandable. Invisible threads run from *Peter and the Wolf* to the poetic images of Marshak, Kvitko, Kharms, and the witty and amusing drawings of Bidstrup and Soifertis. The unexpected comparisons of the commonplace with the fantastic make us think of *The Old Genie Khottabych*. Prokofiev's tale about courage and friendship told in a vivid and poetic manner is consonant with the children's perception of the world, and moreover, in mood and imagery it is also consonant with their own literary, artistic and musical creativity (little children very often try to compose music—from small pieces to large "narratives"). *Peter and the Wolf* is their tale. And it is not surprising that its enchanting music has inspired Yakov Akim to write this poem:

> *From a hollow in an old tree,*
> *From a pool with duckweed grown,*
> *Comes this kind and songful story*
> *Using notes for stepping stones.*
> *Playing in it is a quartet,*
> *Then an oboe and bassoon,*
> *All about a boy called Peter*
> *And a big, bad, hungry wolf.*
> *In this music there are hidden*
> *Fields and meadows, beasts and birds,*
> *And a little logwood cabin*
> *In the forest, 'mid the firs.*
> *Everybody in this story*

Has a voice you'll memorise:
For the duck will quack the oboe,
For the wolf will growl the horns.
There are many more surprises,
But I shan't divulge them all.
It's your fairy-tale, make haste then,
Enter its enchanted world!

Prokofiev wrote after the première of his symphonic fairy-tale at a matinée concert of the Moscow Philharmonic Society on May 2, 1936: "... the performance was no good, and *Peter and the Wolf* attracted little notice." But on May 5, only three days later, the music was repeated much more successfully on the stage of the Central Children's Theatre, and after that its popularity grew very quickly. Here are some of the reviews: "The music, while losing none of Prokofiev's newness and originality, is easily appreciated by the youngest listeners" (D. Kabalevsky). "The characterisations of the personages are clear, vivid and expressive. The music is very easy for children to listen to, and one should expect it to become a fixture in the children's musical repertoire" (A. Isakov).

Indeed, the images are so vivid and the artistic impression so charming that *Peter and the Wolf* appeals to children and grownups alike.

The "career" of this symphonic fairy-tale was as unique as it was lucky. People were so keen on hearing and performing this music that transcriptions and arrangements were made for chamber orchestras, and disc recordings of it were issued over and over again. In the first Soviet set of records (there were no long-playing records at the time) the text was read by Vera Maretskaya; later a long-playing record was made and the text was read by Nikolai Litvinov.

In the United States, a set of records was put out with S. Koussevitzky conducting the Boston Symphony Orchestra.

In Kabalevsky's cycle of talks on music, recorded by the "Melodia" firm, *Peter and the Wolf* is discussed at considerable length.

The music, remarkable for its plasticity, may have been made for the ballet, and in 1940 Adolph Bolm choreographed it for the Ballet Theatre in New York. The American press gave it a warm reception. The *Musical Courier* wrote on March 1, 1941 that the interpretation was extraordinarily impressive. In 1959

A. Varlamov staged *Peter and the Wolf* as a one-act ballet on the Bolshoi Theatre second stage. (The television film was based on this talented production.) In 1960, the puppet show *Peter and the Wolf* staged by the People's Puppet Theatre of Bulgaria won the gold medal at the International Festival of Puppet Theatres.

Unfortunately, the publication of the fairy-tale without the music can hardly be called a success. The very soul was gone from the fairy-tale once it was deprived of its wonderful music and the composer's basic idea (that the story was only a pretext for the music) was distorted. That was how *Peter and the Wolf* was brought out by the Detsky Mir Publishers in 1960, and by Alfred Holz Verlag (GDR) in 1958. In the latter publication there were at least such redeeming features as the excellent illustrations by F. Haaken (splendid from the polygraphic point of view as well), and a supplement of sheet music giving the melodies of the main themes. The result was a well-designed "guide" to the symphonic fairy-tale in place of the tale itself.

Prokofiev's very dynamic tale peopled with interesting imagery naturally attracted the attention of film makers. One American critic said that it calls to mind Walt Disney's best creations, and shortly afterwards Walt Disney did make a cartoon of it. But it was not one of his best.

Nor was the animated puppet cartoon produced in 1958 by Soyuzmultfilm (directed by A Karanovich) at all consonant with the pattern of imagery and falls even more hopelessly short in artistic impact. Still, it is to be hoped that a worthy screen adaptation will be made one day.

Three Children's Songs

The songs included in this small vocal cycle were composed in different years. The first one called *Chatterbox* was written to Agnia Barto's well-known verses in 1936, almost simultaneously with *Peter and the Wolf*. The *Sweet Song* to verses by N. Sakonskaya was composed a year later, and in 1939 Prokofiev wrote the *Little Pigs* to verses by L. Kvitko (translated from the Yiddish by Sergei Mikhalkov). The cycle was written for professional performance (soprano), and intended for a children's audience.

Like *Peter and the Wolf*, the song *Chatterbox* was written for the Central Children's Theatre where the singer was accompanied by the orchestra for which the arrangement was made by the composer himself. Prokofiev dedicated the song to Natalia Satz.

Agnia Barto's verses gave the composer plenty of scope for a contrasting presentation of the images, and this prompted him to use a rather developed form of rondo.

Here is the main theme (refrain) of *Chatterbox*:

Every new episode, following it, begins with a "rush of words" as it were. The fast melody, which seems purposely to allow no pause for breath, gives a marvellously humorous musical equivalent of chatter.

These episodes, however, cannot be called recitative. They are rather fast little songs with a clear-cut rhythm, and there is something in them of the gay and catchy Russian folk ditties (*chastushka*). The accordion-like accompaniment, especially in the second episode, enhances this impression.

In the fourth episode, the music sounds quite unexpectedly like a comically parodied sentimental love song from a musical comedy. The composer seems to hide a smile as he "plays up" the chatterbox's "terrible" worries:

146

The expressiveness of the intonations and the abrupt change
of imagery makes us recall Moussorgsky's *Seminarian*. But in
this latter work, the state of the student's complete stupefac-
tion from cramming is brilliantly conveyed through the "mut-
tering" refrain, sharply contrasting with the flowing melodies of
the episodes.

To really appreciate the innovational merits of the rondo-like
Chatterbox we should remember how the development of children's songs progressed in those years. This is what Dmitry
Kabalevsky said on the subject: "Songs for children are generally written as ditties, and this has become quite a tradition.
There is no question that the ditty is one of the most easily
assimilated forms, but it does not follow from this that composers should write ditties and nothing but ditties.... If, in the text,
there is some line of development that has a beginning and an
end, this in itself conflicts with the form of ditty as the music
here, identical in all the couplets, is denied development that
goes naturally with the development of the song's plot."
Prokofiev's *Chatterbox* does not suffer from this defect
at all.

Prokofiev himself referred to this "small sketch", as a "song
for children and about children, sung to the accompaniment of
a piano or a small orchestra." The fact that there is a variant
with an orchestral accompaniment does not, of course, make
the variant with the piano accompaniment of secondary importance (like a piano score for an opera or a ballet that falls short
of the orchestral score in artistic merit). What is more, it was
the variant with the piano accompaniment that earned the song
its popularity. It is to be regretted that the orchestral variant
has not been published till this day. And it is all the more
regrettable because the modest composition of the orchestra (a

flute, a clarinet, and strings) makes the accompaniment easy to perform.

The *Sweet Song* has an interesting story, and this is what Natalia Satz has to say about it: "The Central Children's Theatre decided to take part in a very worthwhile and quite novel undertaking. The idea was to place the designing of wrappers on sweets, chocolates, and so forth put out for children, on a higher artistic level, to turn chocolate boxes into toys, and to use them for the popularisation of new songs, verses and fairytales. It occurred to someone to draw Sergei Sergeyevich into the venture, and he agreed readily enough. He did hesitate for a moment, wondering if it was 'proper' for him to do so, but then he told himself that it was. 'After all, Mayakovsky became all the more of a Mayakovsky because he did not turn up his nose at writing ads.' And so, Sergei Sergeyevich agreed to write the *Sweet Song* for us. I remember how he said with his kind and shy smile: 'As for the lyrics, let the poetess who didn't make a go of *Peter* and who I was so nasty to at the time, write the words. She'll make a success of the *Sweet Song*.' It was a wonderful suggestion, and N. Sakonskaya was delighted with it."

The song begins very timidly with a reiterative motif made up of two sounds, and the main melody unfolds, as it were, from this insinuative piano introduction.

The melody is rendered dance-like by the lucid accompaniment which, for the most part, is in staccato. The hilarous solemnity of the refrain provides a contrast in imagery:

For another contrast there is the "toy-march" accompaniment in the third and fifth couplets.

In this charming sketch Prokofiev comes stylistically close to the psychologically subtle vocal miniatures of Moussorgsky, in the way he combines declamation with an expressively flowing melody.

* * *

The first page of *Sweet Song*, written in Prokofiev's hand bears a few indications for its future orchestration which, like that of *Chatterbox*, was done specially for concerts arranged by the Central Children's Theatre. (We know from N. Satz that the score of *Sweet Song* perished in a fire that broke out in the theatre.) The notes made by Prokofiev on his manuscript suggest that he meant to provide the whole cycle with an orchestral accompaniment.

The *Three Children's Songs* are much more frequently performed separately than as a cycle. There are many reasons for this. For one thing, *Chatterbox* is a developed vocal work, it is much longer than the other two and can well be performed independently. For another, this song is intended for a mezzo-soprano, while the other two are written for a higher voice. And last, though by no means the least, *Sweet Song* and *Little Pigs* are addressed to the youngest listeners, for such is their imagery, the subject matter and the intonational peculiarities of the melodies, whereas *Chatterbox* is intended for a more "mature" children's audience.

At the conference in 1935, a year before the appearance of *Chatterbox*, D. Lokshin said: "Children have an enormous craving for different genres.... Soviet composers have produced too few humorous songs." Prokofiev's brilliant contribution can therefore be hardly overestimated.

Peter and the Wolf and *Three Children's Songs* were a prelude, shall we say, to the *Winter Bonfire Suite* in which Prokofiev combined vocal and symphonic music with poetic declamation into a single whole.

Winter Bonfire

This suite for reciters, a boys' choir and symphony orchestra was Prokofiev's last composition for children. He wrote it in 1949, practically at the same time as his oratorio *On Guard of Peace*. In both works Marshak's poems were used, and both were composed at the request of the music section of the All-Union Radio.

There are eight movements, and a text is recited before the first seven. The suite tells the story of Moscow Young Pioneers going on a visit to their village friends.

The first movement, called *Departure*, begins with a fanfare of French horns. The jolly whistle and the puffing of the steam engine is wittily rendered. And all at once the fanfare becomes the beginning of a lovely melody. Written in C major (Prokofiev's favourite tonality in which all his music for children except the *Three Children's Songs* begins) it conveys the ingenuousness of the children's emotions, great inner energy, and the joyfulness of childhood.

The intonations of popular Soviet songs are treated here with admirable finesse and originality. They do not upset the colour scheme of Prokofiev's own melody, and at the same time they bring some new tints into it.

These intonations are heard even more clearly in the middle episode of the first movement (*Departure*). Here one can say with assurance that a definite genre—that of a Young Pioneers' song—has found a new embodiment.

A short reprise brings listeners back for a moment to the initial theme of *Departure*.

The second movement is called: *Snowfall*.

The serene, tender music reminds us of *Morning* (from *Children's Music*). With its watercolour lucidity it harmonises beautifully with Marshak's verse.

These placid colours prevail in the initial melody of the second movement, but in the middle of it the music becomes more emotional. Played by the flutes and the bassoon, with the celesta's silvery tones providing the background, it is like an expressive vocal duet and preludes many of the lyrical pages in Prokofiev's Seventh Symphony, the slow part in particular.

The third movement is called *Waltzing on Ice*. Prokofiev introduced this light genre (fancy, music played at the skating rink!) into the body of a developed vocal-and-symphonic composition, and produced a highly poetic and amazingly fresh piece of music.

There is a small, sweetly sounding introduction, and then comes a lyrical, and blithely joyful theme.

In the next episode (the waltz is written in the form of a rondo), the music sounds light, graceful and tender.

The main theme recurs, after which comes the second episode and though the music is faintly wistful it is dance music nonetheless.

The third movement ends with the initial theme which takes on a certain solemnity in the finale.

This is a typically Prokofievan youth waltz. There are the same lyrically radiant colours in his other works written in this genre—for instance, in some movements of the symphonic suite *Waltzes*, in *Pushkin Waltzes*, and in the waltzes from the ballet *Cinderella* and the Seventh Symphony. M. A. Mendelson-Prokofieva recalls that once, listening to Glinka's *Waltz Fantasie* over the radio, Sergei Sergeyevich said that actually his waltzes had been inspired by this favourite one of his. In Prokofiev's *Waltzing on Ice* the intonations typical of Russian waltzes in Glinka's day are all but absent (except, perhaps, in the theme of the second episode). The affinity lies in something else: in the artlessness of the emotions, the chastity of the imagery and a striving for the same purity and vividness in the orchestral colours; also, in the completeness of the narration and the harmonious finish of each separate episode.

Now we come to the fourth movement. The main theme, flowing freely and majestically as though infused with the breath of Russia's infinite spaces, anticipates one of the main melodies in the Seventh Symphony, the secondary theme of the first movement.

The music goes straight on to the march rhythms of the fifth movement, called *Young Pioneers' Rally*. This is the only movement where a children's choir is included, singing a march-like melody the first four bars of which are almost a quotation (also in the same tonality) from the cavalry song *Across the Bridge* (to a poem by A. Prishelets) included in Prokofiev's collection *The Songs of Our Days* written as far back as 1937. The difference occurs only in the further development of the melody. Thus, the colour range of this children's suite has been enriched and extended by this reinterpretation of "grown-up" imagery. It must be said, though, that the theme of the *Young Pioneers' Rally* is unquestionably more expressive emotionally and more flexible than the preceding one.

The *Bonfire* theme concludes the fifth movement. Actually, the fourth and the fifth movements make one single whole.

The main melody of the sixth movement called *Winter Night* echoes the music of the second movement. Like *Snowfall* the melody is radiant and serene.

The seventh movement *On the March* calls to mind the *March* from *Children's Music* but the imagery is less "childish", there is more spirit, even mischief, in the melody, and the rhythm is more buoyant.

Two other themes are set in contrast to the main one: the first is even jollier, boyishly perky; and the second is calm and songful, echoing the other lyrical melodies of the suite.

The main march theme, appearing for the last time, flows right into the eighth movement called *The Return*. This very short movement is entirely built on a recurrence of the main theme of the first movement *Departure*. Thus, the first and the last movements provide a "frame" for the whole suite both in imagery and theme.

* * *

In *Winter Bonfire* the verses and the music seem to complement each other as equivalent components of a single artistic whole. In this sense, the text here is much more important than in *Peter and the Wolf*, and also there is more of it. The suite, therefore, is perceived as a musical-literary composition which is largely due to the artistic merits of Marshak's verses, apart from their compositional importance.

The dramaturgy of the suite is very clear-cut. Besides the correctly found balance between the music and the text, the contrasting imagery in the movements also plays no little part in this. As in *Children's Music* profound meditation and radiant lyricism (in the second, fourth and sixth movements) are contrasted to the poetry of action (say, in the first, fifth and seventh movements). In the opinion of V. Berkov this developed dramaturgy of the suite brings it close to an "original symphony".

The link between *Winter Bonfire* and the oratorio *On Guard of Peace* does not stand to doubt as regards the ideas inspiring the music, the imagery, and occasionally the intonations as well. The main images of childhood in the oratorio *We Don't Want War, Doves of Peace* and *Lullaby* are related to the emotional key of *Winter Bonfire*, but in the former work they are included into a far wider range of imagery as required by an epic narrative.

As in *Peter and the Wolf* there is a certain amount of portraiture in *Winter Bonfire*, but it is of a more generalised nature here. The romantic landscape of the Moscow countryside in winter and the vibrant picture of the children's bonfire are rendered in the score through the prism of profound emotional experience.

The suite includes a boys' choir whose part is not too difficult to perform. The composition of the orchestra is rather modest, and playing time is half that of *On Guard of Peace*. All this taken together and, above everything else, the beautiful sunny music, makes *Winter Bonfire* a very popular work to perform.

Ever-Growing Recognition

When you take a retrospective view of Prokofiev's music for children what amazes you is the genre variety of these works for all their relatively small number. There is his cycle of piano pieces (with a variant in the form of a symphonic suite), a small vocal triad, and then a symphonic tale and a suite for reciters, choir and orchestra.... The genre breadth distinguishing Prokofiev's work for "an adult audience" is as much in evidence in his compositions for children.

The character of the music's expressiveness is another salient feature. In all his compositions Prokofiev always sought the most impressive imagery and the most vivid expressiveness. As for his music for children, here he invariably had his musical

153

imagery tell a definite story. Of course, programme music existed before Prokofiev too. But as we have seen in *Peter and the Wolf, Three Children's Songs, Winter Bonfire* and to some extent in *Children's Music* as well, Prokofiev extended the expressive possibilities of programme music by giving it a musically and dramatically developed plot. It is in fact that presence of a plot in *Three Children's Songs* that has (together with its purely musical merits, of course) earned the cycle its well deserved popularity. A point that should be stressed is that Prokofiev does not force his subject matter on the listener. In *Children's Music*, for instance, the name of the composition combined with the imagery of the music gives free run to the children's imagination, and it is by no means binding upon the listeners to take the title of each separate piece as the only possible interpretation of the content.

Prokofiev's musical language cannot be called primitive or simplified, and what is more, to quote L. Gakkel: "he has no intention of sacrificing a single trait peculiar to his style. These traits are moreover sharpened, as though brought to a focus in the small space of a children's piece of music." And that is why Prokofiev's music though definitely and directly addressed to children finds an appreciative adult audience as well. The vividness of the imagery in *Children's Music* enabled the composer to use two of the pieces in this collection in his ballet *Tale of the Stone Flower*.

Prokofiev never "adapted himself" to an audience. "There is an element of insincerity in this," he used to say, "and no good ever comes of it." But at the same time he always saw the task before him very clearly, and knew exactly to whom he was addressing his work.

"He felt the heartbeat of time," Ilya Ehrenburg said about him. His pen, it may well be said, knew no temporal or spatial bounds. He gave his own, original interpretation to the old Russian folk song, the passionate Italian tarantella, the buoyant Young Pioneer march, and to the urgent sound of the Novgorod tocsin. His command of so many different genres and intonations is there in his music for children as well (in particular in the collection *Children's Music*). Such a breadth of creative range is, of course, perfectly in accord with the psychology of a child's perception of the world and with the emotional character of a child's rich imagination which is equally responsive to fantasy, adventure, and heroism.

What really decided the children's audience in favour of Prokofiev's music and the reason for their wholehearted acceptance of it must be sought in the composer's remarkably keen and sensitive grasp of the intonations of the day and his ability to render the pulse-beat of the busy and many-faceted life about him. Symptomatically, in his music for an adult audience, he also turned again and again to modern popular songs, creatively embodying them in his music, as witness his vocal cycles *Six Songs* Op. 66, *Seven Songs* Op. 79, *Seven Popular Songs* Op. 89, and the suite *Songs of Our Days* Op. 76.

As a composer of children's music Prokofiev is an innovator, tirelessly seeking for a fresh melodic intonation that has not been overused, for new, original harmonies, for the subtlest shades of orchestral colours. He also tried to find an unconventional structure of the form for his compositions. In this respect, the most striking examples are *Peter and the Wolf* and *Chatterbox*. The originality of Prokofiev's images usually presupposes an originality of their structural representation.

Last but not least, a distinctive merit of the music is that children can perform it or take part in its performance, and not just listen to it. The youngest pianists can play pieces from *Children's Music*, boys and girls can act or dance in *Peter and the Wolf*, boys can sing in the choir of *Winter Bonfire*—and is there a better way of learning to appreciate one's favourite music?

Among the compositions written for children by Russian and foreign classics—Prokofiev's predecessors—we would mention Schumann's *Album für die Jugend*, Tchaikovsky's *Children's Album*, the songs, operas and plays by Caesar Cui, Grechaninov and Satz, Ravel's opera *L'enfant et les sortilèges* and his ballet *Mother Goose*, and songs for children by Brahms, Tchaikovsky and Lyadov.

Prokofiev was a convinced innovator, but he did not ignore the experience of his predecessors and at moments was quite close to them. The imagery of *Children's Music* shows an occasional closeness (in *Morning* and to some extent in *Tarantella*)to the moods of Tchaikovsky's *Children's Album*, while *Remorse* from the same collection) tends towards the subtle psychologism of Schumann's album.

In its turn, Prokofiev's work had a beneficial influence on the development of music for children both in the Soviet Union and elsewhere in the world. Prokofiev's traditions are being creatively developed by many Soviet composers. Dmitry Kabalevsky's cantata *A Song of Morning, Spring and Peace* resembles *Winter Bonfire* in its pattern of imagery, its joyful mood, energy and radiant lyricism. The same is true of *Our Garden*, a cantata by the Estonian composer A. Pärt. This composition, like *Winter Bonfire* (written for a children's choir and symphony orchestra) has a definite story to tell, while the subject matter of Kabalevsky's cantata is of a more generalised character.

Peter and the Wolf also had its followers. That same year, 1936, the same theatre staged L. Polovinkin's musical tale called *Volodya the Musician* about a little boy and his violin. An interesting, skilfully written composition by Benjamin Britten called *The Young Person's Guide to the Orchestra* is variations and fugue on a theme of the English classic Henry Purcell. Britten's aim is the same as Prokofiev's in *Peter and the Wolf*— to introduce children to the instruments comprising a symphony orchestra. The latter work, however, is admittedly superior to the former in the vividness of its musical images and their genre variety.

Peter and the Wolf has paved the way to the development of programme symphonic music intended for the youngest listeners. The basic idea here is to "people" the music with musical characterisations of personages, known from fairy-tales and real life.

Thirty years after the appearance of *Peter and the Wolf*, composer I. Morozov (on the suggestion of the Moscow Children's Musical Theatre, directed by Natalia Satz) wrote a symphonic tale called *Dr. Aibolit and His Friends* basing it on the musical themes of his own ballet of the same name.

The lasting worth and vitality of Prokofiev's music for children lies first of all in the direct artistic impact it has on the audience to which it is addressed—the most sincere and fair minded audience of all.

5

REMINISCENCES
AND STATEMENTS
BY PROMINENT
CULTURAL FIGURES

Yuri Tyulin

ON THE PATH TO RECOGNITION

Reminiscences

Interest in the work and life of S.S. Prokofiev and in his highly original personality is as great as ever. A great deal has already been written about him, but the reminiscences of his contemporaries can still add new touches to the picure of him as an individual.

I had the good fortune to become closely acquainted with Prokofiev when we were still young—in 1911. I was at university then and about to enter the Conservatoire, while Prokofiev, who was nearly three years my senior, had already completed the composition course and acquired a reputation as a talented composer of an entirely new trend. At that time he was diligently studying the piano in A.N. Yesipova's class and conducting in N.N. Cherepnin's class. But the difference in our positions did not affect our relationship. He was a simple, nice, affable friend, and I never saw him behave towards any of his acquaintances as their superior, as a rising star towards "mere mortals". His faith in himself was seen only in his bold and independent advance along his creative path. There was not the slightest trace of conceit or arrogance in his relations with his friends.

He always had a natural gaiety, and stood out for his original wit and the remarkable inventiveness of his repartee. He seemed to look at life, at people and their behaviour, from an unusual angle and found something unexpected, and often amusing, in everything. This frequently took the form of sheer mischievousness, the mischievousness of a happy youth, which was also somewhat childish—his spontaneity, his extraordinarily healthy psyche, and his happy childhood spent in the countryside, left their mark on everything about him. And all this was so marvel-

159

lously reflected in his early works. At that time he was a carefree young man, who did not appear to concern himself in the slightest with serious problems. He even seemed frivolous, and many people did not take him seriously—people who did not know him well and did not understand his profound concentration and enquiring mind, did not understand his quickly maturing talent, his sense of purpose and his real talent for looking into the future which led him unerringly to world fame, were somewhat condescending to him.

Prokofiev, of course, had faith in himself: it was no accident that he used Andersen's fairy-tale to create his work on "the ugly duckling" which is autobiographical in essence.

In spite of the fame which he acquired, Prokofiev found little approval in the musical world, particularly in Conservatoire circles. He had to fight hard for his ideals, to defend them with great persistence.

Prokofiev lacked true recognition and support not only among the teachers, but also among the students.

The student composers also included "rebels" who challenged academic dogma or at least felt uncomfortable in its steel grip. But their desire to "experiment" was limited almost entirely to "Scriabinism", which enjoyed tremendous popularity among young people in the latter years of the great composer's life and for a considerable time afterwards. The most ardent "innovators" among the young sought after all manner of spasmodic rhythms and complex, refined harmonies of a "Scriabinesque" nature, regarding melody and themes as something old-fashioned. They believed the future of music lay in the development of Scriabin's ideas embodied in *Prometheus* and the projected *Mystery*. If one is to speak of "modernism" at that time, this is basically how it was expressed.

There could be no question then of an interest in impressionism, and certainly not of an interest in Stravinsky or Prokofiev. Certainly not. For how did the "high-minded" young people regard the work of these composers? As intellectually impoverished, a betrayal of high ideals. Prokofiev in particular was a kind of football-player in music, a musical sportsman, who encroached upon the sacred tasks of music and dragged it down from the sublime to the mundane.

I am quoting only extreme views here, but they reflect to some extent the general attitude to Prokofiev.

He was mercilessly attacked from both sides—from the right

by traditional academism, and from the left, by the "progressive" younger generation which, it must be said, was serious and high-principled in its way, but lacked the common sense and true intuition so characteristic of Prokofiev.

To my mind Prokofiev's greatest achievement lies not in his struggle with the traditional academism, but in the fact that he rescued the music of that time from the impasse of hedonistic decadence.

* * *

From my very first acquaintance with it Prokofiev's work was a real revelation to me, and although I expressed this in a quiet, restrained way, he recognised in me a "sympathetic soul" and responded with warmth. For all his independence and self-confidence, he still felt the need for creative contact. Prokofiev played his works readily without the slightest embarrassment to all who were interested even when he encountered a critical attitude towards himself. If they evoked certain bewilderment, he would play them again. And if people did not like them after a second and third playing—well, they had simply not understood them. In this respect he was entirely lacking in false pride and never took offence. His approach to the appreciation of his works was largely a businesslike one—the audience must be won over and to this and all the necessary measures taken. When the Yurgenson Publishers refused to print his Opus 12, Prokofiev went straight to Moscow, arranged to visit the "boss" at his home, and played him the pieces until the publisher agreed to take them.

Prokofiev was on good, even friendly terms with many people, not only musicians, but with a few rare exceptions he had no very close friends—it was not in his nature. In particular, he could not stand the "heart-to-hearts" and the "psychological conversations" to which many young people of our generation were so addicted. This again speaks of Prokofiev's well-balanced, healthy personality, which was not given to psychological reflection.

He was always businesslike, but also found time to relax, take up sport (it was at the Sokol gymnastic club that we first met), indulge his passion for chess, meet his friends, and sometimes even "hang around" as if he had nothing to do—but all in moderation. It was impossible to see how he managed to do all this and work on three special subjects at the same time—composition, the piano and conducting. He was helped not only by his great talent, single-mindedness and rare self-discipline, which had been cultivated in him since childhood, but also by another feature of his character, a most unusual one—his passion for rationalisation. He was always inventing special ways of attaining maximum efficiency in everything he did and avoiding the unproductive expenditure of time and energy. Thus, for example, though much later, he worked out a special system for indicating the instruments in his scores. In accordance with these strict intsructions and under his supervision other people were able to do the purely technical work of writing out scores. It is typical that he used his frequent train journeys (as he himself told me) to work on a future score, thereby saving valuable time.

This penchant for rationalisation made Prokofiev argue that transposing instruments should be written in C, and with good reason: this would make it much easier for musicians to read scores, especially if they had no special training for this. Prokofiev told that this idea had occurred to him in a train when he was looking at a Berlioz score and it took him a long time to realise that four differently transposed French horns simply formed C major triad. This annoyed him, for he was very proficient at score reading.

After Prokofiev had graduated from the conducting course at the Conservatoire, he studied the organ under Professor Y.Y. Gandshin (this is not widely known). And immediately it transpired that his piano at home had been re-equipped: it had been raised up and given a pedal keyboard. I do not know whether such an invention exists anywhere else. This passion for rationalisation contributed to Prokofiev's remarkable productivity not only in composition, but in all other work.

Prokofiev got on well with people, particularly his friends, but his dealings with them were more of a businesslike nature. He often visited people or invited them home, not for idle conversation, however, but to show them something new or for some other serious reason.

In relation to the conservative group of musicians, however, his behaviour was different. Here he was defiant, sometimes challenging. This encouraged people to compare him with the Futurists (poets and artists) of the time, but in fact he had nothing at all in common with them. His defiance was always gay and joking, I would even say childlike. Unlike many of his fellow-students he had no clashes with Conservatoire, dogmatic teaching, but simply took from it all that he needed and rejected the rest without thinking about it twice.

The lightness of his character sometimes turned into a spontaneous, I would even say childish, mischievousness. I remember one "prank" which could only have been played by Prokofiev in his young days. In 1912 he was to play Liszt's sonata h-moll in the Smaller Hall of the Conservatoire at a student evening. Nikolai Shtember (who studied with Prokofiev in Yesipova's class) and I settled down to listen with the score (we did not know this sonata at the time). Suddenly we realised that Prokofiev was not following the score properly. We turned over the pages and saw that he had left something out. This happened again and again—the sonata was played in a very condensed form. We went into the dressing room. Prokofiev was walking about happily, looking pleased with himself.

"Well, what did you think of it? "

"You made a lot of cuts! "

"Oh, yes! " he replied lightly, as if nothing special had happened. "Anna Nikolayevna [Yesipova] insisted that I should play, but I could not do it properly—my finger hurt, so I left out all the difficult passages. Lyapunov was sitting in the front row and every time I made a cut, he wriggled three times in his seat! "

Later, when Prokofiev was more mature, this feature of his character enabled him to endure with ease the most difficult trials, which would have caused others a great deal of suffering.

In 1916 Prokofiev was to conduct his new work *Ala and Lolli*. We went to the first rehearsal (with A.I. Siloti's orchestra) together. While he was dressing at home, there was a telephone call. I heard him answer: "Yes, yes, do come. The concert is going to take place. Do you know that the price of rotten eggs and apples has gone up in St. Petersburg? That's what they'll throw at me! "

At the rehearsal (in the Mariinsky Theatre) I sat alone in the auditorium, following the score. Prokofiev went up to the orchestra without a trace of excitement, but you can imagine what a great moment it was. He writes in his memoirs that the orchestra hindered his work. In fact, it was far worse: the orchestra tormented him, by openly demonstrating its hostility.

There was no room for the two harpists in the orchestra pit, so they sat on the stage and kept asking him questions in an irritated tone. During their pauses they covered their ears with the wide collars (then fashionable) of their dresses. But Prokofiev continued his work with the orchestra with patience and concentration, as if nothing had happened, and came out after the rehearsal, serious but satisfied.

"Everything is all right," he replied to my anxious question.

You could not help but marvel at his self-possession.

* * *

You can imagine how much boldness, self-confidence, composure, stamina and real courage it takes to go abroad and try to win recognition for your works. Prokofiev wrote to B.V. Asafyev from London that his concert had been a great "success": there had been a lot of reviews of which only two were favourable. He did not win recognition easily—it took a vast amount of hard work and was a truly heroic achievement.

I remember N.N. Cherepnin, one of the few musicians who supported Prokofiev, saying to me in 1917: "Prokofiev must be able to hold a baton in his hands and conduct an orchestra well, because no one will be the first to play his works. It is quite essential that he should know how to conduct, because, believe me, he is going to conquer the whole world."

This far-sighted prediction has turned out to be quite correct. Prokofiev possessed all that was required for such a conquest: not only great musical talent—creative genius and brilliant piano-playing, but also a remarkable personality.

Myra Prokofieva

FROM MY REMINISCENCES

"To dear S.S.
'magician and sorcerer' (p. 25)
from a 'sensitive musician' (p. 28)
June 14, 1940
Eisenstein."

This is the inscription in the book *The Soviet Historical Film* which Eisenstein presented to Sergei Sergeyevich. It contained an article by Eisenstein "Alexander Nevsky" and one by Sergei Sergeyevich "Music in the Film *Alexander Nevsky*".

In his article Eisenstein referred to Sergei Sergeyevich as a "magician and sorcerer" (p. 25).

"I remember my meetings with S.M. Eisenstein with great pleasure," wrote Sergei Sergeyevich (p. 28). "Eisenstein is not only an unusually gifted producer, but also a sensitive musician. Usually, after finishing rehearsals, we invited Eisenstein at the moment when the music was about to be recorded. He always found some detail which should be brought out, some dramatic effect which should be highlighted, thereby improving the quality of our work. Eisenstein's respect for music is so great that he was sometimes willing to move the film of the action forwards or backwards to preserve the unity of the piece of music. It need hardly be said that working in such conditions was a great pleasure!"

Their joint work on the film *Alexander Nevsky* marked the beginning of the great professional friendship between Sergei Sergeyevich and Sergei Mikhailovich.

In the summer of 1939 Eisenstein suggested that Sergei Sergeyevich should write the music for a film about the Ferghana Canal. In a letter of July 30 from Kislovodsk, where Sergei Sergeyevich was resting and orchestrating the opera *Semyon Kotko,* he informed Eisenstein of the reasons which made it impossible for him to agree to this proposal.

165

A conversation about a new professional meeting took place in the spring of 1941. It was then that I made the acquaintance of Sergei Mikhailovich.

In May we went to Kratovo, near Moscow, Eisenstein's dacha was not far away. One day we came back from a walk and noticed some strange objects on an armchair on the terrace—a piece of iron and a stone. We could not imagine where they had come from. The explanation was an unexpected one—Sergei Mikhailovich happened to mention to Sergei Sergeyevich that he had come to see us and, finding that we were out, had left his "visiting card"—iron—*Eisen* and a stone—*Stein*.

During his visit to us Sergei Mikhailovich talked most enthusiastically about his new idea—he was about to start work on an historical film about Ivan the Terrible and suggested that Sergei Sergeyevich should write the music. Sergei Sergeyevich was most interested in the proposal. At that time he was writing the ballet *Cinderella* and the music for the film *Lermontov* with a scenario by K. Paustovsky (produced by A. Gendelshtein). At the beginning of June he sent two acts of the ballet (with the exception of a few scenes) to the Kirov Theatre in Leningrad. "Although the tale of Cinderella exists in all countries, I wanted to treat it as a real Russian fairy-tale. Cinderella herself not only as a fairy-tale character, but as a real person who feels and even suffers," Sergei Sergeyevich wrote later in one of his letters.

On June 7 there was the first broadcast of the radio arrangement of the opera *Betrothal in a Nunnery* (*The Duenna*). The opera was to be put on at the Stanislavsky Theatre and Sergei Sergeyevich attended rehearsals.

On June 22 the Great Patriotic War broke out. Sergei Sergeyevich immediately stopped work on the ballet and film. His one thought at this time was how to find a direct response to the terrible events which were taking place.

On July 8 his *Song of the Brave* with words by the poet Alexei Surkov had its first performance on the radio. On July 17 he completed the orchestration of the *March* (Op. 88) and started planning the symphonic suite. And whereas three months ago when we were rereading *War and Peace* Sergei Sergeyevich had spoken of Tolstoy's work merely as a possible subject for an opera, now, after long and hard reflection, he decided to write this opera. "The pages about the Russian people's struggle against Napoleon's hordes in 1812 and about his army being driven off Russian soil had somehow become very close to me." "I was obsessed by the idea of writing an opera on the subject of *War and Peace*, although I realised what a difficult task this was. Obviously such a vast amount of material could not be contained in a single opera. The more thoroughly I read the novel, the clearer it became to me that the opera must be based on the events concentrated around 1812, and that the beginning should be omitted."

Sergei Sergeyevich treated Tolstoy's work with the greatest care, remaining true to the original in conveying the main idea, the central events and the characterisation, and in recreating the spirit of the novel, the atmosphere of the times, in the opera. He also considered it essential to retain Tolstoy's text as fully as possible.

Realising that he would have to omit many fine passages in the novel, Sergei Sergeyevich sought to make the future opera a single whole and pictured it to himself as *War* and *Peace* only. He flatly rejected suggestions for other titles for the opera. He also objected to the proposal that each part of the opera should have a different title, when the question arose of spreading the production over two evenings.

"I am categorically opposed to any titles for the two parts of the opera. Why should part one be called *Andrei Bolkonsky*, and not *Natasha Rostova* or *Pierre Bezukhov*? This is arbitrary and could encourage a wrong interpretation of the main idea. There are no such titles in Lev Tolstoy. It is important to stress that the opera is a *single whole* and is divided into two parts only because it will not fit into one evening. We must keep the general title *War and Peace*, without subtitles."

Sergei Sergeyevich informed the Arts Committee of his plans and met with warm support. He decided to work with me on the libretto. In July we drew up a detailed plan of it. Unlike the initial draft plan written by Sergei Sergeyevich in April, the opera now consisted of twelve scenes, beginning with the one in Otradnoye. Of these twelve scenes two—the seventh and the eighth—were later omitted from the opera. Scene seven (a very short one)—"A Russian Army Guard Post"—was to portray a fierce clash with the French who crossed the Russian border at night; scene eight—"Napoleon's Tent"—Napoleon's meeting with Balashov sent to him by Alexander I. These scenes, which preceded "On the Eve of the Battle of Borodino", were later replaced by "On the Shevardin Redoubt" (now scene 9).

At the beginning of August we bade farewell to Eisenstein and set off for Nalchik in the Caucasus with a group of musicians, actors, and artists. Here our group found accommodation at the town hotel (where we stayed) and also not far from the town, in Dolinskoye. I remember that one day we went to Dolinskoye with Vladimir Ivanovich Nemirovich-Danchenko. Having learned that Sergei Sergeyevich was planning to write an opera *War and Peace*, Vladimir Ivanovich immediately advised him among other things not to portray battles on the stage, because this was rarely successful. He expressed the desire to read *Betrothal in a Nunnery* and Sergei Sergeyevich gave him the score. Later he discussed the opera with Nemirovich-Danchenko.

Sergei Sergeyevich began to write *War and Peace* on August 15. I cannot call to mind any other occasion in our life together when he spent so much time, so much spiritual energy, on a work. Dmitry Borisovich Kabalevsky writes: "The production of *War and Peace* on the stage was Prokofiev's most cherished dream. 'I am prepared to reconcile myself to the failure of any of my works,' he said shortly before his death, 'but if you only knew how much I want *War and Peace* to see the light of day'."

Sergei Sergeyevich's attitude towards the opera can also be seen from his letter to A. A. Fadeyev, whom he often met while working on the oratorio *On Guard of Peace*.

"...The question of why *War and Peace* is not put on is of great concern to me, not so much because this is one of my most cherished works on which I worked for almost ten years, as for the reason that in writing the opera *War and Peace* I strove to write an ideologically committed work that would be needed by our people."

In Nalchik Prokofiev wrote six lyrical scenes dealing with the life of the main characters in peacetime, their thoughts and feelings, hopes and aspirations. We tried to construct the libretto of these scenes in such a way as to convey the gradual, increasing awareness of the approach of war. Usually we began by examining my text of the scene in question, then Sergei Sergeyevich wrote the music, and in the course of the work, if it was necessary, he would either insert changes and additions in the text or ask me to do so.

As well as the opera Sergei Sergeyevich was writing other works. In Dolinskoye he played *The Year 1941* suite to

N. Y. Myaskovsky, P. A. Lamm, S. Y. Feinberg, and V. V. Nechayev. The orchestration of the suite was completed on October 12.

Sergei Sergeyevich's songs about the Kabardinian-Balkar heroes were first performed on the radio on October 19.

The local arts department arranged for newly arrived composers to hear recordings of folk songs, and Sergei Sergeyevich began to write his Second Quartet on Kabardinian-Balkar themes with great enthusiasm. He very much hoped that when the inhabitants of Nalchik heard the quartet they would recognise their native music.

Sergei Sergeyevich continued to think about an opera based on Leskov's *The Spendthrift*, the idea for which had first occurred to him in February 1940. At that time he wrote a detailed plan of the libretto covering several sheets of an exercise book. On February 11, 1940, he wrote to his great friend Boris Nikolayevich Demchinsky in Leningrad:

"I need your advice and views very much. I have found Leskov's play *The Spendthrift*. At first glance it seems cheap and commercialistic. But then you see that it could be cleansed and elevated: the conversations about money could be omitted, and the good characters uplifted and expanded. Then you would have the splendid language, vividly drawn characters and a number of dramatic situations which could be moulded into something quite powerful.

"Do read it, please. I expect to be in Leningrad on 18 and 19 February. You and I could have a talk—or earlier, if you are coming to Moscow...."

In Nalchik Sergei Sergeyevich wrote a short plan of the libretto. As we read Leskov he would write down words and expressions which he found interesting. At the same time he wrote a plan for the Third Suite from the ballet *Romeo and Juliet*.

Sergei Sergeyevich often took part in concerts for the public with other musicians and actors. I remember seeing O. L. Knipper-Chekhova, V. I. Kachalov, A. K. Tarasova, I. M. Moskvin, M. M. Klimov, V. N. Ryzhova and V. O. Massalitinova standing in the wings, keyed-up and excited, waiting to go on the stage. Their repertoire included works by Chekhov, L. Tolstoy, Gorky, Ostrovsky and Shakespeare. The following musicians took part in the concerts: A.B. Goldenweiser, K.A. Erdeli, B.O. Sibor, S.Y. Feinberg, V.V. Nechayev, N.L. Dorliak and A.L. Dolivo. Sergei Sergeyevich usually played the Gavottes Op.

12 and Op. 25, the Prelude Op. 12, the Etude Op. 2, No. 4, *Fugitive Visions, Old Granny's Tales* and the March from the opera *Love for Three Oranges*. He often went with other actors to the hospitals. Performances for the officers and men of the Red Army were particularly rewarding.

At the end of November we moved to Tbilisi. Here, as in Nalchik, Sergei Sergeyevich concentrated mainly on the opera. He wrote the scenes "On the Eve of the Battle of Borodino", "Moscow", "The Smolensk Road", "The Meeting of the Wounded Prince Andrei and Natasha in a Peasant House in Mytishchi" and "On the Shevardin Redoubt". (I have listed them in the order in which Sergei Sergeyevich wrote them. He began writing "On the Shevardin Redoubt" in January, then put it aside and returned to it in April.)

In his work on the scenes dealing with the events of the Patriotic War of 1812, the Russian people's struggle and its victory over the invader, the scenes in which the main characters were the Russian army, peasant fighters and partisans, Sergei Sergeyevich strove to depict the people's suffering, anger, stamina and courage, its love for the Motherland. At the same time he wished to emphasise how closely the fate of the characters in the preceding scenes was linked with the events which they were experiencing, "... to emphasise the profound changes that took place in their mind and character in connection with the danger which threatened the Motherland". In the library and reading-room we found material about 1812, and Field-marshal Kutuzov. We read Tarle, a guidebook to the places where the Battle of Borodino was fought, collections of Russian folk songs, proverbs and sayings of the period, notes by the poet and partisan Denis Davydov (which provided the text for Denisov's aria and, in part, for the Epigraph). In the collection *The Expulsion of Napoleon from Moscow* we found a suitable text for the choral episodes in the scenes "On the Eve of the Battle of Borodino" and "Moscow" (the central part of the choir at the beginning of the scene—"Hark! ... the foreign locusts have descended upon us" and the soldiers' choir "In the old, Suvorov Way"—in the scene "On the Eve of the Battle of Borodino"; and the choir of the people of Moscow "On a dark, moonless night" in the finale of the "Moscow" scene. Sometimes I had to write the text after Sergei Sergeyevich had composed the music. In this case he gave me fixed dimensions in accordance with which the verse was to be written (based on the

170

texts of folk songs). At first he did this by indicating where the strong and weak syllables should come $(-\smile)$, but this turned out not to be sufficiently precise and two more signs were necessary: strong-weak $(\overset{\smile}{-})$ for syllables where there was a stress but not the main one, and very strong $(=)$ for strong syllables which completed the sentence. In addition he put some weak syllables in brackets $(\smile)$: this meant that I could use this syllable or not, as I wished, in other words, Sergei Sergeyevich could either add another note here or, the reverse, join two notes over one syllable. I have described this in detail because the same system was used in work on the operas *Betrothal in a Nunnery*, and *A Story About a Real Man*, and in some unfinished stage works.

War and Peace was completed in April. Long before this Sergei Sergeyevich had shown it to N.Y. Myaskovsky and P.A. Lamm, played it willingly and frequently to friends and acquaintances, and was glad to have their opinion. He played it at home, and at the Myaskovskys' and the Lamms'. Among those present I remember N.Y. Myaskovsky's sister, Valentina Yakovlevna, and Sofia Alexandrovna and Olga Pavlovna Lamm, the Alexandrovs, the Shaporins, the Nechayevs, the Knippers, A.B. Goldenweiser, N.L. Dorliak, A.V. Gauk, A.L. Dolivo who had come to Tbilisi on S.I. Shlifshtein's business, and the artist I.E. Grabar who was extremely fond of Sergei Sergeyevich's music.

O.L. Knipper-Chekhova and V.I. Kachalov and his wife, N.N. Litovtseva came to our home to hear *War and Peace*. Sergei Sergeyevich introduced them to the libretto, then played the scenes "Otradnoye", "At Hélène's", and "Moscow". They liked "At Hélène's" and the waltz very much and found the "Moscow" scene powerful and moving. They expressed surprise that Pierre was a tenor. Sergei Sergeyevich explained this partly by the fact that "Tolstoy's Pierre has a slight lisp". Much was said about the importance of the future opera be g well acted, not just well sung.

Varvara Osipovna Massalitinova particularly v anted to hear the scene "In the Akhrosimova Mansion"—she was to play Akhrosimova in the stage version of *War and Peace* to be put on at the Maly Theatre. The actress thought it might help her work on the part if she heard Sergei Sergeyevich's music.

Theatres began to take an interest in the opera. The director of the Kirov Theatre in Leningrad, Y.M. Radin, who was working in Perm at that time, made enquiries about it. For several evenings Sergei Sergeyevich played *War and Peace* to V.R. Rappoport, head producer of the Baku Opera Theatre. On March 2 there was a hearing of *War and Peace* in Yerevan, where Sergei Sergeyevich had gone in connection with his concerts.

As in Nalchik Sergei Sergeyevich gave frequent performances of his works in Tbilisi, adding the Second Piano Sonata, *Diabolical Suggestions*, the dance of the Antillo girls from the ballet *Romeo and Juliet*, and pieces from the cycle *Children's Music* to those that had been performed earlier. Sometimes he played his melodies for violin and piano with Y.M. Guzikov. Sergei Sergeyevich's works were also performed by Nina Dorliak (romances to words by Anna Akhmatova), A.L. Dolivo (the songs about the Kabardinian-Balkar heroes, "My Country Grows" to words by A. Afinogenov, etc.), and B.O. and N.B. Sibor (the sonata for two violins).

In March Sergei Sergeyevich received a letter from Eisenstein: "The facts: *Ivan the Terrible* is to be filmed. I shall probably begin at the end of the winter....

"The composer is allowed a free hand all round."

N.M. Sliozberg, who had arrived on business from the film studio, delivered a letter to Sergei Sergeyevich from Eisenstein dated March 3 and an invitation to visit Alma Ata.

We decided to accompany N.M. Sliozberg on his return to Alma Ata. Sergei Sergeyevich was looking forward to the meeting with Sergei Mikhailovich. In March, at the request of the All-Union Society for Cultural Relations with Foreign Countries, he wrote an article about his work on the cantata *Alexander Nevsky*. This article contained the following reference to Eisenstein:

"It was extremely interesting to work with Eisenstein because he is not only a brilliant film director, but also has an excellent feeling for music. This expressed itself, firstly, in the very concrete and picturesque musical tasks which he set me, and secondly, in the understanding with which he accepted the music I had written."

At the beginning of April Sergei Sergeyevich sent the score of the opera to the Arts Committee in Moscow. On May 3 he began to orchestrate the opera—the scene "At Hélène's", then "Otradnoye" and "In the Akhrosimova Mansion".

Sergei Sergeyevich was delighted to receive the following letter from Dmitry Dmitrievich Shostakovich:

"May 4, 1942. Kuibyshev

"Dear Sergei Sergeyevich,

"I am taking advantage of the opportunity to sent you greetings and best wishes.

"On a visit to Moscow I was fortunate to have a look at *War and Peace*. Unfortunately this look was rather brief and hasty. I was most impressed. I will not attempt to give an analysis. But I think the first four scenes are really splendid. They made me gasp with delight as I played them through and I repeated some passages several times, which also slowed down my reading; I did not have time to play it all. Everything that takes place before the Battle of Borodino is very powerful. I liked the scene "The French in Moscow" less. However, I would not be categorical about this, as I had so little time to study it.

"With a cordial handshake

"D. Shostakovich

"P.S. I should be glad to have a word from you. My address is: Flat 2, 2a Vilonovskaya, Kuibyshev. Tel: Novaya ATS, 2-22-73.

"My wife sends you greetings

"D.S."

Sergei Sergeyevich replied to Dmitry Dmitrievich as follows:

"Dear Dmitry Dmitrievich,

"Many thanks for your kind letter. I was extremely pleased by your comments on *War and Peace*: for I was not at all sure whether you would like my opera. Shlifshtein came to Tbilisi in February and gave me the score of your Seventh to look at for three minutes. It was your original manuscript on Istanbul paper, but all sort of music was being played at the time, so all I could do was admire some of the patterns, without studying it properly. Then we tried to pick up radio broadcasts of the performances in Kuibyshev and Moscow, but without success, and even went to ask for an explanation from the management of the local radio station. So the pleasure of hearing your symphony still awaits us....

"...I shall be going to Alma Ata shortly, where I expect to receive letters with suggested changes from the Committee, who commissioned the work. In the meantime I am arranging for instruments the scenes which are not likely to be affected by these suggestions. Do write to me at the following address: c/o

173

Central Film Studio, Alma Ata, Kazakh SSR. What are your plans? What are you working on now?

"With a cordial handshake. Best wishes to Nina Vassilyevna.

"Yours SP"

At the same time as writing *War and Peace* Sergei Sergeyevich also worked on other compositions in Tbilisi.

On December 10 he played his quartet at the Nechayevs'. Those present were N.Y. Myaskovsky and his sister, P.A. Lamm and his family, and V.O. Massalitinova.

In April Sergei Sergeyevich resumed work on his Seventh Piano Sonata, begun in 1939 at the same time as the Sixth. To quote Sergei Sergeyevich, he "could not see for a long time how to handle certain features of it". He said, "on playing the sonata through after a long interval, I could not immediately understand what I had written." It needed time to "see it properly, understand why it was written like this and not in some other way". Sergei Sergeyevich used to say that often on returning to a work which had been put aside at first you "cannot see why it was put like that and not differently, but then you take a proper look and realise that is the way it should be". His work on the sonata was completed on May 2.

Shortly before our departure a representative of the Children's Film Studio, who was visiting Tbilisi, asked Sergei Sergeyevich to resume work on the film *Lermontov*. On May 25 Sergei Sergeyevich wrote the following letter to the director of the film, A.A. Gendelshtein, then in Stalinabad. [Now Dushanbe.—*Ed.*

"Dear Albert Alexandrovich,

"I am very glad that Lermontov has come to life, but sorry that Filanovsky appeared a few days before I was due to leave for Alma Ata. I had to hurry to get the music for the ball written. Nevertheless I managed to write the numbers you requested. They have been done in such a way that after playing the number to the end you can start again from the beginning and end at any point you like. This will leave you free to decide the length of each piece. Filanovsky informed me of your wishes point by point and I took note of them, which can be seen from the minutes of our meeting. He will be informing you of some of my comments. I beg you to keep the first scene in the theatre: it is very effective. I managed Fenella's reminiscences with the subsequent references to the girl very well. I shall work on the other numbers in

Alma Ata and await news from you."

At the same time Sergei Sergeyevich sent Gendelshtein a telegram saying that he would give the representative of the Children's Film Studio two waltzes, a polonaise, a galop and Fenella's reminiscences.

On May 29 we left for Alma Ata. It was sad to say good-bye to the friends we had got to know so well over the last ten months.

On the way to Alma Ata we spent a few days in Baku and Tashkent. On 1 June there was a hearing of *War and Peace* in the Baku Opera Theatre. We did not know whether the opera would be produced here, but our warm, friendly meeting with the theatre company left some most pleasant memories. "I send you cordial greetings and remember Baku and the warm reception from the State Opera Theatre with great pleasure," Sergei Sergeyevich wrote to V.R. Rappoport at the beginning of August from Alma Ata with a detailed description of his work on *War and Peace.* He had heard Niyazi's opera *Hosrof and Shirin* for the first time with great interest.

In Tashkent we stayed with the poet Vladimir Alexandrovich Lugovskoi, taking advantage of his hospitality. Lugovskoi read us the text of his songs for *Ivan the Terrible.* Sergei Sergeyevich found that he read "with great rhythmic vigour" and said he wanted to remember Lugovskoi's reading and understand his basic ideas before composing the music.

On arrival in Alma Ata we went to stay at the hotel of the House of the Soviets where many people who worked for the Central Associated Film Studio were living at the time.

Eisenstein was delighted to see Sergei Sergeyevich. He was completely absorbed in the film. "First he described the scenario, then we went through the whole of it together, and he told me in vivid detail how he imagined the music."

Eisenstein showed Sergei Sergeyevich his most interesting sketches for the film. He asked him to think about the main themes and musical characterisations, and gave him a list of main themes covering twelve pages of writing paper and dated July 14, 1942. The place and nature of each theme were indicated precisely. I shall quote the following examples:

"1. 'The storm approaches'—the main theme of *Ivan the Terrible.*

Treated like the scene of an approaching storm.

a) In the 'Overture':
    the birth of this theme

out of a chaos of voices and noises
(to the words 'A black cloud has risen').
b) Ivan appears to receive
the envoys ('Ivan the boy').
c) The end of the scene over the coffin
of Anastasia.
Finale of Part I.
2. The Song of the 'Blue Ocean'
with words.
A Schlager that can
be sung.
a) The nurse sings to the little Ivan.
b) Appears in Ivan s speech in
the Assumption Cathedral—sadly.
c) Appointment of Kurbsky
for the Livonian campaign
(after the scene of Ivan's illness).
Part II
The march of Livonia (cavalry
at the gallop. They reached the ocean.
The ocean at Tsar Ivan's feet).
3. Kazan song
('Forge cannons of copper, Ye founders')
A Schlager that can be sung.
a) Preparations for Kazan
2 couplets
then alternate with
the couplets of Foma and Yerema.
3rd couplet. Orchestra.
b) Night and dawn
(lyrical culmination: blessing of the warriors).
c) Sung in militant fashion—
an assault. Combination with Foma
and Yerema (Kurbsky rushes off).
4. Oprichniks' vow
a) As singing in the Oprichniks' Chancery.
b) As a semi-recitative—
At the death of Vladimir Andreyevich.
c) In dance form—whistling by Staden
d) In the Basmanov father and son scene—
as a background
Fyodor—whispering."

Sergei Sergeyevich pondered on the material for the film and orchestrated the opera. At the beginning of July he received detailed letters from the Arts Committee—its comments on the opera. The letters praised the lyrical scenes. With regard to the folk scenes, Sergei Sergeyevich was requested to consider strengthening the dramatic and heroic elements and shortening the everyday episodes, and concerning the opening of the opera doubts were expressed as to whether *War and Peace* should open with a lyrical scene. From the letters Sergei Sergeyevich learnt that S.A. Samosud was very interested in the opera.

The folk scenes had to be reviewed. Sergei Sergeyevich examined the scene "On the Eve of the Battle of Borodino" and decided to make some changes in the conversation between Denisov and Prince Andrei: their dialogue now led up to Denisov's impassioned arioso. A new episode was inserted—the arrival of the inhabitants of Smolensk, Vassilisa and Matveyev, who give the home guard a bitter, wrathful account of the destruction of their native town by the enemy. The scene of the women bringing food was deleted.

Sergei Sergeyevich decided to consult Eisenstein and gradually played the whole opera through to him. In the meantime Eisenstein received a telegram from Samosud inviting him to assist with a production of *War and Peace*. In order to consider possible changes, Sergei Mikhailovich requested the libretto and was thus prepared in advance for each successive meeting.

With regard to the lyrical scenes, I remember Sergei Mikhailovich frequently telling Sergei Sergeyevich that he could not "forgive" him for not writing a scene of the ball when Natasha dances with Prince Andrei. In considering changes to the folk scenes, they both sought to give them unity and strengthen the dramatic element. In this connection, apart from the insertion of new episodes, much attention was given to deleting prosaic details which slowed down the action.

In the scene "On the Eve of the Battle of Borodino", Eisenstein suggested that the scores of Vassilisa and Matveyev be supported by a choir. Sergei Sergeyevich agreed that this would produce a more powerful effect. Sergei Mikhailovich was very fond of Prince Andrei's monologue, "But I will tell you". Under the influence of his insistent pleas Sergei Sergeyevich expanded this monologue slightly, by adding "He who fights the hardest, he who spares himself least, will wrest victory from the foe". When Eisenstein first heard Prince Andrei's monologue, he asked "What will be the equivalent of the Andrei theme in Ivan the Terrible?" and immediately replied himself: "The Oprichniks' Vow," which he asked him to write as soon as possible. Each meeting began by Sergei Mikhailovich "demanding" that the Prince Andrei theme be played. Only after that would he proceed to the business in hand.

In the "Moscow" scene it was decided to take out the two French songs with which it had originally opened and the scene in which the Muscovites read Napoleon's edict. The scene was now to begin with Ramball's words "Moscow is empty" and his conversation with Bonnet.

Sergei Mikhailovich suggested the addition of two new episodes in the fire scene—one showing French actors wearing costumes and make-up and running away from the fire and the other the arrival of Napoleon and his marshals who are confronted by the fire and the wrath of the Russian people. (There was also a plan to have Napoleon and his marshals meet a procession of Muscovites carrying the bodies of the executed.)

In the last scene—the Smolensk Road—Sergei Mikhailovich suggested a "more howling prelude". He was attracted by the idea of a snowstorm—a blizzard and the retreating French army which the Russian people are driving from their native land. Sergei Sergeyevich worked very hard on this "howling" prelude. He told me, "It's even worse with the snowstorm, than when I got stuck on the orchestration of the moonlit night in *Semyon Kotko*. I want to achieve the greatest possible effect, to have devils, Baba Yagas, whirling about in the air." It was based on the material with which the scene had opened before, but was expanded and orchestrated "with screaming and whistling". In order to speed up the action, he and Sergei Mikhailovich decided to omit the partisans' conversations before the attack and the scene after the battle. Sergei Sergeyevich rewrote the music of the battle. It was decided to write an aria for Denisov after his words "The foe is vanquished." Pierre learnt of the fate of Prince Andrei and Natasha from Dolokhov, instead of Denisov in the first version. Incidentally, Sergei Sergeyevich told me several times how sorry he was that Pierre's words "A rusty door opens and out wafts the scent of long forgotten happiness" were omitted in the performance. Sergei Mikhailovich also suggested omitting the female choir which precedes the finale, in order not to slow down the action. He often said that he pictured the opera's finale as an extremely majestic scene.

When Prokofiev and Eisenstein discussed the opening of the opera, they found themselves in disagreement. Sergei Sergeyevich thought it essential to have a choral prelude of an epic nature about the "multitude of tongues" which had come to Russia, which he wanted to call the Epigraph. Sergei Mikhailovich suggested beginning the opera with a very short scene of Tilsit in the form of an introduction: the two emperors embracing, Russian and French soldiers, banners, and shouts of "Peace! Peace! " Sergei Sergeyevich objected that "this was cold", that he could not see "how this could be done interestingly in music", and that the opening of the opera was so important. The, discussion became so heated that it almost caused a tiff. But after a while Eisenstein accepted Sergei Sergeyevich's idea and even advised him to take a look at Suvorov's words for the Epigraph.

In November Sergei Sergeyevich wrote to S.I. Shlifshtein of the Arts Committee:

"...As you already know from my telegram, I have finished revising *War and Peace.* This revision follows the plan which I described to Solodovnikov in Alma Ata in August and which he approved. The changes were later agreed upon by Eisenstein who provided me with some interesting ideas. Their main purpose, to delete the everyday scenes and replace them with dramatic and patriotic episodes, would seem to have been achieved. At least, the "war" part of the opera now has much more dramatic tension. All that remains is to write a choral prelude on the theme of which will form a kind of epigraph to the whole opera. I already have the plan and part of the text, and hope to write it soon."

The management of the opera theatre in Alma Ata asked Sergei Sergeyevich to write a ballet. He did not want to begin work on a new ballet before completing *Cinderella.* He was much more attracted by the idea of writing an opera based on Kazakh folk music which he found remarkably original and beautiful. Sergei Sergeyevich decided to write a lyrico-comic opera about a jolly barber, beloved by the people.

During Prokofiev's stay in Alma Ata in the summer of 1942 the management of the Opera Theatre suggested that he should write a ballet. Sergei Sergeyevich did not want to embark on a new work before he had completed *Cinderella*. (By then two acts were almost complete.) He expressed the desire to write an opera using Kazakh folk music, with which he had been acquainted for some time from A. Zatayevich's collections. I remember that the critic D.L. Talnikov took part in these talks.

We began studying Kazakh stories, legends, songs and proverbs. There gradually emerged the theme of a bold, quickwitted barber, a cruel khan, true love and undying friendship. The content of three acts of the future opera was written in September.

In late 1942 and early 1943 we went to Moscow in connection with public performances of Prokofiev's new works. In reply to questions about future plans, Sergei Sergeyevich mentioned a lyrico-comic opera *The Horned Shah* (otherwise known as *Khan Buzai*) among the compositions on which he was proposing to work in the immediate future.

After returning to Alma Ata, he arranged for instruments *War and Peace*, made some changes in *Betrothal in a Nunnery* in connection with the Bolshoi Theatre's intention to produce the opera, and wrote the cantata *Ballad of the Unknown Boy*. At the same time he devoted a great deal of time to his new plan; studying Zatayevich's collections, getting acquainted with the orchestra of Kazakh folk instruments and Brusilovsky's operas, and visiting the Kazakh Drama Theatre.

He read *Essays on the History of Kazakh Literature* by Mukhtar Auezov and Leonid Sobolev (*The Literature and Art of Kazakhstan*, Alma Ata, 1939, Nos. 8-9), copying down names connected with Kazakh folklore, descriptions of folk songs, their nature (wedding songs, lyrical songs on themes from everyday life, spells and incantations, comic songs, etc.).

On April 2, 1943, Prokofiev wrote to N.Y. Myaskovsky and his sister Valentina Yakovlevna:

"I am now collecting all sorts of Kazakh material for a rather large work. There is so much of interest, a whole sea, q ite untouched! "

In April the Presidium of the Kazakh Soviet Socialist Republic invited Sergei Sergeyevich to take part in an evening to commemorate the anniversary of Vladimir Mayakovsky's death.

"Your work is, without a doubt, very akin and close to the poet's work," read the invitation. "This is why we are requesting you to take part in the evening by performing some of your compositions which are best suited to the programme.

"We trust you will agree, bearing in mind also that the proceeds from this evening will be donated entirely to the fund to help the children of soldiers at the front."

The concert was held on April 26 at the Opera Theatre. Sergei Sergeyevich played a Prelude, the Gavotte Op. 25, and the March from the opera *Love for Three Oranges*—works which he had once played to Mayakovsky.

Prokofiev decided to spend the summer in Perm, where the Kirov Opera and Ballet Theatre had been evacuated from Leningrad, to continue work on *Cinderella*. Shortly before his departure he wrote the content for a new scene of the opera *Khan Buzai*—"The Dream".

In Perm, while awaiting the arrival of the librettist N.D. Volkov and the ballet-master K.M. Sergeyev, Prokofiev orchestrated the *Ballad of the Unknown Boy* and finished his Sonata for Flute and Piano begun in Alma Ata.

Ary Moiseyevich Pazovsky and the director of the theatre Yevgeny Mikhailovich Radin spoke to Sergei Sergeyevich not only about *Cinderella* but also about the possibility of including the operas *War and Peace* and *Betrothal in a Nunnery* in their repertoire. As author, he was invited to say who he would like to see in the main roles. He attended performances at the theatre, making notes on the programmes about this or that singer.

The theatre also expressed an interest in producing the *Tale of the Buffoon* (*Who Out-Buffooned Seven Buffoons*), and Sergei Sergeyevich played excerpts from this ballet to L. Yakobson, I. Sherman and P. Feldt in September.

Work on the libretto of the new opera also continued. In the autumn of 1943 we returned to Moscow. Sergei Sergeyevich resumed work on the opera *Khan Buzai* in 1946, when he completed the ballet *Cinderella*, wrote the Fifth Symphony, the Eighth Piano Sonata, music for the film *Ivan the Terrible*, and the Ode to the End of the War.

Sovietskaya Muzyka, No. 8, 1962

Svyatoslav Richter

ON PROKOFIEV

I had more encounters with Prokofiev's music than with the composer himself. I was never particularly close with Prokofiev the man. I was shy. For me he was all in his works, earlier as well as now. Acquaintances with his compositions were acquaintances with Prokofiev himself. Thus it is about them that I can say more. Yet at the same time, in playing Prokofiev, I exhaust to a certain extent that which I could say about him in words (herein lies the difficulty of my position). But I will remember a few bright moments of my personal meetings with Sergei Sergeyevich all my life.

The first meeting. The first thing I associated with Prokofiev's name was how everybody played the March from the *Love for Three Oranges.* A novelty that everyone liked very much. And when Prokofiev came to Odessa and played his compositions, everyone concluded that the only good thing was that march. He played a great deal, all evening, but they waited for only the march. And the musicians said: "Yes, wonderful, wonderful" ... but everything centred around the march. It was published in a cover with little circles, squares (new! futurism!).

I was 12 years old. All of us—Papa, Mama, and I—lived in Odessa. Papa taught at the Conservatoire. I liked to sit at home and sight-read operas at the piano—from beginning to end. Once Papa took me with him—Prokofiev was going to perform in the Conservatoire's hall.

It was a winter day. It was dim in the hall. Before the public appeared a tall young man with long arms. He wore a fashionable foreign-made suit—short sleeves, short pants—and probably because of this it seemed that he had grown out of it. And all in checks, like the cover of *Three Oranges*.

I remember that the way he bowed seemed very funny to me. He sort of bent in two—crack! Besides, his eyes didn't change their expression, stared directly ahead, and therefore gazed somewhere at the ceiling when he straightened up. And his face didn't seem to express anything at all.

Then he played. I remember I was impressed by the way he played everything without pedal and in a very "polished" manner. He played his own little pieces, and each one was like an elegant delicacy in a strictly thought-out menu. This was very unusual for me and greatly differed from what I had heard earlier. I was still a child and to me everything he played sounded the same (then even Bach's works sounded all the same to me).

The march came at the end.

The audience was pleased. So was Prokofiev. He bowed with a peculiar, pleased look, reminding me of a circus juggler, or a character from Hoffmann.

Then I knew nothing about him. No, I knew from the talk of musicians that he had written a certain Classical Symphony. That the Classical Symphony was good, very good. That it was a model for new composers.

And also, that the Odessa composer Vova Femelidi, who had written the opera *The Break-up* and the ballet *Carmagnole*, was under the influence of Prokofiev. Afterwards I became convinced of this, but then he struck me as original. And that is all. I knew nothing of Prokofiev himself. One would think that he had "gone out of fashion" and was forgotten.

I knew that there were such composers as Rachmaninov, Puccini, Křenek (in those years the operas *Turandot* and *Johny Performs* were in the repertoire of the Odessa Opera Theatre), and even Pfitzner (I had the piano score of *Palestrina* at home). I knew of Stravinsky—I had heard *Petrouchka* twice—and knew of Shostakovich—I had looked over the piano score of *Lady Macbeth*. But I knew nothing of Prokofiev.

And so 10 years passed without Prokofiev.

Moscow. In 1937 I came to Moscow, became a student of H. Neuhaus, and immediately found myself immersed in a genuine musical life. Completely new horizons opened up before me. I found out "what" Myaskovsky was. Shostakovich's Fifth Symphony appeared—this was a great event. People were talking about Prokofiev in the Conservatoire.

One sunny day I was walking along Arbat Street and caught sight of an unusual man. He had a defiant air about him and passed by me like an apparition. He was wearing bright yellow shoes and a checked suit with an orange-red tie.

I could not help turning around to look at him—it was Prokofiev.

Now I could always meet him. Though I hardly knew him, this had become an everyday possibility; I lived with the Neuhauses, and Neuhaus and Prokofiev lived in the same building. This was the atmosphere of that life—Prokofiev lived here.

You could hear the phrase: "Those boys there are so charming.... They are Prokofiev's sons: the older one and the other, a real little doll! Charming! " You could always meet Prokofiev's wife—an elegant woman in a dark-blue beret, with an impatient look on her face. I saw them together at concerts. Once we were returning home from a concert in the Large Hall of the Conservatoire. Neuhaus, Anatoly Vedernikov, and I. Emerging from the Kurskaya Metro station, at the turn to Chkalov Street, Neuhaus joyfully exclaimed:

"Ah, Sergei Sergeyevich, hello! "

They walked ahead, talking. Prokofiev was saying something about Richard Strauss. It seems to me that he was speaking ironically about his ballet *The Legend of Joseph*. Neuhaus didn't agree. Anatoly and I walked along behind, observing them and joking at their expense—who Neuhaus looked like and who Prokofiev, in general, babbling indecencies, excusable at that age.

I still treated Prokofiev's music with caution. More correctly, I still had not "fathomed" it. I always listened with interest, but remained passive. I was "brought up" on romantic music and this "hampered" me. It seemed to me that the latest thing in new music was Richard Strauss.

When Prokofiev's cello concerto appeared in 1938, I was, quite unexpectedly, asked to rehearse it with the 'cellist Berezovsky. I regarded this as I would any other work which I had to do in order to make some money. I went to Berezovsky's on Krivokolenny Lane, on the fifth floor, for two months. This was just another job for me. Berezovsky, on the one hand, was pleased with the commission; on the other, this music was alien to him. He shrugged his shoulders, sighed, became distressed over the difficulties, but studied the music and was quite nervous about it. I can't say that I liked the concerto, but I already felt that this work aroused an interest in me.

When we first performed the concerto in a smoke-filled room at the Composers' Union, which was situated at that time in a "gothic" little building not far from Arbat Street, it received an enthusiastic reception: "A real event. Just like the Second Violin Concerto." There was a lively, positive public debate. Wishes of success were expressed to Berezovsky. No one doubted that the work would be a tremendous success. "This is a new page." Nevertheless the work soon suffered a set-back.

When we came to play the concerto for Prokofiev, he opened the door himself and led us into a small canary-coloured room. Sketches of the scenery from, it seems to me, *Three Oranges*, done in pencil or Indian ink, hung on the walls. He immediately shouted at the children: "Go into the other room, children! Don't bother us here! " Then he sat down. Berezovsky looked terribly confused. Probably because of this Prokofiev didn't particularly want to discuss things with him; he sat at the piano himself and began to show him: this way and that way ... I stood to the side, completely "out of the picture". Prokofiev was businesslike, but not pleasant. Berezovsky's questions probably irritated him. I was pleased that his demands coincided with my views. He wanted that which the music demanded—nothing more! Berezovsky had a tendency for sentimentality, and he couldn't find a place to use it anywhere. To show off his tone in at least one small passage! But, as if on purpose, such passages were not sentimental at all. I didn't even once sit down at the piano, and we left.

Berezovsky passed into the hands of Melik-Pashayev, who conducted the concerto. I don't know how they worked together.

I went to the première and sat in the amphitheatre. I hid in a corner and was nervous. Simply for the work, and for Berezovsky also, of course. The ground was pulled out from under his chair, so to speak, during the performance. Melik-Pashayev took highly uncomfortable and, moreover, wrong tempi. It seems to me that he missed the inner essence of the work.

185

It was a complete failure. They bowed haphazardly, and on
that everything was over.

A new attitude. Soon after, Prokofiev conducted a concert of
his own works. *Egyptian Nights*, the Second Violin Concerto
played by Busya Goldstein, the suite *Ala and Lolli*, and the
suite from the ballet *The Buffoon* were performed. Again it was
"interesting".

But the work which compelled me to like it and, through it,
Prokofiev in general, turned out to be the First Violin Concerto.
Later I met many people whose love for Prokofiev also began
with this work. It seems impossible to me to love music and not
to be captivated by it. You can compare its effect with the
sensation you get when you first open your window in spring-
time and restless sounds burst through it from the street. I fell
in love with the concerto even before I knew the violin part. I
simply listened to Vedernikov practising the accompaniment.
From that time on, I welcomed with amazing delight and even
with envy each of Prokofiev's works that I came to know.

Enchanted by the Violin Concerto, I decided to play one of
Prokofiev's compositions. I even dreamed about playing the
Second Sonata. And so I decided to learn it. The sonata turned
out to be completely different from what I had dreamed about.
I learned it on the second course, in 1938. I studied it without
any particular pleasure.

It was then that I met Sergei Sergeyevich in the Composers'
Union. Anatoly Vedernikov and I played through Stravinsky's
Oedipus Rex on two pianos. Vedernikov played the orchestral
part and I—the choral. The performance was organised seriously, with recitation. Before this something had taken place in the
hall, a meeting, I think. Many composers were present. Someone asked Prokofiev: "Are you staying to listen?" "What for,
without an orchestra and choir? No, I am leaving." Nevertheless, they talked him into staying. We played well and with
feeling. A few young composers left demonstratively. When we
finished, Prokofiev came up to Vedernikov who was sitting at
the first piano. I could see that he was pleased and he said that
it was good and that he hadn't expected it to sound like that on
two pianos.

The performance of his Third Symphony in 1939 left a
tremendous impression on me. The composer conducted. I

hadn't felt anything like it in my life while listening to music. The impression was staggering; it was like the end of the world. Prokofiev uses super-intensive means of expression in the symphony. In the third movement, the Scherzo, the strings play such an abrupt figure that it seems to fly just like flakes of ash, as if something was burning in the air. The last movement begins like a sombre march—grandiose masses gape and topple over—"the end of the Universe". Then after a calm everything begins with redoubled force, accompanied by the funereal sound of bells. I sat and didn't know what would become of me. I wanted to hide. I looked at my neighbour. He was wet and red.... Shivers still ran up and down my spine during the intermission.

Once Neuhaus came and said: "This is what Sergei Sergeyevich is like! Always something new up his sleeve! There was his *Romeo*. Now he has written an opera, and a magnificent one! I was at the rehearsal—marvellous! "

This was *Semyon Kotko*.

The première of the opera was a momentous event in my life. One of those which in the full sense of the word attracted me to Prokofiev.

After that a whole crowd of us students went three or four times, though the performances and production left a lot to be desired.

It was also then that I saw the film *Alexander Nevsky*, and it was actually the music that left a lasting impression on me. Earlier, film music had never impressed me to such an extent. This time it literally overwhelmed me.

In general, it seems to me that after his Fifth Concerto Prokofiev found his style, which was new, yet very easy to understand and even popular. I consider *Semyon Kotko* to be one of these works. At the same time it is one of the richest and most perfect of Prokofiev's creations and, without doubt, the best Soviet opera.

In *Semyon Kotko* Prokofiev continues to follow the path charted by Moussorgsky. Many composers developed this trend (Debussy, Janáček), but I think that Moussorgsky's direct descendant in the field of national folk musical drama is our Prokofiev.

He carries his musical design, coming from the intonations of human speech, to the utmost prominence. Listening to the opera you begin to live a common life with the work, which breathes youthfulness, like in that time, that period of history which is portrayed in it.

This composition is so perfect and easy to understand that its appreciation depends only on the listener's willingness to listen. And there is always such a listener. This is my deep conviction. You only have to have a real chance to hear this pearl of operatic literature.

That evening, when I first heard *Semyon Kotko*, I understood that Prokofiev was a great composer.

The Sixth Sonata. A circle of serious musicians used to gather at the Lamm's, in an old, dark Moscow apartment, filled chiefly with music. The main nucleus consisted of Moscow's composers and prominent musicians of the older generation. Myaskovsky was always there—taciturn, infinitely tactful. If his opinion were asked, he spoke like one who knew the subject, though quietly and at the same time as if it didn't concern him. Pianists and conductors were often invited, the circle gathered regularly, as if carrying on the tradition of the Russian musical circles at the time of Balakirev.

It was all informal. The main thing—playing in 8 hands. Tea and boubliks were served. Pavel Alexandrovich Lamm did all the arrangements for piano. For every Thursday he contrived to prepare something new.

Neuhaus took me with him.

Something special was expected—Prokofiev was supposed to come.

Rather too gloomy... A spot on the wall... Very soon I found myself at the piano playing Myaskovsky's Thirteenth Symphony. We played in 8 hands, from manuscript. I sat with Shebalin, Nechayev—with Lamm.

Prokofiev entered the room. He came not as a regular, but as a guest—this could be felt. He looked as if it were his birthday, but ... a little overbearing as well. He brought his sonata and said: "Well, to work! " At once: "I'll play."

...He was younger than many, but everyone felt that he meant to say: "Though I am younger, I am as good as any one of you! " His somewhat haughty attitude towards his associates didn't, however, extend to Myaskovsky, to whom he was particularly attentive.

Prokofiev behaved businesslike, professionally. I remember

how he heeded the advice of Neuhaus, who considered that the bass A couldn't sound for 5 bars, and he rewrote the passage.

It seems to me that he played his sonata twice and left. He played from manuscript and I turned the pages for him.

Prokofiev did not even finish playing but I had already decided that I would play this sonata.

When later, during the war, I heard him play the Eighth Sonata, he already didn't play as well as then.

The remarkable clarity of style and structural perfection of the music amazed me. I hadn't heard anything like it before. The composer, with barbaric audacity, breaks with the ideals of the romantics and includes the shattering pulse of the 20th century in his music. This is a magnificent sonata, classically well-balanced in spite of all the sharp corners.

The sonata also interested me as a performer; I thought: as I had never played anything like this I should try my hand at it. Neuhaus agreed. When I went home to Odessa for the holidays I took the music with me.

Papa admitted the merits of Prokofiev's music, but it was too extravagant for his ear. "Terrible," he said, "like being slapped in the face all the time! Again smash! Again ... it takes aim: bash! "

I recall that I studied it with great pleasure. I learned it during the summer and played it at a concert on the 14th of October.

This was my first non-student public performance. And what a responsibility! Neuhaus included me—a student of the 4th course—in the programme next to himself. He played Myaskovsky, Alexandrov, and Y. Krein in the first half; I played Prokofiev in the second. Three small pieces: the rondo from *The Prodigal Son*, the *Pastoral Sonatina*, and *Paysage* were like a prelude to the Sixth Sonata. I was terribly nervous before the concert. I locked myself in a classroom and practised for ten hours at a time during the last three days. I remember that I wasn't satisfied with my playing at the concert, but the sonata was a very great success. The audience was a specific one—musical. It was unanimously "for", not one "against". It liked both the sonata itself and how I played it.

The Fifth Concerto. Prokofiev crossed the entire hall, smiling, and shook my hand. In the artists' room he said: "Maybe the young musician will play my Fifth Concerto, which has been a failure and never been successful anywhere? Maybe he will play it and the public will like it? "

I didn't know the Fifth Concerto, but it immediately interested me. When I got the music I didn't like it very much. And Neuhaus somehow didn't approve of the choice. He advised the Third. In general, the concerto had a somewhat undermined reputation. I looked the Third Concerto over. I had heard it many times. There was a recording of Prokofiev playing it. It was considered the best, but for some reason I wasn't attracted by it. I looked it over again, and again I thought: no, I will play the Fifth. Once Prokofiev said it, my fate was sealed.

In February of 1941 I went to Odessa and took the score of the Fifth Concerto with me.

A month later I returned to Moscow with the prepared concerto. Prokofiev wanted to hear it. We met at the Neuhaus' where I played the concerto over twice with Anatoly Vedernikov.

Prokofiev came with his wife and the room filled with the strong scent of Parisian perfume. He straightaway began to tell some unbelievable stories about the life of gangsters in America. They were told in Prokofiev's inimitable style—businesslike and with humour.

We sat at a small table under which our legs didn't fit and drank tea with the invariable Neuhaus slices of ham.

Then we played.

Prokofiev was pleased and, standing in front of us behind the two pianos from where he had conducted, he pulled two chocolate bars out of both pockets simultaneously and presented them to us with a grand gesture. There and then we agreed on the dates of the rehearsals.

He sat me down at the piano at the very first rehearsal so that the orchestra could become accustomed to the piano part. Prokofiev's conducting gestures "suited" his works like nobody else's so that the musicians, who understood little in this music, played quite well anyway. Prokofiev gave his instructions plainly and directly: "Kindly do this and that.... And you—be so kind as to play it this way." In general, he was naturally demanding. There were three very productive rehearsals in all.

The day of the concert grew closer. Prokofiev was to conduct the entire programme.

The suite *Lieutenant Kizhe, The Scythian Suite*, the Fifth

Concerto and, finally, the *Classical Symphony* were to be performed.

The order of the programme seemed strange to me and I didn't like it very much. I wanted *The Scythian Suite* to be at the end.

I arrived earlier at the Tchaikovsky Hall and stood and listened. Nervousness, uncertainty and the strong impression from *The Scythian Suite* were all mixed up in my mind. I thought: now I will go on to the stage and that's it ... the end ... won't be able to play anything.

I played accurately, but I remember that I wasn't pleased with my performance because of my nervousness.

There was no usual applause after the first movement, as usually occurs, and I began to think (I looked at the hall and saw sour faces in the first row) that nobody understood anything. There was a sort of chill ... and the hall was rather empty. And just recently I had played Tchaikovsky's concerto to a full house.

And yet the concerto was a great success. We were called back many times and Prokofiev said: "How strange, look, a success! I would never have thought.... Hm... Hm..." And then all of a sudden: "Aha! I know why they are applauding like that—they are waiting for a Chopin nocturne from you! "

I was extremely happy. At 22 I had decided to become a pianist and now, at 25, I was playing a work which no one but the composer had performed. At the same time I had a feeling of dissatisfaction both from the great nervousness I had experienced (try to play the Fifth Concerto and you will understand) and maybe from the premonition that I wouldn't play it again for a long time—almost 18 years! ...

The Seventh Sonata. Soon the war began, separating all of us. I didn't meet Prokofiev again for a long time.

I prepared for a concert, my first solo concert in Moscow, which had been scheduled for October 19, 1941. Posters were pasted all over the city. Because of my nervousness I didn't notice what was happening around me.

Before this I had played a Bach concerto for piano and orchestra, the Schumann concerto, the Brahms quintet and the Bach double concerto with Anatoly Vedernikov. But the nervousness about my first recital literally made me shiver.

The concert was postponed—the time was inappropriate. It took place in July of 1942. The programme included Beethoven, Schubert, Prokofiev, and Rachmaninov. And so, in my first solo concert I played Prokofiev—the Second Sonata. I didn't play well.

Approximately at that time the opera *War and Peace* appeared. An extraordinary event! An opera based on Tolstoy's novel! This seemed impossible. But since Prokofiev had undertaken it, you had to believe.

We played the opera to a group of musicians, again with Vedernikov. Shostakovich was among the listeners.

The winter days were overcast, and darkness came early.

At the beginning of 1943 I received the music of the Seventh Sonata. I became engrossed in it and learned it in four days.

A concert of Soviet music was being prepared and Prokofiev wanted me to perform his new sonata. He had just returned to Moscow and lived in the National Hotel. I came to play the sonata for him. He was alone. There was a piano in the room, but everything began with the pedal not working and Prokofiev said: "So what, let's fix it...." We crawled under the piano, fixed something under it, and in a moment bumped foreheads so hard that we saw stars. Sergei Sergeyevich later recalled: "But we fixed the pedal after all, didn't we! "

The meeting was a businesslike one; we were both involved in the sonata. We spoke little. I never had any serious talks with Prokofiev. We limited ourselves to laconic indications. True, I was never alone with him other than that time with the Seventh Sonata. And when a third person was present, it was always that third person who spoke.

The première of the sonata took place in the October Hall of the House of Trade Unions. I was its first performer. The work was extremely successful. (Later, too, the sonata was invariably a success everywhere except in one city—Kiev. This was also the case with the Second Sonata.)

Prokofiev was present at the concert and was called on the stage. When almost all the audience had left and mainly the musicians had remained (there were many: I remember Oistrakh, Shebalin...), everyone wanted to hear the sonata a second time. The atmosphere was elevated and at the same time serious. And I played well.

The listeners particularly keenly grasped the spirit of the work which reflected their innermost feelings and concerns

hostakovich's Seventh Symphony was similarly welcomed at
at time).

The sonata immediately throws one into the anxious
tuation of the world losing its equilibrium. Anxiety and un-
ertainty reign. Man is witnessing the riot of the violent forces
f death and destruction. However what he had lived by before
id not cease to exist for him. He feels, loves. Now the full
ange of his emotions bursts forth. Together with everyone and
verything he protests and poignantly shares the common grief.
he impetuous, advancing race, full of the will for victory,
weeps away everything in its path. It gains its strength in
truggle and develops into a gigantic life-affirming force.

The Seventh Sonata was to be performed in the Sovinform-
ureau, where various new works were premièred during the
var. Political and official Moscow gathered in Kalashny Lane in
n old mansion. Writers read their works. The atmosphere was
ot very auspicious: the grand piano was all carved and gilded,
ut the keyboard practically didn't work. I didn't play well. I
lmost completely became lost in the second subject.

Sergei Sergeyevich said later: "Something happened there...
But that doesn't matter. You got out of it cleverly. I was
lready worrying that you were on the point of ... how would it
nd."

I recall S. S. in a different situation, when he seemed almost a
oy. I always noticed his interest in unusual and strange
phenomena. There was something of the boy or adventurer in
his. In 1943, when I first played his First Concerto, he
ittended the rehearsal. After it he suddenly said:

"Do you know what an amazing thing I saw.... When you
began the final octaves, the empty chairs around me moved in
he same rhythm.... Just think, the chairs also... How interest-
ng! ..."

That year I went on my first tours, during which I played
Prokofiev's Fourth and Seventh sonatas, among other works.

The Eighth Sonata. The next important meeting with Prokofiev was my acquaintance with his Eighth Sonata in 1944.
Prokofiev played it in the Composers' Union and its first
performance in concert was given by Gilels.

Prokofiev played it twice. After the first time it was evident
that this was a remarkable composition, but when I was asked

whether I was going to play it I didn't know yet what to answer.

It was difficult for Sergei Sergeyevich to play. He didn't have his former confidence and his hands fluttered limply over the keys.

After the second hearing I definitely decided that I was going to play the sonata. Some people sniggered: "What outdated music, don't tell us you want to play that? ! "

It is the richest of all of Prokofiev's sonatas. It has a complex inner life with profound contrapositions. At times it seems to freeze, as if listening to the inexorable march of the times. The sonata is somewhat heavy to grasp, but heavy with richness— like a tree heavy with fruit.

Along with the Fourth and Ninth it remains my favourite work. Gilels played it magnificently in his recital in the Grand Hall.

The All-Union Piano Competition was about to take place, and my closest friends strongly urged me to take part. I included the Eighth Sonata in my programme.

I didn't have my own apartment at the time and lived at Vedernikov's near Moscow.

I was supposed to play last, but I somehow got mixed up and arrived an hour late. Everything was over. Prokofiev waited, waited for a long time. Many were leaving but they returned when they learned that there would be a continuation. Sergei Sergeyevich also returned. He was very strict in such cases but this time he simply said: "Ye-e-s ... an hour late... Well, we'll have to hear the sonata anyway." He was interested in hearing his own work.

I remember that the Eighth Sonata left a great impression on Gedike: "You know, Slava, this music really is good. What a magnificent sonata! "

I had one more incident with Sergei Sergeyevich, a most punctual man. I was to play the Sixth, Seventh, and Eighth sonatas in a subscription concert of Prokofiev's works in the October Hall of the House of Trade Unions. Nina Dorliak and I had just returned from Tbilisi where concerts begin at nine o'clock in the evening. They phoned us at eight and asked what the matter was, why we weren't coming. It was Victory Day— the 9th of May. City traffic was stopped. The streets were teeming with people. We lived in Arbat Street. I arrived at the House of Trade Unions only at 9.15 p.m. Sergei Sergeyevich waited with the rest. When the concert was opened and the Sixth Sonata announced, an elderly, intelligent-looking man stood up in the middle of the hall and said: "This is the most swinish trick of all! " and left. He had waited for an announcement that the "concert was cancelled".

Sergei Sergeyevich was pleased that the concert took place. As to my being late, he taunted me, but good-naturedly.

He had greatly changed from the last time I saw him. He had become gentle and condescending. True, I was never late when I went to him on business. Here he would have certainly been very angry. When we made arrangements he would say: "Well, and what about the time? " He emphasised that you had to be punctual.

The Flute Sonata. The "Akhmatova Cycle". After the Seventh Sonata Prokofiev wrote the Flute Sonata which he later remade into a violin sonata because the flutists didn't hurry to perform it. Now all violinists play it. It is now known as the Second Violin Sonata, but it is far better in its original version for flute.

Its first performance wasn't in concert but at an audition of works by the State Prize Committee in the Beethoven Hall of the Bolshoi Theatre. I played it with Kharkovsky. It didn't receive any award. After that we played it often in concerts and it was always a success.

This sonata was performed in a concert of Prokofiev's works in 1945, in which I played for the first time for Nina Dorliak, who sang the "Akhmatova Cycle".

The programme of the evening turned out to be heavy. Melnikova sang the "Russian Songs". She sang well. H. Tsomyk played the Ballade for Cello. I played the Sixth Sonata at the end.

Generally, Sergei Sergeyevich's works were played in concerts continuously. You couldn't imagine Moscow's musical life without his music.

Prokofiev worked indefatigably. He tirelessly enriched the treasure-house of modern classics.

Nikolina Gora. On his birthday, when I visited him for the first time at Nikolina Gora, Prokofiev told me:

"I have something interesting for you." And he showed me the sketches of the Ninth Sonata. "This will be your sonata...

Only don't think that it will be for effect... Not to amaze the Grand Hall."

Truly, at first glance it seemed quite simple to me. I was even a little disappointed.

I somehow cannot describe that most vivid and interesting day. It was my first really close meeting with Prokofiev, in his home, amongst his friends. I couldn't suppress my confusion. Everything seemed to pass me by.

I remember that there was talk of *War and Peace* and the *Tale of the Stone Flower*. That they should be staged. I remember the early spring, the highway turnoff to Nikolina Gora, the trip by boat across Moskva River (there was no bridge), and Sergei Sergeyevich coming to meet us in the garden, the elegant breakfast, given for the first time on the cool veranda—very charming—the scent of spring....

Another meeting. The year 1948 came around. I personally don't understand the attitude to Prokofiev's work in that period.

On January 28, 1948, my concert with Nina Dorliak was to take place (the programme included Rimsky-Korsakov and Prokofiev). Everything was successful in that concert: the programme, the performance....

That was a great success for Sergei Sergeyevich. The audience called for the composer and he came on stage, thanked Nina Dorliak, and said, smiling: "Thank you for reviving my 'deceased' works."

The Illness. Then I remember the ill Sergei Sergeyevich. The Kremlin Hospital.

Myra Alexandrovna and I visited him in the ward. He was alone, and somehow completely grown soft. The tone of his voice was extremely offended. He said: "They won't let me write.... The doctors won't allow me to write..."

Myra Alexandrovna soothed him. "Seryozhenka.... Seryozhenka." As you would talk to a sick child—soothingly and monotonously.

He complained that they kept taking his paper away, but that he wrote and hid the small paper napkins under his pillow....

This in no way tallied with the idea of this giant of Russian music. You didn't want to believe reality: the man, creative energy itself, was so helpless.... It was difficult to reconcile oneself to this.

Then we visited him for a second time, a month later. Prokofiev was getting better. He was allowed to write. He joked, related something. He was sweet, pleasant, and serene.

He accompanied us to the stairs and when we reached the bottom, he waved good-bye to us ... with his foot. There was something boyish about him, as if a naughty schoolboy were before us.

60 years old. In 1951 he celebrated his sixtieth birthday.

On his birthday Prokofiev was ill again. A concert was arranged in the Composers' Union two days before and he listened to it over the phone. I played the Ninth Sonata for the first time. This sonata is radiant, simple, and even intimate. I think that in some respects it is a domestic sonata. The more you hear it, the more you come to love it and feel its magnetism. The more perfect it seems. I love it very much.

A Great Musician. While Sergei Sergeyevich was alive you could always expect a miracle. As if you dwelt in the domain of a magician who might at any moment present you with fabulous riches. Swish-h-h! and then you get your *Stone Flower* or *Cinderella.*

I can't forget the impression from one of his best compositions—the little *Toast.* This is a work of genuine inspiration....

I recall, as you would a good, severe drawing, the concise but very vivid suite *The Year 1941....*

I will never forget the first performance of the Fifth Symphony in 1945, on the eve of victory.... This was Prokofiev's last performance as a conductor. I sat close to the stage, in the third or fourth row. The Grand Hall was probably lighted as usual, but when Prokofiev stood up, it seemed as if the light poured directly on him from somewhere up above. He stood like a monument on a pedestal.

And then when Prokofiev mounted the podium and silence set in, artillery salvos suddenly thundered.

His baton was already raised. He waited, and until the cannon fire ceased, he didn't begin. There was something very significant, very symbolic in this. A sort of common borderline had come for everybody ... and for Prokofiev as well.

The Fifth Symphony conveys his full inner maturity and his

retrospective view of the past. He looks down from the heights at his life and at everything that was. There is something Olympian in this....

He rises to the full stature of his genius in his Fifth Symphony. At the same time it has time and history, war, patriotism, victory....

Victory in general and Prokofiev's victory. And here he triumphed completely. Earlier he had always triumphed as well, but here, as an artist, he triumphed for all times.

Prokofiev himself considered this work to be his best.

After this Prokofiev became a composer "of age". The final act of his life began. This was felt in his music. Very lofty. Maybe the loftiest.... But the final one....

I learned that Prokofiev had died on the morning I left Tbilisi by plane for Moscow. And we had to land in Sukhumi. Unprecedented, heavy snow was falling ceaselessly on the black palms and the Black Sea. It was terrible.

I thought of Prokofiev, but... I didn't grieve.

I thought: but after all I didn't grieve the death of Haydn, or ... Andrei Rublyov.

David Oistrakh

IN MEMORIAM

I was a student of the Odessa Music Institute when I first made the acquaintance of Sergei Prokofiev's music and later of the composer himself. That was in 1925-1926. In preparation for my graduation examination I had been searching for a suitable programme. I wanted something brilliant and at the same time not too well known. In this I was encouraged by my tutor, Professor P. S. Stolyarsky, who was always very much interested in new music for the violin. This interest communicated to me. Not satisfied with what I found in the music shops of Odessa, I wrote to Moscow, and one day I received along with the usual parcel of music, Five Melodies for Violin and Piano and the First Violin Concerto by Sergei Prokofiev.

At that time Prokofiev's music was the subject of much discussion both in the press and in the musical world generally. The Leningrad Academic Opera Theatre had just produced his opera *Love for Three Oranges*. The Moscow Persimfans Ensemble was giving whole recitals of his music. The violinist Joseph Szigeti had been introducing Prokofiev's D-major Violin Concerto to Soviet audiences with much success. I did not know a single note of the concerto but had heard much about it from visiting Moscow musicians. Some of them praised it highly, others were frankly irritated by it. That alone whetted my curiosity about the new work and I eagerly commenced to learn it.

I cannot say the music appealed to me at first. It contained far too much that was strange and unusual at the time, both as regards the material itself and its treatment. But the more I worked at it, the more I liked it. Its melodious themes, fantastic harmonies, novel technique and especially the radiant mood of the whole music delighted me. It made me think of a landscape flooded with sunshine. That indeed is how I pictured to myself the beautiful opening of the concerto and the melodious finale.

When I began to study the concerto (simultaneously with Five Melodies) I had not heard anyone play it before. There were no gramophone recordings in those days and all I knew of Prokofiev's music were a few of his piano compositions and a sextet which our local musicians played. All this, of course, made my task no easier. But the natural desire of a young musician to tackle something new spurred me on, and in the spring of 1926 I played the concerto at the graduation examinations. That was the first time it had been performed in Odessa.

Opinion was divided. Some people liked the concerto very much, others thought the music affected and accused the composer of nihilism and pseudo-innovation. This was the case with nearly every new major composition of Prokofiev. Nevertheless interest was tremendous.

At about the same time the pianist K. N. Igumnov came to Odessa on a concert tour and introduced the public to Prokofiev's Fourth Sonata and the *Old Granny's Tales*. Shortly before this the Entr'acte and the famous March from Prokofiev's opera *Love for Three Oranges* had been performed by an Odessa orchestra conducted by Malko, who also introduced the local music-lovers to Prokofiev's *Classical Symphony*. Prokofiev's music began to appear more and more often in concert programmes.

Before long, in February or March 1927, the composer himself came to Odessa and gave two recitals of his works. This was a sensational event. The recitals were given in the Odessa Opera House, and the large hall was filled to overflowing long before the concert began. Practically every musician in town, all the veteran music-lovers and a host of young people came to hear the famous composer. The concert was a resounding success. For some reason I felt as excited as if I were the hero of the day. The impression made on me, not so much by the music, which by that time I had learned to understand and appreciate, as by the performance, was unlike anything I had ever experienced. What struck me about Prokofiev's playing was its remarkable simplicity. Not a single superfluous gesture, not a single exaggerated expression of emotion, no striving for effect

The composer seemed to be saying, "I refuse to embellish my music in any way. Here it is. You may take it or leave it." There was a sort of inner purity of purpose behind the whole performance that made an unforgettable impression.

I do not recall exactly what he played at those recitals, apart from the sonatas, the Second and Third, and I believe, the Fifth. Of the smaller works I remember the famous Toccata, *Old Granny's Tales*, a great many short pieces from his earlier works, and a few new things, like the Scherzo and the March from the *Three Oranges*. Coming after the dynamic Toccata, which he played with great inner force (while outwardly appearing perfectly calm and unmoved), the lyrical *Fugitive Visions* made a deep impression. One of them, the piece in C major, with its beautiful lyrical episode in the middle, still rings in my ears. The tempestuous, defiant Prokofiev at such moments became as touching as a child. The fact that Prokofiev could be poetic and moving came as a surprise to many who, until they heard his music performed by himself, had refused to believe that it could have any emotional depth and content.

In this connection I should like to touch briefly on some of the difficulties of Prokofiev's music, and specifically his violin music, from the standpoint of the performer. It is music in which nothing can be omitted, not a single turn of the melody, not a single modulation. It requires the strictest attention to every detail of expression, a fine, but not overrefined, execution of each individual intonation, as in the case of well-enunciated singing. The chief thing is that it does not tolerate any artistic liberties. The best performance of Prokofiev's music, or of any other good music for that matter, is one in which the personality of the performer does not obtrude in any way. That is precisely what one could say of Prokofiev's playing.

After the recitals there was a banquet for Prokofiev at which local musicians gave renderings of his music. I was chosen to play the Scherzo from his Violin Concerto. I was naturally much thrilled at the prospect of meeting the composer in person, and it was with mingled feelings of happiness and shyness that I, then a lad of 18, awaited the day of the performance. At last it came. Little did I suspect how sadly it was to end for me.

The cream of Odessa public was assembled in the Scientists'

Club where the banquet for Prokofiev was to be held. In the place of honour right in front of the platform sat the composer himself. As I played I observed his face grow darker and darker. When I had finished, the audience applauded, but not Prokofiev. Instead, he stepped on to the stage, paying no heed to the hubbub in the hall, sat down at the piano and, turning to me with the words: "Young man, you don't play it right at all," proceeded to show me how the piece ought to be played. My debacle was complete.

Many years later when I knew Prokofiev quite well I reminded him of the incident and of his Odessa concert tour in general. To my surprise he remembered everything down to the smallest detail, including the programmes and the number of encores, and Chishko, the Ukrainian composer and singer with whom he performed *The Ugly Duckling* at the banquet, and "that unfortunate young man" whom he had given "a fine drubbing", as he put it. His genuine embarrassment and distress when I told him that I was that young man showed me how warm and human he could be.

A cherished memory is that of my performance of Prokofiev's First Violin Concerto at a concert of his works, with the composer conducting. Prokofiev was in no sense a professional conductor. His movements were rather awkward, and he waved his hands in a stereotyped manner. Nevertheless the orchestra under his baton played splendidly. Everything sounded simple and natural, without the slightest artistic affectation. As I played the concerto I felt the music burgeoning with fresh colour. The musicians in the orchestra, as I later learned, experienced the same sensation. The music poured forth with delightful ease, every man felt as if he were playing solo that night and played with a fervour that was communicated to the other musicians.

By this time (1939) I was seeing Prokofiev frequently. We usually met over the chess-board, for he was a passionate chess fan and could sit for hours over a game. We were both frequent visitors at the international chess tournament that was being held in Moscow at the time with the participation of Lasker, Capablanca and our Botvinnik. And later when we were neighbours we held our own blitz tournaments. As a rule, Prokofiev was the initiator and it was amusing to see the boyish enthusiasm with which he would draw all kinds of colour diagrams of victories and defeats, his frank delight when he won a game and his equally frank grief when he lost. I still have the invitation ticket to our match arranged by the Central Art Workers' Club in 1937. It was a "full dress" affair, with time limits, judges, and, of course, an audience. We spent sleepless nights, worrying over the games, as if we were competing for the world championship. For some reason our tournament remained unfinished—we played only seven out of ten games.

* * *

His mind was always occupied with new compositions. When asked sometimes to settle some dispute about the reading of a passage in one or another of his compositions he would have some difficulty in replying. He had finished with that work and passed on to something else.

When I first heard his Sonata for Flute, shortly after it was written, it occurred to me that it would sound very well on the violin. I felt that this beautiful piece of music ought to live a fuller and richer life on the concert stage. I approached the composer with the suggestion that he write a violin version of it. Prokofiev was interested in the suggestion. We arranged to meet and talk the matter over. It was the first time I had seen Prokofiev at work and it was a revelation to me: I had never believed it possible to work with such speed and efficiency. He asked me to make two or three versions of each passage in the score that required editing, numbering each one carefully. As I submitted the pages to him, he marked the version he considered suitable and made a few pencil corrections here and there. Thus in no time the violin version of the sonata was ready.

I remember the day in the summer of 1946 when I drove out to Prokofiev's country house in Nikolina Gora to hear a new violin sonata he had written (it figures as No. 1 in the list of his works). "You must come," he had said over the phone. "Nikolai Yakovlevich has also written a violin sonata. So you will have a chance to hear two new sonatas at the same time."

I arrived punctually at the appointed hour. Before long, Myaskovsky who lived nearby, joined us, and we sat down to listen to Prokofiev's sonata. If I am not mistaken Myaskovsky

was also hearing it for the first time. Before beginning to pla
Prokofiev enumerated all the movements, after which he play
the whole sonata through without pausing. It made a powerf
impression, in spite of the fact that his performance was son
what "shy". One felt that this was truly great music, and inde
for sheer beauty and depth nothing to equal it had been writt
for the violin for many a decade. Myaskovsky had only o
word for it: "A masterpiece," he said. "My dear fellow, y
don't realise what you have written! " he kept saying to P
kofiev. He was obviously deeply moved.

Then Nikolai Yakovlevich was to play his sonata. However,
was decided to make a short break during which Myaskovs
went to his home, while Prokofiev showed us (my son a
myself) around his garden....

Later when I and my partner L.N. Oborin, the pianist, w
learning to play the sonata we visited the composer many tin
and he gave us a great deal of invaluable advice. One could s
that this work was very dear to him. He took obvious pleasu
in working at it with us, making suggestions concerning bc
the character of the movement and the inner meaning of t
music itself. For instance, about one passage of the first mo
ment where the violin plays passages running up and down t
scale, he said that it should sound "like the wind in a gra
yard". After remarks of this kind the whole spirit of the son
assumed a deeper significance for us. Never have I been
completely absorbed in a piece of music. Until the first pub
performance I could play nothing else, think of nothing else.

*　*　*

Prokofiev's music for the violin, and his attitude to the vio
as an instrument, is a subject worthy of special study. But ev
a list of the works written for the violin will suffice
appreciate the magnitude of his accomplishment in this fie
two concertos, both of them now part of the repertoire
leading world violinists; two sonatas, one better than the oth
a sonata for solo violin, Op. 115, written as an exercise
violin students but suitable for concert performance by a unis
of violins (as the author intended). Prokofiev's name has beg
to figure more and more frequently on concert programm
alongside names like Tchaikovsky and Glazunov. His works

tracting the attention of all who love and appreciate Russian
usic.

It is with a sense of deep gratitude and emotion that I recall
y association with the great composer. His dedication to me
f the F minor Sonata No. 1 I consider one of the momentous
ents in my artistic career.

March 1954

MY GREAT FELLOW–COUNTRYMAN

I first heard Sergei Sergeyevich Prokofiev in 1927 in Odessa. His image of composer and pianist has remained with me throughout my life. I remember the tall figure at the piano, the special, distinctive "sweeping" manner of playing peculiar to Prokofiev alone. He performed his piano miniatures—*Old Granny's Tales, Fugitive Visions*, pieces from Op. 12 and sonatas....

Next came 1935. It was a great event for us students—Prokofiev was playing in the hall of the Odessa Conservatoire. (Well-known artists visiting Odessa often performed for the students.) Sergei Sergeyevich played his arrangement of Schubert's waltzes for two pianos with one of the students, and also some of his own works.... It was an unforgettable experience.

These are two fleeting memories from my youth. They were followed by Moscow in the 1930s and 1940s, where we all met and listened to Sergei Sergeyevich and his splendid new works. This was the most intensive period of Prokofiev's life as a composer, when he produced so many magnificent works. Each of them attracted great attention of performers. I remember how we rushed to get our hands on the Seventh Piano Sonata when this fine work appeared in 1942. I studied it from the printer's proofs—white notes on blue paper. When I left the piano the lines of music stayed in my mind's eye because of the unusual print....

In 1944 Sergei Sergeyevich invited me to give the first performance of his new Eighth Sonata.... I became totally absorbed in my work on this composition. The Eighth Sonata is a profound work demanding a great deal of emotional tension. It impresses one by the symphonic nature of its development, the tension, breadth and charm of the lyrical passages.

I had to study the sonata from the manuscript and was a frequent visitor at Sergei Sergeyevich's home. I would play to him from the rough draft of the work, and he would check certain passages, making corrections in the text. Sometimes he sat down at the piano himself and showed me, without playing the passage in full, what he wanted above all from the pianist.

I also met with Sergei Sergeyevich in connection with another work—the Third Concerto for Piano and Orchestra. I cherish the memories of these meetings.

Prokofiev had the ability of finding something new where everything seemed to have been said. Thinking of this characteristic feature of his, I recall a profound idea he once expressed on the fate of music. He was speaking of two types of composers. "There are mule composers," he said, "and composers who give off plentiful shoots." Prokofiev blazed new trails with his work, opening up new horizons for modern music. We musicians are constantly aware of his role as an innovator. By his original thinking Prokofiev encouraged musicians to be original too.

Prokofiev's music is the proud possession of world culture. The anniversary of his death found me in Paris. On the evening of March 5, 1954, leading representatives of the French music world assembled in a concert hall to pay homage to the great composer's memory. It was a very warm, cordial occasion.

A famous French actor read out a tribute of respect to Prokofiev's memory, which had been signed by many French composers. This was followed by a concert at which Prokofiev's works—romances, a quartet and piano pieces—were performed. I was among the performers. The tokens of respect shown for our great fellow-countryman were extremely moving.

January 7, 1959

PROKOFIEV PLAYS IN MOSCOW

For the generation of musicians whose conscious life in art began in the 1920s, Sergei Prokofiev's first concerts in Moscow were a truly unforgettable event. The titanic power of Otto Klemperer, the brilliant technique and indefatigability of Egon Petri, the inspired, subtle skill of Joseph Szigeti, none of these were to have such far-reaching consequences from the artistic point of view.

The composer arrived in Moscow in the second half of January 1927 when the concert season was in full swing. Shortly before his arrival there were some memorable concerts in the Grand Hall of the Moscow Conservatoire by young Soviet pianists who had been selected to take part in the First International Chopin Competition in Warsaw. They included Lev Oborin, Dmitry Shostakovich, Yuri Bryushkov and Grigory Ginsburg. At that time the first of the concerts to commemorate the centenary of Beethoven's death were being held in the Smaller Hall of the Conservatoire: Konstantin Igumnov played at one of these concerts (sonatas Op. 22, 28, 81, 109 and 110); and at another (sonatas Op. 57, 90, 111 and the 33 variations on the theme of Diabelli). Shortly before, the Italian composer and pianist Alfredo Casella had given some interesting performances of his own works, including a number of new compositions.

I first heard Prokofiev play at a Persimfans concert on January 24, 1927; this was probably the composer's first performance after his return to the Soviet Union. Accompanied by the Persimfans, Prokofiev played his Third Piano Concerto; the programme also included two orchestral suites—from the ballet

Tale of the Buffoon Who Out-Buffooned Seven Buffoons and from the opera *Love for Three Oranges*, which was about to be put on by the Bolshoi Theatre. There was a most festive atmosphere in the Grand Hall of the Conservatoire, where the concert was held; nearly all of the Moscow music world was there. Prokofiev's appearance was greeted by thunderous applause and a musical fanfare.

Prokofiev's playing at the concert was remarkably original, integral and clear. Many of us had expected a tempestuous, daring, superficially striking Prokofiev. But instead we heard a pianist who played austerely, laconically and very simply. He enchanted the audience by the freshness, energy, vividness and remarkable integrity of his performance. The rhythm was clear-cut, the sound resilient and full, the phrasing clear and brilliantly moulded, the accents sharp and rapidly alternating. Yet there was no harshness or unnecessary noise in the playing. We were listening to a performance full of exhaustible creative energy, optimism, and wit, which was at the same time organically integrated and structurally well-balanced. We were listening to a pianist who played not only with remarkable forcefulness and rhythmical fervour, but also with warmth, sincerity, poetic softness, the ability to handle the melodic line fluently and smoothly. I shall always remember, for example, the emotional impact of the lyrical passages in the Third Concerto—the secondary theme of the first movement, the slow variations of the second, and, particularly, the middle of the finale which impressed one by the beauty of its melodic development. These passages were just as impressive as, say, the well-known fast passages in the first movement or the sharply stressed, brilliant, rapid variations in the second. Only very few musicians could equal Prokofiev in integrity and conviction of performance.

As an encore he played several small compositions: I remember, in particular, the gavotte from the *Classical Symphony* (played with great restraint, clarity and subtlety, but also with considerable rhythmic freedom and whimsy) and the *Toccata* (with its steady, measured semi-quavers and hypnotic dynamic crescendo). In this piece Prokofiev again demonstrated his brilliant technique and strong will as a pianist.

A few days later Prokofiev gave his first recital in Moscow—a chamber concert organised by the Association of Modern Music in the hall of the State Academy of Artistic Sciences, which then had its premises in Kropotkin Street (No. 32). By some

14-230

miracle I and a few of my Conservatoire friends managed to get in.

The relatively small hall, with windows on both sides, was packed with what seemed to be all the leading lights in the arts. Prokofiev played two of his piano sonatas (the fairly well-known Third and the completely unknown Fifth) and the *Toccata.* I do not know whether it was the more in intimate size of the hall or the friendly and receptive audience, but this time Prokofiev played with special inspiration and skill.

His recitals in the Grand Hall of the Conservatoire which took place shortly afterwards and included the Second, Third, Fourth and Fifth piano sonatas, *Fugitive Visions, Old Granny's Tales*, pieces from Op. 32, the *Toccata*, the march from the opera *Love for Three Oranges*, and also Schubert waltzes arranged by Prokofiev for two pianos, the part of the second piano was played by S. Feinberg), merely confirmed the impressions of his talent as a pianist.

In his playing Prokofiev developed each idea with the maximum of expression. The laconism, austerity, and integrity of his performance were combined with freedom and boldness, the choice of the characteristic and specific with spontaneity, the vividness and precision with an abundance of devices. Those who for some inexplicable reason insist that Prokofiev played somewhat coldly and awkwardly, casting accents about at random, are profoundly mistaken. No! He played poetically, with a childlike chastity, a remarkable purity and modesty. And those who maintain that grotesque elements and prankishness dominated his playing, are equally not quite right. Prokofiev was undoubtedly a past master in this sphere, but he was equally proficient at manifesting sincere poetic feeling. But in his playing this feeling was always embodied in restrained forms, without affectation and false exaggerated emotion. Everything bore the imprint of serenity, concentration, serious reflection, occasionally slightly softened by notes of gentleness.

Prokofiev's physical appearance was most in keeping with these inner qualities of his: he was extremely original. When playing he would sit remarkably still, without making any unnecessary movements. Even in the most breathtaking crescendoes and extremely rapid passages he remained imperturbable. At the same time his hands flew over the keyboard with remarkable ease. It is difficult for anyone who has ever seen and heard Prokofiev at the piano to forget his characteristic pose, his manner of playing, and his face in profile (sometimes impenetrably calm, sometimes extraordinarily mobile).

And one other point. Prokofiev played with extraordinary ease, without the slightest tension. One could even say at times that he played gracefully, elegantly, although there was enough force and drive in his playing for two or three pianists.

Under his hands the musical fabric of the work came to life, breathed, grew, melted away and was reborn. He had the same feel for harmonic colour as for melodic combinations.

Prokofiev's playing was never slovenly, sketchy or rhythmically loose. He liked well-defined strokes, sharply outlined and clear, he liked to play in "close-up". At the same time his playing revealed a whimsical pattern of details which were never exactly repeated. Everything about the performance was harmonic, everything followed logically and consistently from what had gone before.

Prokofiev stressed the peculiarity of the melodic contours with rare skill: in his playing, as in his creative work, he proceeded not from the colour, but from the expression and the emotional content and imagery of the work. It is this imagery that determined the wealth of colour in his music.

In this connection I remember another concert by the Persimfans at which Prokofiev played (in the Grand Hall of the Conservatoire at the beginning of February 1927). It was then that Muscovites first heard his Second Piano Concerto which literally stunned us, young musicians, by its novelty, boldness of expression, and power and richness of content. The composer played with great verve (perhaps even greater than in the case of the Third Concerto), with a kind of elemental sweep and power. Everything shone, sparkled, seethed under his fingers. Each twist of harmonies, each bend of the melody, each shift of the rhythm had an exquisitely beautiful and, most important, uniquely Prokofievan ring about it. I shall never forget, for example, the tireless race of the scherzo, or the marvellous main theme of the concerto, against a background of sad alternating fifths and fourths, or, finally, the grandiose cadence in which Prokofiev achieved an extraordinarily powerful effect. No subsequent performances of the concerto (and it has been played by some excellent pianists) have approached this one by the composer in terms of the powerful, vivid highlighting of the psychological element and imagery. One need hardly say that it was a tremendous success. The enthused audience insisted on one encore after the other. It would literally not allow Prokofiev leave the stage; there was no end to the curtain calls.

One might also mention his splendid repeated performance of the Third Piano Concerto, his brilliant playing of the piano sonatas and small pieces, and also his excellent performance of a number of small pieces from Op. 4 (*Diabolical Suggestions*) and Op. 12 (the march, gavotte and prelude). Here was a pianist "by the grace of God", a pianist of rare harmony and perfection, who also possessed the gift of poetic inspiration. When we reflected on what this inspiration really was, we inevitably came to the conclusion that in the case of Prokofiev it was the "subjective deepening" of works written by him earlier. It bore the expression of his creative personality, his artistic "ego", which, in the final analysis, determined the lasting value of his performances.

Sovietskaya Muzyka, No. 8, 1962

Dmitry Rogal-Levitsky

MEETINGS WITH THE ARTIST

...By the early 1920s Prokofiev's name was known all over the world and his music was frequently performed abroad. At that time he was, undoubtedly, a most fashionable figure, and his remarkably popular works had an irresistible influence on budding composers. The name of Prokofiev possessed a kind of magical force, attracting to it all those who were interested in the development of Russian music.

* * *

I returned to Moscow (from evacuation) at the beginning of April 1943. When Sergei Sergeyevich returned, I do not know exactly, but at the end of October I was unexpectedly summoned to visit Prokofiev and Radin at the Moskva Hotel.

Quite unsuspecting, I arrived at the appointed time. Sergei Sergeyevich had a room on the tenth or twelfth floor. As soon as I knocked, he invited me to come in.

"Right on the dot! " he greeted me. "That's good. I like punctuality and hate wasting time...."

I bowed in acknowledgement of this flattering remark. Prokofiev did not give me time to utter a word.

"Now about the reason why I decided to trouble you. I have a great request to make of you...."

I listened in amazement. Prokofiev had a "great request" to make of me? Surely not. He had not probably expressed himself properly, or he was joking. But the situation became clear as soon as he resumed.

"The point is this. The Mariinsky Theatre is planning to produce my ballet *The Buffoon Who Out-Buffooned Seven Buffoons*. Do you know it? " he asked quickly.

"I know the suite from the ballet, but have never seen or heard the ballet itself."

"It doesn't matter.... Well. The only orchestral score, my manuscript, was destroyed in Berlin during the bombing. A search was made for it at my request, but it was not found. I suspect, although I cannot be sure, that it was burnt. There was a copy of this score in Kiev. A.I. Orlov staged it there and, judging by all accounts, this copy was also destroyed during the nazi invasion."

"Perhaps it is still somewhere in the theatre basement? " I ventured timidly.

"That's unlikely. The nazis made such a thorough job, that hardly a thing was left. But now the situation is as follows. We need a new orchestral score, and I am asking you to undertake the task of restoring it...."

Restoring the *Buffoon*! Was he joking! My orchestral language was as far removed from Prokofiev's as Mars from Venus or, to put it better, as Venus from Saturn! What could there be in common between us? I was most embarrassed and kept silent. Sergei Sergeyevich perceived my confusion and continued:

"There is nothing special about it. I have given the matter considerable thought and have decided to request your assistance. You are an accurate and conscientious person, the only person to whom I can entrust this work..."

"But, Sergei Sergeyevich, aren't you afraid that I might spoil your work and do something wrong. After all, it's not what I am used to...."

"I know. That's why I am asking you. I will help you with advice...."

He rose quickly and went to his desk.

"Here, take this. It is the published orchestral score of the suite from the *Buffoon*, and this is the piano score of the whole ballet. Everything in the suite is also here in the piano score, but a great deal is scattered about in the different scenes, and it will need a lot of work to piece everything together...."

"I really do not know what to say," I objected, hesitantly. "Frankly I am afraid to take on something like this."

"There's nothing to be afraid of. Just do as you like, I'll agree to everything in advance. But I am so busy with new works at the moment, that I simply have no time to even think about the *Buffoon*. If I were to start orchestrating the ballet myself, it would probably turn out to be quite different.... That is what I am afraid of. You will do it the way it should be done. You will have my score to guide you all the time...."

"But what if I get carried away and begin to make changes even in your score, what then? " I asked somewhat provocatively in the hope that this consideration would restrain Prokofiev from such a rash step.

"What of it? If you find it necessary to make some changes—for the better, I trust—I shall not object. In other words, I give you *carte blanche*, do what you like."

"Very well, Sergei Sergeyevich! It only remains for me to thank you for your trust, which I have hardly deserved. But anything may happen. If I find myself in difficulties, do you promise to help me at least by giving advice? "

"I have already promised that. I would suggest that in such an event we meet personally. Ring me up, and I will always find a few minutes for a talk. Does that suit you?" he asked quickly.

"Entirely," I replied. "But wouldn't I be pestering you too much? "

"Try not to. We shall have very little time—only a few minutes on each occasion. That is my only condition. So, in those few minutes we shall have to decide questions which would take hours under different circumstances."

We were both silent. Prokofiev was pondering over something, and I was still puzzled as to why he had turned to me for help and not to one of his friends.

"By the way," he said, emerging from his thoughts. "Have you spoken to Yevgeny Mikhailovich yet? "

"No, not yet. My meeting with him is scheduled for tomorrow...."

"Oh, that's excellent. Good-bye! Don't be afraid, take your courage in both hands ... everything will be all right...."

We parted warmly, and I went away torn by the most conflicting thoughts. Naturally, it was a serious matter to have merited such high trust from Prokofiev. But the complexity of the task was an equally serious matter. Prokofiev's orchestration was highly original: he had his own distinctive tastes, many habits which were peculiar to him alone, and, in general, a great deal which was not to be found in other composers, myself in particular. Thinking along these lines I eventually came to the conclusion that there were no insuperable obstacles; all I had to do was get to the heart of Prokofiev's score and then everything would be all right.

The next day I set off again for the Moskva Hotel to see the director of the Mariinsky Theatre (which had already been renamed the Kirov Theatre.—*Ed.*), Yevgeny Mikhailovich Radin. He greeted me with the most refined courtesy....

"Have you seen Prokofiev? "

"Yes, I saw him yesterday," I replied.

"And did he inform you of our request to work on his ballet the *Buffoon*? "

"Yes, he asked me to help him and take on the work. It is very difficult for me to comply with this request...."

"But the request is from Sergei Sergeyevich himself," Radin remarked.

"I was compelled to give my consent. I could not refuse Sergei Sergeyevich."

"That's splendid! I did not doubt that you would agree. Thank you at least for this, and now..." After a short pause, Radin continued:

"Now let's talk about the business side. We shall sign a contract with you as soon as I get back to the theatre. In accordance with the established routine, I should be grateful if you approach Abram Abramovich on all matters concerning the music. He is with us now. What will you need? " he enquired.

"Only paper for the time being, if possible the same sort as I used in Perm...."

"And what else? "

"What else? " I replied. "Nothing, I think, except for a legal arrangement with Prokofiev...."

"He has already talked to me about that. Your name will be on the posters for the orchestration. You can be sure of that."

On November 12, 1943, I began work on the *Buffoon*. First I made a careful study of the music for the ballet, then I began to examine the orchestrated score of the suite and look for the passages to which it corresponded. It was not until January 5, 1944, that I eventually started the orchestration of the *Buffoon*.

It went well and I worked on it almost every day, leaving time only for my teaching at the Conservatoire. I had to copy long passages from the existing orchestral score; I studied them carefully and made some insertions which I marked with arrows—at the beginning and the end of the insertion. Sergei Sergeyevich also kept his word and never refused to see me. I worked quickly and consequently our meetings became increasingly "compressed". But Prokofiev remained true to his promise. Whenever I rang him up and asked him to appoint a time for us to meet, he replied:

"Of course! At three o'clock sharp. We shall have seven-and-a-half minutes. Is that enough? " he asked, and waited for my reply.

All I could do each time was agree and hope that the specified number of minutes would be increased. Prokofiev might get interested in my work and want to take a more detailed look at it, and he might suggest something new or give me some ideas for the orchestration. Yet each time I arrived he took out his chronometer, looked at it and said:

"We have seven-and-a-half minutes at our disposal, as we agreed...."

He would glance rapidly through my piece of orchestration, pausing a little longer on the places where I wanted his advice, and occasionally adding a few pencilled notes to the text of the score.

"I think it was like that, if my memory does not deceive me...."

I never trespassed on Sergei Sergeyevich's time and was always extremely punctual. My questions were short and to the point, and his answers quick and sharp. But on one occasion I felt completely at a loss, quite incapable of coping with what appeared to be an insuperable problem. After ringing Prokofiev up and receiving permission to visit him on the twelfth floor at a strictly appointed time for eleven-and-a-half minutes, I decided to be clever and arrive three or four minutes earlier. It was a difficult problem, and I was not sure that we could solve it in such a limited time.

I knocked at the door. Sergei Sergeyevich quickly let me in, walked up to his desk and looked at the chronometer.

"Aha! " he smiled. "You are not as punctual as usual to-day...."

"No," I replied. "I have a very difficult problem, and I decided to trouble you a little earlier...."

"I am afraid that is impossible—I'm busy. Take a glass and

pour yourself some orange juice. It's very rare these days. By the time you are through with it, I will be at your disposal...."

I was somewhat perplexed—eleven minutes was too little, and I really did not know what to do. Nevertheless Prokofiev continued writing and paid no attention to me. When the appointed time came, he invited me most cordially to his desk.

"Show me how I can be of help to you...."

I opened the score quickly and pointed to the place which was troubling me.

"Ah! " Prokofiev drawled. "I thought so. There were parallel triads of three clarinets here. They came in one after the other, like this..."

Prokofiev snatched up his pencil and began to write in the second parts quickly.

"This is how it went, see... And the same here... Is that clear? "

"Yes, of course..."

"What else? " Prokofiev hurried me.

I showed him another place which worried me and gave him an enquiring look. Prokofiev examined the music carefully, thought for a minute, then said gustily:

"That's easy. There was another passage like this, only in a slightly modified form. Compare the two passages and you will get the right answer...."

I said nothing.

"I'll find you the passage now," Prokofiev continued, flicking rapidly through the score.

"Here we are, look! It's quite simple... Isn't it? "

"Yes," I agreed, without understanding what he meant. "But will you please mark the place with a piece of paper: I will work it out at home, so as not to take up your time..."

Prokofiev tore off a strip of paper, placed it in the score, and closed the music.

"Well, there we are! That's all for today... Incidentally, do you have any of my works? " Prokofiev enquired.

"Not much to speak of if you mean orchestral scores," I replied cautiously.

"What would you like to have? " he continued.

"Frankly, the score of *Alexander Nevsky*..."

"Haven't you got it? "

"I was out of Moscow when it was published, so, unfortunately, I missed it."

"Yes, that's not easy..." Prokofiev murmured. "I'll try... Perhaps I can get it for you..."

I thanked him for his kind promise to help me find the orchestral score of *Alexander Nevsky* and left.

This time the work went comparatively easily. I made rapid progress. In early February or late January I again went to see Prokofiev at the Moskva (this was my last visit to him at this hotel, because in accordance with some rather unclear regulations he had to be moved from the Moskva to the Metropol Hotel).

When I entered and spread out my orchestral scores and the piano score as usual, Sergei Sergeyevich, while looking through the music, announced suddenly:

"I have got *Alexander Nevsky* for you."

"Really! " I exclaimed in amazement. "I am most grateful to you...."

Prokofiev did not move. He looked carefully through the orchestral parts and grunted his approval. When we had finished our business and I had clarified all the points which interested me, he opened his desk, took out the score and handed it to me, saying:

"Here, take this score as a memento of our work together."

I was most touched by this kind gesture. When I returned home and began to look at the gift I saw Sergei Sergeyevich's firm handwriting in Indian ink in the top right-hand corner of the title-page:

"To Dmitry Romanovich Rogal-Levitsky,

"In memory of our pleasant meetings during work on the *Buffoon*,

"S. Prokofiev
January 30, 1944"

After this delightful event (naturally I cherish the score with Prokofiev's autograph) our meetings continued, but were now held in the Metropol Hotel.

Time marched on relentlessly. I was working very hard, although I was already feeling not only very tired but also rather worried—all my enquiries addressed to the theatre either remained unanswered or the answers were very vague. After finishing some of the opening scenes, I turned to the end of the ballet and began work on the fifth or sixth scene. Things went well again and my meetings with Prokofiev became less frequent—I did not want to trouble him with trifles and was now proficient enough myself to do without his help for the most part.

On March 16, I was unexpectedly summoned to the Bolshoi Theatre, and had to begin work immediately on a new orchestration of the National Anthem.

When musical circles heard of my participation in this work and the favourable comments on it by the Government, Prokofiev began to joke about it and once referred to me publicly as the "state orchestrator".

"Well," he said jokingly, "now there is nothing to fear, I am quite sure that the *Buffoon* is in reliable hands, the hands of the 'state orchestrator'."

But the "state orchestrator" did not manage to resume work on the *Buffoon*....

(At one of our meetings) ... when we were about to say good-bye to each other ... Prokofiev did not seem to be in a hurry, so I immediately took advantage of the opportunity.

"Sergei Sergeyevich! May I ask you a question?"

"Of course! What is it? " he enquired.

"Have you received anything from Yevgeny Mikhailovich? "

"From the theatre? No, nothing. Why? "

"Neither have I—not a letter, a telegram or a contract...."

"A contract? " Sergei Sergeyevich asked in surprise. "Are you working without a contract? "

"Yes. I always do...."

"My dear man! You are naive! Who would work without a contract? ..."

"I'm used to trusting people," I remarked timidly.

"That is most praiseworthy, of course, but all the same you should never work without a contract... Stop work immediately and wait until you get a contract."

"I had to stop work on it on March 16, and today is April 21...."

"That's good, then. Let them send a contract, then you will resume work. Why waste time."

"Perhaps they have changed their minds about staging your ballet? Have you heard anything to this effect? "

"All I know is that Lopukhov refused to put on the *Buffoon*, it seems. He thinks he is not up to it now...."

"There you are... That means they don't know what to do themselves. But they could have notified us about it in some way. Don't you agree? "

220

"Of course. Try asking them by letter. Don't you correspond with someone at the theatre? ..."

"Yes, Ashkenazi."

Naturally, I did not write either to the director or to Abram Abramovich, and ceased the work. The theatre had evidently been unable to find a producer and had quietly given up its plan. Following Sergei Sergeyevich's advice, I did not resume work on the score of the *Buffoon*, and thus it remained unfinished. As far as I can remember, I had not completed the sixth scene and not started the third. Many years later I frequently intended to complete the work, but somehow there never seemed to be time. Besides, I was now out of practice, which made it difficult to concentrate on the ballet.

* * *

On one of my visits, fairly late in the evening, Prokofiev was most welcoming and did not look at the chronometer. He greeted me with the joyful news that he was particularly pleased with himself that day—he had just finished a very important and complicated section of *War and Peace*, so he was quite free.

"Take a look, if you would like to! This is the completed page of my manuscript..."

He handed me several sheets of music paper covered with music written in his firm hand. The manuscript was an extremely detailed score written on several lines, as many as ten or more in places. Everywhere there were notes indicating which instruments should play which passages.

"How complicated! " I could not help exclaiming.

"Not at all! " Prokofiev objected mildly. "All that has to be done now is to write out the parts on separate sheets of music and everything will be ready. I usually indicate the minutest details in a score like this, and Pavel Alexandrovich simply follows my indications! " he concluded gaily.

"But what if Pavel Alexandrovich gets confused and makes a mistake? " I asked cautiously.

"It's out of the question. Everything here is so clear and comprehensible that it's impossible to make mistakes." I looked closely at the manuscript. The smallest details really were indicated...

"But this way of writing must take up a great deal of time, doesn't it? " I persisted.

"Not at all," said Prokofiev. "One page of my score takes less time to write than a page of your orchestral score with all the transposing instruments."

"Perhaps so," I replied. "A page of my score usually takes from one-and-a-half to two hours to write."

"Mine takes much less! By the way, why don't you use my method of writing—in C? It's so convenient."

"Probably for you only, Sergei Sergeyevich, because you are used to it. It seems more complicated to me. For example, I cannot hear French horns written in C in the G and F clefs."

"Really! That is strange! I have grown so accustomed to this way of writing that I doubt whether I could use the old method any more..."

"Quite possibly," I remarked.

"I should so like to persuade you to write in C. It is so convenient! " Prokofiev said gaily.

"And I should like to entice you back to the old 'way of truth' ," I replied in the same jocular tone.

"No hope of that! " Sergei Sergeyevich said concluding our talk, and went off to rummage among a pile of magazines.

"Would you like to see the last photograph of Rachmaninov? This is an American magazine which has just arrived in Moscow."

"Of course," I replied and went over to him.

"Here we are. Look how much he changed just before his death..."

Rachmaninov's face really was unrecognisable. There were enormous bags under his eyes, the face was covered with deep wrinkles, and there was something depressed and sad about his slightly Mongolian countenance usually so austere.

We were both silent as we reflected on this last picture of the composer.

"Perhaps it was not a very good photograph? " I asked, refusing to believe the cover of the American magazine, so neatly printed in colour.

"I don't think so. Probably he really did look like that," Prokofiev replied quietly and became pensive.

"What do you want to ask me? " he enquired, suddenly.

"Nothing, now," I replied. "The photograph has upset me so much that I have even forgotten the purpose of my visit. But, look. What should I do here? "

Sergei Sergeyevich looked at the music, thought for a moment, then replied:

"Do what you like. You know everything now, you have picked up my manner perfectly...."

"I still cannot get used to the piano..."

"But it is so convenient! " he replied, laughing, and took a bowl of wrapped sweets from the table.

"Here, have a 'Mishka' or 'Romashka'—they're very good..."

I picked up one and took my leave. This time our meeting had not been very successful.

* * *

In the last five or six years of Sergei Sergeyevich's life, I saw him rarely and only by chance, at concerts or theatres. He was always most friendly and cordial towards me, asking for a detailed account of my activities, but saying little about himself. He obviously disliked talking about his work at length, and in this respect he was rather reticent than open. Nevertheless, in spite of this lack of contact, a humorous episode took place which might well be regarded as an "encounter by correspondence". At that time, from 1944 to about the first half of 1948, the State Music Publishers frequently requested my services as an external editor. It was then that I received the orchestral score of the suite from Prokofiev's opera *Semyon Kotko* to edit. The manuscript had been copied out in Prokofiev's beautiful handwriting and carefully checked by him. My editing therefore was limited to removing graphic inaccuracies which were accepted by foreign publishers and had long been used by Sergei Sergeyevich. The octave divisi of the strings in high registers looked particularly ugly. It was not simply that his method of writing was difficult to read and took up a lot of space, but at that time the publishing house was counting each kopeck. This type of notation added greatly to the cost of engraving. Guided by these considerations I not only reduced a large number of musical symbols, but also removed all the unnecessary ligatures. Having introduced changes, which made the score much easier to read, I came across some additional lines at the bottom of the score for the trombones which were for some reason written in the alto clef, instead of the tenor or bass. Since I knew that

Sergei Sergeyevich did not use a very convenient tenor clef, I transposed these notes, which were difficult to read and play, into the bass clef.

After reading through the first proofs most attentively, I sent them to Prokofiev who quickly returned them, having carefully restored the whole of his manuscript. I rejected all Sergei Sergeyevich's changes, allowing only obvious printing errors to be corrected, read through the second proofs, and again sent them to Prokofiev. He again restored his manuscript and signed the proofs for the press. It is most strange that he twice restored the alto clef, so unsuitable in the given circumstances, and was obviously determined to have his own way. But I changed it back again and sent the score to the printers. The published score looked quite impressive, and evidently Prokofiev accepted it as *fait accompli.*

Shortly after the publication of the suite from *Semyon Kotko* we happened to meet in the foyer of the Grand Hall of the Conservatoire. As always, Prokofiev greeted me cordially, with a smile, then immediately got down to business.

"Why did you reject all my corrections? " he asked unexpectedly.

"Sergei Sergeyevich," I replied. "I was only acting in keeping with the financial requirements of the publishing house—we are trying to cut down on the engravers' work these days. You should have accepted that."

"I did! " Prokofiev replied gaily. "But the way I wrote is the way it is always done abroad..."

"I know that. Although, frankly speaking, there is not much point in writing octaves with diverging tails—it takes up more space and it is harder to read..."

"It only seems to you so. We are used to writing that way... Still, I am not going to argue—the published score looks quite nice..."

"Well, there you are! " I replied. "That's exactly what I wanted, a pleasant appearance. Please don't be offended... It is an excellent publication, just take the figures, for example!"

Prokofiev smiled.

"Oh, very well! Have your own way! " and we parted friends.

* * *

... During the last five months of Sergei Sergeyevich's life I intended to visit him on many occasions, but did not take the liberty, knowing not only about his illness but also about how busy he was—at that time Prokofiev was finishing some piano pieces and working on the completion of his new ballet *The Stone Flower,* which was already being rehearsed, in preliminary form, at the Bolshoi Theatre. So it happened that I postponed my intention to visit Sergei Sergeyevich until eventually the day came with the news of his sudden death....

Then I sincerely regretted that I had not agreed (at our last business meeting) to spend a few (more) minutes with Prokofiev. His moving and affectionate request should have been granted no matter what the circumstances. Now that he has departed from us, I can only reproach myself for this intractability. But every cloud has a silver lining. The lesson which I learned in late 1952 and early 1953 has not been lost on me. I made it a rule never, in any circumstances whatsoever, to refuse anyone who came to me with a question or a request—one never knows what may happen...

Sovietskaya Muzyka, No. 4, 1968

Boris Pokrovsky

WORKING ON *WAR AND PEACE*

Sergei Prokofiev's operatic works are extremely varied and lamentably rarely performed. The tendency of our theatres to limit their repertoire for years on end to a few good operas which are firm favourites with the public enables companies to work hard and seriously on these works. But the exclusive nature of this principle means that we lose a whole range of operas, mainly those which are not certain to have a long run on the stage. Yet they include many interesting works. Prokofiev has operas which cannot yet be called "popular", although there are no grounds for claiming the reverse. But today, unfortunately, many of them never appear on the stage. The most frequently produced are *War and Peace*, *The Duenna* and *Semyon Kotko*, and abroad—his *Love for Three Oranges* and *The Flaming Angel* (a work which I regard as a most powerful anti-clerical tragedy). *The Gambler* and *A Story of a Real Man* for some reason attract less attention, than they undoubtedly deserve.

This is necessary to broaden the public's knowledge of opera, to promote the creative development of performers, and to advance the study of Prokofiev's operatic works as a whole. The latter is essential for the creation of the opera of the future.

It would be wrong to say that theatres do not show an interest in Prokofiev's work, but it is a fact that the specific features of his musical dramaturgy are little studied. This is partly due to the old, philistine view of Prokofiev as the rabid formalist, the mischief-maker who flouts convention and whose music is unnecessarily intricate, involved and "unvocal". We, theatre people, often have only an empirical idea of the regularities in Prokofiev's operatic dramaturgy and are often the victims of subjective views about the author, instead of really understanding his work. Yet we often go from one extreme to the other. Having recognised Prokofiev we sometimes turn him into a model of infallibility, thereby depriving ourselves of the right to note his shortcomings, making it impossible for us to divine the author's idea and help to give it embodiment on the stage. The living features are lost, leaving only dogma. (Incidentally, this applies not only to the interpretation of Prokofiev's operas, but also to the music of other celebrated composers).

However, the specific features of Prokofiev the man also explain a great deal in his work. It is most important to have a practical knowledge of the opera theatre (in this article I am speaking solely from this standpoint)—of when, how and why a composer wrote this or that opera, scene or episode.

I regard the fact that the composer began writing *War and Peace* in the trying days of the Great Patriotic War in 1941, as the most decisive factor in the production of the opera, in finding the "core", the essence in the treatment of this work.

Late one evening in a room on the first floor of the administrative building of the Bolshoi Theatre behind drawn curtains ("black-out" regulations), in the light of two army paraffin lamps the composer, with a coat thrown over his shoulders, played the lyrical scenes with Natasha Rostova to S. Samosud and me. The music brings to life the pastimes of the Kuragin circle, Pierre's psychological quests, Karatayev's philosophy, Tikhon Shcherbaty's rollicking ditties, ... portraying all manner of people.

Prokofiev's main interest in this "war theme" is human characters and destinies in all their variety and incompatibility. Countless hordes of people swarmed into the opera, dressed in foppish hussar's pelisses or bast sandals, with unkempt bushy beards or glasses through which peered tired, intelligent eyes, in plumed cocked hats or peakless caps, in simple bonnets or elaborate hairstyles, with lorgnettes or axes, pitchforks or kid gloves.

It is easy to understand the confusion of a producer confronted by this mass of people with such different languages, social standing, characters and mode of thought and feeling. I became quite panic-stricken when I tried to organise these characters into an orderly system, "threading them" onto through action. The characters did not fit in with one another, the events began and ceased of their accord, the plot was constantly interrupted.

"Let's abridge it," Samosud said to me.

Yet as soon as I suggested omitting something, I heard:

"Oh, but listen. That's such an original character. Quite unlike anything or anyone else! "

Indeed, the whole opera was an encyclopaedia of characters and types, but...

"How can we possibly have Natasha and Andrei Bolkonsky meeting only in his death scene? " I asked.

Everyone saw to their amazement that this really was the case. What was to be done? .

"*War and Peace* is impossible without Natasha's first ball," I said. "That is where Natasha and Bolkonsky fall in love with each other. That is where you meet most of the "peace" characters..."

"So you want to lengthen the opera instead of thinking about shortening it? " Samosud laughed.

"And it is also absolutely vital to have a scene of the council of war in Fili! " I insisted.

Here again Samosud gave the charming laugh which often drowned many arguments and problems. Drowned them, but did not solve them.

Samosud talked persistently to Prokofiev about the need for the new scene (now scene two). I was not present, but according to the information I have, the composer was not very keen on the idea of a "banal opera ball" with polonaises, waltzes and mazurkas. (Oh, these producers!) However... Shortly afterwards I received from Moscow (the opera was being produced in Leningrad) an addition to what is now scene eleven. (This scene is full of remarkably accurate sketches, more than half of which are not included in the version now presented by theatres). It was a remarkable episode and character study: French soldiers singing a song and chatting casually as they pasted Napoleon's edicts. And there were some more such characters, not "linked" to the main plot, but magnificent and essential from the point of view of high drama, characters who helped to reveal the "seamy side" of the events taking place, and the terrible truth of life with its contrasts and grimaces...

But what was a producer to do with the opera? What could he do when the composer, after being asked to write an important scene to put the plot "in order", added some episodes which made the opera even more complicated? Without giving a thought to the theatrical organisation of the plot, Prokofiev was obsessed by his "idée fixe": entirely dissimilar people and characters have been brought together in the chaos of events; they are many and diverse, and all of them are "simmering" in the terrible cauldron of war. Those who saw the first performances of the opera will remember the final scene, full of vividly drawn characters of peasants and partisans. Here we meet Tikhon Shcherbaty, Vassilisa, and the partisan Denisov. With deep regret we omit the choir of fleeing peasants from scene eight, although the dramatic "purpose" of this episode is obvious: together with the "excursion" into the sphere of the hero's inner life (Andrei Bolkonsky) to give the groans and wails of the peasants ("The cattle is bellowing...") against the background of the war rhythms of the night before the battle.

...If it were possible to perform all the episodes now omitted from the opera we would be amazed at their subtle logic and significance. But they are omitted because of the inexhorable requirements of the theatre. When, in the first Leningrad production, we presented the opera during two evenings, this was an artistic failure, although it was in keeping with the author's idea. The way in which the audience perceives a work is a most important, decisive factor. One must not forget the whole in one's concern for detail. This was our argument. But in our concern for the whole, we lose the most important feature of Prokofiev's plan—to create a kaleidoscope of characters, phenomena, facts, to bring together diametrically opposed feelings and events. War turned life upside down, mixing up everything on earth; it has torn the veils from people's faces, showing their true characters; it has smashed social barriers, ranging people according to another principle—the ability to love.

...Nevertheless the composer did write the second scene—the ball scene with a polonaise, a mazurka, the introduction of the characters, the arrival of the Emperor and ... a waltz. "Something like Glinka's *Waltz Fantasie*," Samosud "ordered" on the telephone, winking at me as if to say: "The composer's not very happy!"

It was not long before another package arrived during a rehearsal. Samosud, who was present, immediately put the music on the piano for the pianist and conducted as if he knew it by heart. It was a waltz. And to this day it is played like that in all theatres with the addition in the middle of Natasha's and Bolkonsky's remarks, which we ourselves inserted at a rehearsal, because I had to "link" the music of the waltz to these two characters dramaturgically.

It was a waltz for Natasha, and Natasha alone.... You cannot imagine the waltz without Natasha, or Natasha without the waltz. It is a facet of her character. It is only natural, therefore, that in scene eight when the dying Andrei Bolkonsky is recalling his moments of happiness, he remembers Natasha, the ball and the waltz. And the moment before his death, when he and Natasha are thinking about the happy past, the waltz sounds again. At first it was played at rehearsals as an "étude" in order to help the actors, and was eventually included in the score. When the composer came to a rehearsal he found it all so natural and logical that the additions were approved without any discussion in the score of the eighth and twelfth scenes. Natural and logical! The great formula of Prokofiev's dramaturgy. And also respect for the logic of the production: the producers want it that way, so let it be like that! It is an old truth that opera music should produce an effect not so much by itself as in the given dramaturgic situation.

The waltz turned into a scenic symbol not only because it was delightful in itself, but also because it became the dramaturgic culmination of the heroes' biography.

...In the first version the "Napoleon" scene was followed by the scene of the fire of Moscow. As already mentioned, I suggested the "war council in Fili". Prokofiev wrote this scene at once, without any objections, probably because the war council provided him with the thing that his pen wanted most of all at that time—a multitude of different characters. Beningsen is unlike Yermolov, Yermolov is unlike Barclai, Rayevsky is unlike anyone and so, of course, is Kutuzov. Each small remark conveys the whole character with his own world, his own weaknesses and his social standing. And all of them are closely linked here by the dramaturgic structure, the culmination of which is Kutuzov.

"Since we have the scene now, we must have an aria for Kutuzov," demanded Samosud. Prokofiev sent in several versions. They were even sung at performances, but they did not satisfy anyone. Finally, we received yet another version of the aria, the theme of which was borrowed from the music for the film *Ivan the Terrible*. This was just right. It conveyed the man's striking character, his states and emotions. It was both the portrait of Kutuzov, and patriotic love for Moscow, for the Motherland. Then the music of the aria sounded in the words of the dying Prince Andrei. And, finally, a new chorus for the finale was based on it. The image was expanded to achieve extreme generalisation of emotions, thoughts and situations.

This artistic process, the course of the creation of the work, enables us to draw conclusions concerning the production which, to my mind, apply to all composers and all operas.

In connection with *War and Peace* I cannot help feeling a certain dissatisfaction with what the theatres have so far done in this sphere. No, I am not claiming that the opera should be treated in accordance with the principle of "sharp forms" (to fit in with the way some people regard its music), Prokofiev's characters are absolutely authentic and lifelike down to the minutest detail.

I also hope that no one is expecting a literal reproduction of the score. I thought it impossible to end scene nine in the way indicated by the author. The ending suggested in the first production has so far remained unchanged by producers. Yet it could without a doubt have two, three or a dozen other versions. This will be decided by time and the development of theatrical thought. However, I believe that the most important task in the staging of this opera, is to reveal the composer's main intention: to show a cascade of characters and events, which are outwardly disconnected but linked by an idea. So far theatres have not fulfilled this task. There are weighty reasons for this, of which all producers should be aware.

...A new opera always puts people on their guard. It is listened to with suspicion and prejudice. During the first production of *War and Peace* Samosud would not let me stage the "epigraph"; he even did not play the introduction. At that time people expected "nightmarish discords" from Prokofiev, and Samosud wanted to "win over" the audience by beginning with the pianissimo of the lyrical scene in "Otradnoye".

Perhaps this is not a matter of principle? It is. A theatrical production has a definite lifetime (not more than twenty years), and we must take the conditions of this period into account for the propaganda of works which we produce and in which we believe.

What the first audiences who came to see *War and Peace* (in the Maly Opera Theatre in Leningrad), enjoyed above all was a spectacle dissociated from the opera, as it were, which brought to life their favourite characters from Tolstoy. They used to say, half-jokingly, half-seriously: "It was good entertainment in spite of the music." This view was widespread even among well-known musicians, whose names it would be tactless to mention here. But we, producers, knew that if it were not for the opera with this very music there would have been no spectacle at all. The production did not exacerbate the attitude of the public towards Prokofiev (at that time!), on the contrary, it toned down, as it were, even ironed out that which was unusual and hard to understand (then!) in Prokofiev's music, and in so doing fulfilled its purpose.

Thus, what appears at first glance to be an "unprincipled approach", turned out to be a wise one. Time passed and it became possible to produce the opera differently. Today nobody is shocked by the "epigraph" in the Bolshoi Theatre production. On the contrary, it determines the form and "core" of the opera.

With time better interpretations of *War and Peace* will be found. But they will be in keeping with their age.

Can we not draw a conclusion from the following fact? I put on the first production in fine, friendly collaboration with Samosud and Dmitriev. I was considerably younger and less experienced than my eminent colleagues. They influenced me, and I was glad to accept this influence. But here is the strange thing: both Samosud and Dmitriev tried subtly to induce me to put on an heroic production, a sort of memorial. While agreeing with them in my mind, I could not produce the opera in this way.

My production was simple, realistic, devoid of expressive *mises-en-scène*, exaggerated emotions and majestic, ritual-like treatment. Although at the time I was very fond of that sort of thing.

My colleagues were surprised, not being able to recognise me, but ... when Dmitriev brought the sketches for the sets and Samosud began conducting, it emerged that both the former and the latter, in speaking about the pathos of the theme and the romantic nature of the characters, had been captivated by true life, by feelings which were so penetrating and yet so simple and close to the hearts of all. Even then, perhaps particularly then, when the fate of our country, our native land, our people, was at stake. What guided us subconsciously? Tolstoy, to a large extent, perhaps, but, above all,—and I am deeply convinced of this—Prokofiev.

In the opera *War and Peace* he is more intimate and humanly delicate than ever.

Galina Ulanova

THE AUTHOR OF MY FAVOURITE BALLETS

I shall try to tell you about Prokofiev as I remember him from the day I first saw him and as I have thought of him so many times since—each time, in fact, I dance the parts of Juliet, Cinderella or Katerina. For Prokofiev's original and exquisitely beautiful music has played a tremendously important role in my life as an artist. Indeed, it would hardly be an exaggeration to say that my whole artistic career has been in large measure shaped by Prokofiev's ballets, and for me there is no contemporary ballet to equal those of Prokofiev. His music lives for me, it is the very soul of the dance, his Juliet is my favourite heroine, the quintessence of that radiance, humanism, spiritual purity and nobility that is to be found in almost everything he wrote.

But let me endeavour to marshal my memories in some semblance of chronological order, though the actual circumstances of my association with Prokofiev are, of course, of less interest than the effect his music had on my art, that music which future generations will indubitably cherish as a living and magnificent heritage of the epoch in which the new Soviet music and the new Soviet choreography began to take shape and develop.

I do not remember exactly when I first saw Prokofiev, I only know that at some point during the rehearsals of *Romeo and Juliet* I became aware of the presence in the hall of a tall, somewhat stern-looking man who seemed to disapprove heartily of everything he saw and especially of our artists. It was Prokofiev.

I had heard that in the early stages of the production, Lavrovsky and Prokofiev had had some heated arguments about the music. Lavrovsky had told the composer that there was not enough music in the ballet for a full-length production and that he would have to add to it. To which Prokofiev had stubbornly replied, "I have written exactly as much music as is necessary and I am not going to add a single note. The ballet is complete as it is. You may take it or leave it."

After much wrangling a way out of the difficulty was at last found by bringing the score closer to the dramatic line of the libretto, and by changing the order of the music here and there. The result is the production as we now know it.

I exchanged barely more than a few words with Prokofiev until the production was nearing completion when it was decided that a formal introduction ought to be made. I shall never forget that occasion. It took place at one of the final rehearsals of the ballet with orchestra in the Kirov Theatre of Opera and Ballet in Leningrad. On the previous day I had undergone a very painful operation on my gum and appeared at rehearsal with my face bandaged and my eyes red with weeping. That is how Prokofiev first met his future Juliet. And since she was obviously unable to dance that day the rehearsal was postponed.

Time was flying, the rehearsals were in full swing, but we were still badly hampered by the unusual orchestration and the chamber quality of the music. The frequent change of rhythm, too, gave us a great deal of trouble. To tell the truth we were not accustomed to such music, in fact we were a little afraid of it. It seemed to us that in rehearsing the Adagio from Act I, for example, we were following some melodic pattern of our own, something nearer to our own conception of how the love of Romeo and Juliet should be expressed than that contained in Prokofiev's "strange" music. For I must confess that we did not hear that love in his music then.

We did not tell Prokofiev anything of this, we were afraid of him. All our doubts, perplexities and suggestions were transmitted to the composer through Lavrovsky. Prokofiev seemed unapproachable and haughty, and we felt he had no faith in ballet or in ballet artists. This last hurt our feelings deeply. Youth and professional pride prevented us from realising that Prokofiev had grounds for distrusting the ballet theatre, for he had had bad luck with his ballets—not one of those he had written prior to *Romeo and Juliet* had survived. I shall leave it to the musical historian to explain why this was so, and continue my account of my acquaintance with Prokofiev.

We were rehearsing the beginning of Act III—the "Lark Scene", we called it, because as Romeo leaves her chamber, Juliet says:

> *Wilt thou be gone? It is not yet near day:*
> *It was the nightingale, and not the lark,*
> *That pierc'd the fearful hollow of thine ear;*
> *Nightly she sings on yond pomegranate tree:*
> *Believe me, love, it was the nightingale...*

Anyone who knows the production will remember, of course, that when the curtain rises Juliet is sitting on a brocaded couch with Romeo kneeling beside her, his head in her lap. The couch stands at the back of the stage some distance from the footlights and, consequently, from the orchestra as well, and hence we who were acting the parts of Romeo and Juliet could not hear it. Suddenly we were startled by a shout from Lavrovsky: "Why don't you begin? " "We can't hear the music," we replied. Prokofiev, who was present, lost his temper: "I know what you want! " he shouted. "You want drums, not music! "

We did not take offence. We invited him to come on to the stage and sit beside us. He did so, and throughout the entire scene he sat on that couch, listening carefully to the orchestra without saying a word. But on leaving he said, still looking very annoyed, "Very well, I shall rewrite the music here and add something."

Slowly the production began to take shape. The acting became more clearly defined, costumes were ready, the pattern of the dance emerged and Prokofiev began to see that we were not altogether deaf to good music and that we did have the power of giving visual expression to that music. And once he had acquired faith in us his attitude changed. Gradually that air of chill aloofness we had so much resented at first disappeared. He began to listen to our remarks with increasing interest and attention, and before long a sympathy which soon turned to warm and genuine affection sprang up between the ballet dancers and the composer. That feeling was all the more precious for having weathered the stormiest periods in the relations between the representatives of two interrelated arts who had begun by fearing they would never be able to understand each other.

That mutual regard was finally sealed when after the first night performance Sergei Sergeyevich, moved and elated by the success, came on to the stage to share the triumph with us. And when at the little supper held later to celebrate the occasion, I proposed a toast ending with the words: "Never was a tale of greater woe than Prokofiev's music for *Romeo*," Sergei Sergeyevich seemed to enjoy the joke more than anyone else. But that was merely a joke.

My first acquaintance with the new choreography had begun with Asafyev's *Fountain of Bakhchisarai*. But whereas in that ballet it was Pushkin's dramatism that determined the idea and dramatic content of the music, Prokofiev's music actually seemed to merge with Shakespeare's poetry. In *Romeo and Juliet*, in spite of the novelty and originality of the music, the fusion of idea and action was on a far higher plane than in the *Fountain of Bakhchisarai*. That is the secret of the success of Prokofiev's ballet, of its unfading freshness.

Prokofiev with his vigorous, dynamic, truly visual music, at once so modern and yet so Shakespearean in spirit and flavour, guided us with a sure hand through the action, investing it with meaning and purpose. His vividly drawn characterisations literally dictated the pattern of the dance, making our task easier.

At first, as I said before, the music seemed to us incomprehensible and almost impossible to dance to. But the more we listened to it, the more we worked, experimented and searched, the more clearly emerged the images that music created. And gradually as we came to understand the music, we no longer found it difficult to dance to; it became clear both choreographically and psychologically. And now if I were to be asked what the music of *Romeo and Juliet* should be like, I would say without hesitation: like Prokofiev's for I cannot now conceive of any other music.

I do not propose to discuss Prokofiev's other two ballets in such detail as *Romeo and Juliet*. As regards *The Tale of the Stone Flower*, for instance, I can do little more than comment on the melodiousness and humanity of the music, and the magnificently developed themes of some of the characters—the Mistress of Copper Mountain, Danila and the villain Severyan. This is not because the exquisite music of Prokofiev's last ballet does not evoke profound emotions and ideas, or does not furnish material for a more exhaustive analysis. On the contrary, perhaps just because that music is so interesting and significant one has to hear it many times, to let it "captivate one", before being able to draw any general conclusions or to understand fully what place it will occupy in one's own career as an artist.

I had to dance Juliet for many years before I fully grasped the role, before I understood, or rather, appreciated the tremendous work the composer, choreographer and the entire troupe had invested in the production. I believe this is true of every genuine work of art such as Prokofiev's ballet.

...I met Prokofiev several times after the Leningrad première of *Romeo and Juliet* during my visits to Moscow for guest performances and, later, for the Leningrad theatre festivals. I saw him several times before the first festival in the home of the artist Nikolai Radlov where I was a frequent visitor. But the charming person I saw there, usually absorbed in a game of chess, was a very different Prokofiev from the man I had been in such awe of, and whom I had even disliked for what I believed to be his haughtiness. This Prokofiev was warm and friendly, simple and natural in his manner.

I shall never forget the first performance of *Romeo and Juliet* at the first Leningrad theatre festival in Moscow. It was a great success. I returned to my hotel, tired and happy, and had barely recovered from the excitement of the evening when there came a knock at the door. To my great surprise it was Prokofiev. "You must come with me at once to the Writers' Club. They are expecting us," he said in a tone that brooked no objection. I went. Williams, Dmitriev and many other people I knew were there. As we entered the large hall we were met with applause and to its accompaniment we marched to the banquet table.

I was much embarrassed when Prokofiev invited me to dance with him. It was an ordinary foxtrot, but he danced it as if he heard some rhythm of his own, beginning the step somehow "off-beat". It confused me, and I missed my step several times. I was afraid I would not be able to catch his rhythm and would end up by stepping on my partner's toes, in short, prove to him that I could not dance! But gradually I caught the extraordinary rhythm and after the first dance everything went well. That was an extremely pleasant evening.

I remember also the winter before the war when I lived partly in Leningrad and partly in Moscow. Y. Radin, the director of the Kirov Theatre, wishing to cement our ballet's good relations with Prokofiev, asked him to write something else for us. One evening he brought Prokofiev with him to my room in the Moskva Hotel. They asked me what part I would like to dance.

"The Snow Maiden," I replied.

"Oh, but Rimsky-Korsakov has written such a splendid *Snow Maiden* that I wouldn't dare to tackle that theme," said Prokofiev. "Suppose we try *Cinderella?* "

He told us why he had not had faith in ballet before *Romeo and Juliet,* why he had not believed that ballet art could give full expression to musical and literary images. But now his attitude had changed completely and he wanted to write rich, full-blooded music for a new ballet.

It was not only Prokofiev's attitude toward ballet that had changed at this time. He himself had changed. He had begun to search for greater simplicity of musical idiom. His search sometimes led him far afield, but his great talent invariably guided him back on to the path of great, genuine human feeling. In this period I learned to appreciate the charm of Prokofiev's personality, the frankness and outspokenness of his manner, his almost boyish exuberance and gaiety which could change instantly to anger when he encountered injustice, vulgarity or incompetence. I believe that without knowing him personally, one cannot help but feel this frankness and sincerity of his—one has only to listen to his music, especially to such compositions as *On Guard of Peace* or the Seventh Symphony.

The war interrupted his plans for a ballet on the theme of *Cinderella.* The next time I met him was in Alma Ata. It was on a sweltering day and he was on his way to his room in the hotel where I too was staying along with many other evacuated artists. A grand piano took up nearly all the space in the room, and sheet music was piled everywhere—on the piano, on the floor, on chairs and on the window-sill. Prokofiev was in excellent form and full of ideas. He was writing the music for *Ivan the Terrible,* composing his *War and Peace,* thinking about *Cinderella* and planning a trip to Perm where the Leningrad Kirov Opera and Ballet Theatre was performing.

It was not until after the war that I began to work on *Cinderella* in the Bolshoi Theatre. I tried to persuade Prokofiev to give *Cinderella* the beautiful theme of the Fairy Godmother, but all my efforts were unavailing. Prokofiev was a man for whom art was sacred and he was incapable of making any compromises. He had created that melody for the Fairy Godmother, that was her theme as he saw it and felt it, and nothing on earth could have induced him to give it to any other character.

The fact that we "fell in love" with *Cinderella* at first sight and that much of it was clear to us from the very outset, or at any rate much sooner than in the case of *Romeo and Juliet*, showed how well we had learned to understand Prokofiev's music. Nevertheless, though it would be unfair to say that *Cinderella* is on a lower plane than the Shakespearean ballet, one could hardly expect the ballet *Cinderella* to be more in relation to the ballet *Romeo and Juliet* than Shakespeare's tragedy is to Perrault's fairy-tale. And although the fairy-tale, too, is immortal, though it too has philosophical depth, passion and humanity, *Cinderella* could never rise to the sublime heights of *Romeo and Juliet*.

When this, his best ballet, was staged in the Bolshoi Theatre the composer was already seriously ill and unable to attend rehearsals. Only rarely, when his health permitted, did we see him at performances.

At this period he lived mostly in the country, at Nikolina Gora. But he was full of creative energy. He and Lavrovsky were now good friends, and he was planning to write a new ballet on the theme of Don Juan. He had nursed the idea for a long time, ever since *Romeo and Juliet* was first produced in Leningrad. With Williams and Lavrovsky he had prepared to carry his cherished dream into effect. But again the war interfered. I believe he intended to take Byron's Don Juan for a model, but perhaps his Don Juan would have been the composite figure familiar from the works of the world classics from Tirso de Molina, Perrucci, Shadwell and Goldoni to Molière, Mérimèe, Pushkin and Blok.

It is curious that though he did not venture to "compete" with the national genius of Rimsky-Korsakov in *Snow Maiden* (although I, for one, am convinced that Prokofiev would have found his own powerful and original version), in the case of Don Juan the fact that such composers as Mozart, Cherubini, Cimarosa and many others had written music on the subject, and Gluck even a ballet, did not deter him.

However, after much thought Prokofiev chose a Russian theme taken from Bazhov's *Ural Tales*. That is how *The Tale of the Stone Flower* ballet was born. As I mentioned before, it will take me far more than the few months that have passed since its first performance to form any more or less conclusive opinion of my work in this, his last ballet.

The terrible thing is that it was his last. One can imagine what a wealth of magnificent music Prokofiev might still have written! His children's suite, the peace oratorio, and his last symphony, so radiant and exquisite, open such breathtaking vistas that one cannot find words to express the bitterness and pain one feels at man's helplessness in the face of Death.

April 16, 1954

Ilya Ehrenburg

HE FELT THE HEARTBEAT OF TIME

In the life and art of Sergei Prokofiev it was the tragic element that was most strongly manifest. This is in no way inconsistent either with his love of life or the philosophical optimism which helped him to emerge on the highroad of history.

At the beginning of the century progressive artists were filled with alarm and anxiety. The obsolete aesthetic standards seemed to them false and evil. Sergei Prokofiev was both an iconoclast and a builder. Beneath the outward calm of this seemingly cold Northerner there surged a deeply passionate nature. He was one of the first to translate the spirit of his stormy age into music.

He grew up in the years before the Revolution, he had a thorough knowledge of classical harmony, he loved real harmony. But greater still was his love of truth in art; he felt the heartbeat of his time. His path in art has much in common with that of Pablo Picasso. Sergei Prokofiev too could work in diverse styles, he too contradicted himself at every step, tried everything and rejected everything, but always remained true to his calling and his artistic conscience.

He renounced the world that had made him famous; he wanted to work for his own people and for the future. He suffered many trials, but he never lost heart, never gave up the fight, and he died young in spirit, uncompromising, true to himself to the end. He was a great man and future generations will not be able to understand that difficult and glorious time which we still have the right to call our own without listening carefully to Sergei Prokofiev's music and pondering over his remarkable life.

1955

Mikhail Botvinnik

PROKOFIEV, THE CHESS–PLAYER

My first introduction to Prokofiev's music occurred at musical lessons that were a regular part of the curriculum in 1923-1926 at school No. 157 in Leningrad which I attended. These lessons were essentially little chamber concerts with explanations by the music teacher. As a rule, we were given classical music, but one day our teacher said that she was going to play something rather out of the ordinary.

She told us about a young composer named Sergei Prokofiev and his original style. "It is impossible to be indifferent to his music," she told us. "Some people believe him to be exceptionally talented, others disapprove of him altogether. When I addressed a gathering of teachers recently and announced that I was going to play the music of Prokofiev I was given an extremely chill reception. I shall play the same piece to you now..."

If I am not mistaken, the name of the piece was *Despair*. It made a deep impression on all of us. Unfortunately, I have never heard it since; if I had I should recognise it at once.

I met Prokofiev in 1936 at the height of the Third International Chess Tournament in Moscow. He was a first-rate chessplayer himself and never missed a match. His position in the tournament was a delicate one and he maintained a strictly neutral attitude throughout, for while his sympathies were naturally with me as the young Soviet champion, he could not wish for the defeat of the ex-world champion Capablanca with whom he had made friends in Paris.

Some months later Capablanca and I shared first place at the tournament in Nottingham, England. When the tournament was over I received a telegram of congratulations from Sergei Sergeyevich. I was naturally very pleased and, without thinking, I showed the wire to Capablanca who was with me at the time. At once I saw that I had made a mistake—from the expression on Capablanca's face I realised he had not received a wire from Prokofiev. Two hours later Capablanca came to me beaming—he had received a telegram too! Of course, Sergei Sergeyevich had sent both wires at the same time, but evidently the Moscow telegraph office clerks had felt that the Soviet champion ought to get his message first!

Sergei Sergeyevich was passionately fond of chess. He took part in the chess activity of the Central Art Workers' Club. Moscow chess-players still remember his rather unique match with David Oistrakh—the winner was awarded the Art Workers' Club prize and the loser had to give a concert for art workers.

I played chess with Prokofiev several times. He played a very vigorous, forthright game. His usual method was to launch an attack which he conducted cleverly and ingeniously. He obviously did not care for defence tactics. His severe illness did not lessen his interest in chess. In May 1949 the well-known chess-player Y. G. Rokhlin and I paid a visit to Prokofiev at his country home at Nikolina Gora. Sergei Sergeyevich was ill in bed and looked very poorly, but as soon as he saw Rokhlin he livened up. "Where is that volume of the 1894 Steiniz and Lasker chess match you promised me? " he demanded. Poor Rokhlin, who had clearly forgotten all about it, was much embarrassed.

In the summer of 1951 Sergei Sergeyevich entered as one of the participants in a demonstration of simultaneous play I was to give at Nikolina Gora. His doctors, however, forbade it, but that did not prevent Prokofiev from following the games with his usual avid interest. I believe that was the last chess contest he ever attended.

1954

Konstantin Sergeyev

AN ELEVATING INFLUENCE

My meeting with Sergei Sergeyevich Prokofiev and his music became the central event of my creative biography and my life as a whole. It took place twenty-six years ago, at the time of the production of *Romeo and Juliet,* the composer's first ballet on the stage of our theatre.

This was in the 1930s. One must know the period well to imagine the atmosphere of creative enthusiasm in which we worked. Young Soviet choreography was on the threshold of some brilliant artistic discoveries. We wanted ballet to discard the "stilts" of fairy-tale plots and turn to the veracity of great, profound, vivid human characters, genuine passions, real conflicts. In this quest, in our day-to-day work together, we formed a firm alliance of like-minded artists—G. Ulanova, R. Gerbek, T. Vecheslova, L. Lavrovsky, A. Lopukhov, E. Biber, and many of our older comrades who had succeeded in finding a realistic treatment, in creating authentic characters in such productions as, say, *The Fountain of Bakhchisarai* or *Lost Illusions* by Boris Asafyev. Prokofiev's ballet was the culminating point of our quest.

Romeo and Juliet. Shakespeare in the language of the dance! It was unexpected, incredible. Many people had doubts about it. And no wonder: the music was complex, strange to our ears, and sometimes seemed unsuitable for ballet. Lavrovsky's choreography was unusual, a far cry from theatrical "prettiness" There were no traditional variations, no numbers in the various genres and rhythms. All this put the troupe on their guard, and the doubts grew. But we, who performed the main parts, were full of enthusiasm: the power and charm of Shakespeare's characters were so magnetic! We needed drama with profound, vivid characters, and the doubts of our comrades did not hinder our work. We were in love with it and, like all lovers, did not notice anything else, or pretended not to. But we needed serious moral support. And at this crucial moment there finally appeared the already famous but as yet unknown to us Prokofiev.

Everyone became very excited when we learnt that the author had come to a stage rehearsal. I remember this rehearsal, which was accompanied by a piano, very well. In the dark, empty auditorium was Prokofiev. On the stage was one of the crowd scenes from Act I. Suddenly the sound of sharp, rhythmic clapping came from the stalls. We did not realise at once what it was. The clapping continued steadily, out of time with the dancing and the piano playing: obviously the composer was demanding a change in tempo. But such a change would also have altered the rhythm of the dance, and that was impossible. Our pianist E. Kushelevskaya looked fearfully at Lavovsky, as if caught between the devil and the deep blue sea. This continued right until the end of the number.

Prokofiev was adamant, and both of them refused to give way. This put us on the alert. We sensed the hardness of his character and, perhaps, the equal hardness, of his rhythm. It was the same at subsequent rehearsals. He had written the music, he thought in these rhythms and would not make the lightest concessions. We even began to feel that Prokofiev had a somewhat "hostile", "irritated" attitude towards ballet.

Disagreements also arose in respect of the orchestration. For example, we felt that certain scenes and episodes were not quite comprehensively orchestrated, that the orchestration was too chamber-like and that this did not suit Shakespeare's dynamic passions. I remember tearing off my wig in despair, quite unable to continue the rehearsal. But Prokofiev thought that if there were only two actors on the stage at a given moment, the orchestra should be "modest" (unlike Wagner, say, who liked supporting a single singer with an extraordinarily developed orchestral part which frequently drowned the voice of the soloist). He was convinced of this, and we could not change his mind.

For a long time I asked Sergei Sergeyevich to give Romeo the chance to dance: for originally the ballet did not contain a single solo variation for my character. Romeo's variation, in which the theme from the Adagio is developed at a quick tempo, is the result of these arguments and requests. We later learned that Prokofiev was opposed in principle to adding new music to a finished score. The composer thought that by the time he had finished a work he was "different"; that he would write differently from what he did before, so he did not want to change anything. It took a real "battle" to have the gavotte from the *Classical Symphony* and the dance of the servant girls (Act I) included in the ballet

Yes, there is no point in concealing it: Sergei Sergeyevich's irritability and stubbornness sometimes upset us. But this was forgotten as soon as all the components were put together and the integrate production by Prokofiev, Lavrovsky, Williams and the whole theatre was presented. The première was a success, and this mollified Prokofiev to some extent. He limited himself to half-jocular, half-serious remarks about the producers.

The ballet *Romeo and Juliet* was then shown in Moscow during a ten-day festival of Leningrad art and was highly acclaimed by both audiences and critics.

I was often asked how did it happen that I parted company so "easily" with the part of Romeo, which was considered to be one of my more successful roles. And, indeed, I danced it for only two seasons, but then war came. (*Romeo and Juliet* could not be presented in Perm, where the theatre was evacuated because of the lack of sets and costumes.) On my return to Leningrad I did not want to dance in the ballet without Ulanova, because I thought that the role of Romeo was choreographically most significant in the duets, dialogues, and, frankly, could not imagine dancing with a different partner. I thought would not find the understanding of the inner choreographic rhythm which had linked me with Ulanova for a long time in various ballets. It was impossible to recapture this harmony, and my Romeo found himself all alone in his prime. Only on one occasion, the Gerbek anniversary, did I dance again with Ulanova as Juliet: we performed two scenes from Prokofiev's ballet..

After the production of Romeo we wanted Sergei Sergeyevich to write a new ballet for us. He refused, saying jokingly that he had been tortured enough as it was. Nevertheless, after while he felt the urge to turn to ballet again. Nikolai Dmitrievich Volkov suggested the plot of *Cinderella* to him (incidentally, it was no easy matter to find Prokofiev a plot: he ever rejected *The Snow Maiden*!)

246

Whereas my first encounter with the composer had been a meeting with a "beautiful stranger", the second time—in our work on *Cinderella*—I met him as an artist of whom I had become very fond, a man of remarkable warmth. This was in 1942, during the war. The theatre had been evacuated, but no difficulties could deter us. Prokofiev was composing music rapidly, with great inspiration. There was no trace of estrangement, irritability or prejudice in him. The composer "had fallen in love" with ballet, and therefore his work progressed swiftly. Together with Volkov and Feldt we met in a small room in the Perm hotel. These were very exciting meetings with the great composer, who was writing a radiant, optimistic work during a period of severe trials.

Outwardly restrained, sometimes even somewhat stiff, he possessed the poetic heart of a wise and yet childishly naïve story-teller. He felt and portrayed most vividly both the highly grotesque scenes of the philistine and court life, and the great, pure love of Cinderella and the Prince. His rich imagination knew no bounds. For the culmination of the ballet, for example, he saw a clock with a huge pendulum which swung to the ominous chords of the music, across the whole stage. It was impossible to look at the composer without smiling. Tall and thin, he became literally transformed when talking about his ideas for the production of this episode which he pictured down to the minutest detail. Then the decor designer and I would give a great deal of thought as to how Prokofiev's idea of the scene could be put into effect.

Mindful of our desire that he should try himself in the role of the traditional ballet (in the best sense of the word) composer, Prokofiev wrote a "real ballet", using our favourite rhythms, tempos and forms—adagios, enchanting waltzes, galops, polkas, and court dances—pavanes and passepieds... This time he readily complied with our numerous requests. "Ask what you will of me while I am writing," he used to say. "Once I've finished, that's that." And in this way, we, representatives of the choreographic art, participated directly in the process of creating the work, instead of having nothing to do with the music once it had been completed, as was the case in the production of *Romeo*. This naturally yielded some good results. As always, Sergei Sergeyevich carefully guarded the musical material, using some of it later in other works.

As an artist, I wanted very much to give the male dance more

247

"space". We tackled this important task together. Great scope was given to the dancing in *Cinderella*, and the Prince was in the air from the first to the last dance. This was my artistic "revenge", and also my début as a choreographer. It was the first time I undertook such an important production (previously I had staged only small concert numbers).

Prokofiev's music called for very precise and laconic thinking. It provided excellent material for the creation of vivid choreographic images and vivid dramaturgical texture of the ballet. This was a splendid training for me and helped me to master the basic principles of professional choreographer's work.

Prokofiev lent an attentive ear to the choreographer's advice. At the same time he demanded a clear, precise "description of the character" For example, at first Cinderella's sisters were to be called Kubyshka and Khudyshka ("squat" and "lean"). I thought that these concepts were not suited to the ballet genre, and the composer accepted my idea of Krivlyaka and Zlyuka ("All Airs and Graces" and "Full of Spite"). When we started discussing the concrete musical and scenic characterisation of Krivlyaka, Volkov and I produced the description: "sugary on the outside and venomous inside". Prokofiev was delighted. He clapped his hands like a child: "Marvellous, splendid! " As always when he was genuinely pleased, he burst out laughing. His was infectious, rumbling, typical "Russian" laugh. The variation was soon written. After the first hearing I had to say in amazement: "I am afraid I do not understand it". It was no usual, traditional variation. But the composer had coped with the "task" perfectly. A few more hearings convinced me of that and now it was my turn to be delighted: I felt how Sergei Sergeyevich had reproduced both the "sugar" and the "venom" in the Krivlyaka variation. And once having felt this, I found the choreography for it. There were many cases like this....

When I began work on the production, some people who regarded Prokofiev as lacking in lyricism doubted whether his music could be combined with my dancing which was essentially lyrical. But I am deeply convinced, and time has proved me right, that *Cinderella* revealed two aspects of the composer's talent: striking grotesque and the most poetic lyricism which we had not sensed so acutely before, perhaps, even in *Romeo*. The qualities which Prokofiev himself possessed to a high degree—poetic feeling, a childlike naïveté and simplicity, and at the same time wisdom—were felt most strongly in *Cinderella*.

I sensed these qualities in my personal encounters with Sergei Sergeyevich too—in Perm, and later in Moscow and at his country house in Nikolina Gora. We always felt the kindness of this delightfully hospitable host, his truly Russian welcome, although in the middle of a heart-to-heart talk he would suddenly make some ironic, caustic remarks about the art of ballet, as if in revenge for the difficulties experienced by him during the production of *Romeo...*

I remember in particular our meetings (together with Lavrovsky) connected with Prokofiev's last ballet *Tale of the Stone Flower*. I liked the music very much, although I found it unusual at the first hearing. By then I was chief ballet-master at the Kirov Opera and Ballet Theatre, and was eager to produce the *Stone Flower*, but the Bolshoi Theatre beat us to it; Sergei Sergeyevich's new ballet was first staged in Moscow and then, three years later, at the Kirov Theatre in Leningrad. The composer was not destined to see this production, but I know that he was most anxious for the *Stone Flower* to be produced in our theatre. Because he had faith in us...

Prokofiev's immortal music has cultivated in me a clear, vivid mode of thinking and the ability to make rational use of means of expression. I am very fond of it. And I believe that many a generation of ballet dancers and choreographers will benefit from its elevating and ennobling influence. I am happy that fate granted me the opportunity to work with this great musician and great man.

Sovietskaya Muzyka, No. 4, 1966

Alexei Yermolayev

DANCING IN PROKOFIEV'S BALLETS

I did not become acquainted with Sergei Prokofiev's music until quite late, after I had danced in the ballets of Tchaikovsky, Glazunov, Asafyev and Glière...

After the first hearing of *Romeo and Juliet* only a few scenes remained in my mind; I was unable to get the impression of the work as a whole due to the complexity of Prokofiev's writing. Previously I had encountered music which required one to listen, Prokofiev's required one to think. This was all the more difficult because my tempestuous character, Tybalt, did not have his own "portrait" theme. He was characterised by the whole music of "enmity". It was most difficult to extract Tybalt's specific features, characteristic of him alone, from this. I found most of the material for work on the part not in the scenes of the brawl in Act I and the duel (Act III), but in the dance with the cushions. The measured rhythm of this music, majestic and awesome, yet passionate and solemn, evoked the mental picture of a grand procession which could be either a triumphal wedding procession or a ponderous funeral one. These apparently mutually exclusive associations provided me with the best key to the portrait of Tybalt, for whom the world is hell, yet who, nevertheless, finds it painfully hard to bid farewell to life and clings desperately to each second left to him...

When I had mastered Prokofiev's complex work enough to feel at home with it, I noticed to my disappointment that the part of Tybalt was treated as pure pantomime. I had "scrutinised" the character to such an extent that I could imagine the way he performs a variation at the ball and saw passion in this variation, passion which was more direct than in the dance with the cushions or the agile feats of the duellist—a series of sharp musical "thrusts", illustrating the street brawl, as it were.

I went to Prokofiev with my discoveries and asked him to write the variation for Tybalt. Prokofiev became interested and questioned me thoroughly about my view of the dramatic pattern of the dance. He said he would definitely write the variation ... but did not.

True, he did not forget my request, for he promised to write without fail a whole part for me in his new ballet as a compensation: I never found out from him which one it was, but personally consider it to be Severyan.

In working on the part of Tybalt I re-read *Romeo and Juliet*, *Othello*, and *Richard III* in search of his character, whereas Severyan, although I associated him with many works from Russian literature, grew mainly out of the music which portrayed this terrible figure of the rich man's lackey and "slaughterer" with Prokofiev's typical precision. The music contains unrestrained bravado, loutish insolence and a brutal hatred of the ordinary working man, it contains the "ostentatious" movement with which Severyan tucks his silken shirt under his belt as a sign that the dancing should begin; it contains the drunken, desperate sobbing when Severyan, moved by the heart-rending melody of the gypsy dancing, is tormented by sorrow and longing, then rages in a drunken frenzy and acts like a rich merchant, throwing money under the feet and in the faces of the dancing gypsies as if attempting to revenge himself upon them for his loneliness....

These two parts were most important for me, particularly Tybalt, who led me to the main roles of my "pantomime" repertoire, such as Guirei...

Irma Yaunzem

RECORDING PROKOFIEV'S MUSIC

I first saw Prokofiev in 1915. A young man came into the canteen of the Petrograd Conservatoire where my friends and I were having a bite to eat in a break between classes. Tall, with fair, gingery hair, an energetic face and bright, intelligent eyes, and dressed in a light, sporting-type suit, he immediately attracted attention.

"That's Prokofiev," my neighbour whispered, "the composer they're all talking about now. Such original music! And what a pianist! "

"Really," another girl broke in. "Call that music? It's just a mixture of modernism and futurism. They're making a fuss about nothing."

At that time Prokofiev's music provoked much heated debate and conflicting opinions....

But it was not until 1932, that I heard Prokofiev play and made his acquaintance. This was in the actors' club which then had its premises in Staropimenovsky Alley in Moscow...

Then, twelve years later, in October 1944, when victory was the only thought in everybody's minds, I met Prokofiev professionally. S.M. Eisenstein was finishing the production of the first part of *Ivan the Terrible* and I was invited to record my voice for the scene of the nurse with the young tsarevich Ivan, where the nurse has to sing a song; the Russian folk character of its melody bore the strong imprint of Prokofiev's distinctive style. The first orchestral rehearsal (conducted by the young A. Stasevich, an ardent admirer of Prokofiev), at which S.S. Prokofiev and S.M. Eisenstein were present, went well. As Eisenstein and the film's musical director R.A. Lukina later told me, they had been looking for someone to sing this song for a long time... Opera singers performed it like an aria, without the traditional folk flavour, while folk singers could not manage the rhythmic pattern or master Prokofiev's peculiar intonations; moreover, they sang with a deliberately "open sound". Eisenstein said that I succeeded in finding both the correct traditional folk manner and the right timbre and pronunciation for an elderly woman. But ... at the second rehearsal, I allowed myself to take a "liberty"—in the middle of the song I sang one note one-fourth lower than in the original. I felt instinctively that this change and the resulting effect were more in keeping with folk tradition and more convincing. The conductor turned pale:

"What? Have you gone mad? " he cried, stopping the orchestra. "That's sacrilege! He'll never forgive you! " But at that moment Prokofiev came out of the adjoining room and said:

"It sounded quite all right. I like it," and immediately amended the score. After the rehearsal I apologised to Sergei Sergeyevich and wanted to explain my reasons, but he smiled:

"There's no need to return to it. I am quite satisfied. It is better like that; in general I do not like making changes in a completed score, but this was an exception."

In Part One of the film, the composer asked me to reproduce a woman's "scream", full of horror and pain, in the scene where Glinskaya is poisoned, at the moment when she runs downstairs. This had to be done against the background of the music, "in tune" with the clarinet, in the same key. In spite of the high tessitura and the unusual nature of making the sound track, the scene was recorded.

Exactly a year later we started to make the sound track for the second part of *Ivan the Terrible*. I was to sing the *Song of the Beaver* which belongs to Yefrosinia Staritskaya (acted by Serafima Germanovna Birman). Serafima Germanovna and S.M. Eisenstein came to my home for nearly all the rehearsals. I had to reproduce the timbre of Birman's voice exactly, capturing all its characteristic features and intonations. We rehearsed with *mises-en-scène* and the text. It was important to ensure that the words and the singing were fully synchronised. Serafima Germanovna was a splendid musical partner. We understood each other without the slightest difficulty. Eventually the rehearsals were transferred to the studio and the recording was made immediately. Prokofiev accepted everything, without a single reservation.

I also met with Prokofiev when I was working on a cycle of Russian folk songs arranged by him—*Green Grove, Katerina, Guelder Rose,* and *Dunyushka,* to which I later added two more delightful songs *My Beloved Is Gone* and *Dream* (which was later recorded on a gramophone record). Sergei Sergeyevich was very interested in my method of working on the song, asked me questions and made some suggestions himself. I remember that, when working on a programme of songs by Soviet composers, I asked S.S. Prokofiev to select some for me. A few days later I received the music from him with a note wishing me success. So, two more songs were added to my Prokofiev repertoire— *Two Brothers* and *My Country Grows,* which were a great success with audiences.

Unfortunately, these songs and Prokofiev's arrangements are heard less and less frequently on the stage. I should like to bring them to the attention of our young vocalists, who are evidently not sufficiently acquainted with the legacy of our great composer.

Sovietskaya Muzyka, No. 4, 1961

LIST OF AUTHORS

Shostakovich, Dmitry Dmitrievich (1906-1975)–Soviet composer.

Kabalevsky, Dmitry Borisovich (b. 1904)–Soviet composer and musicologist, the author of a number of studies on Prokofiev's work.

Karayev, Kara, Abdulfaz-Ogly (b. 1918)–Soviet composer.

Leman, Albert Semyonovich (b. 1915)–Soviet composer.

Khrennikov, Tikhon Nikolayevich (b. 1913)–Soviet composer.

Myaskovsky, Nikolai Yakovlevich (1881-1950)–Soviet composer.

Blok, Vladimir Mikhailovich (b. 1932)–Soviet composer and musicologist, the author of a number of studies on Prokofiev's work.

Karklinš, Ludvig Andreyevich (b. 1928)–Soviet musicologist.

Nestyev, Izrail Vladimirovich (b. 1911)–Soviet musicologist, the author of a number of studies on Prokofiev's work.

Danko, Larissa Georgievna (b. 1931)–Soviet musicologist, the author of a number of studies on Prokofiev's work.

Tyulin, Yuri Nikolayevich (b. 1893)–Soviet composer and musicologist.

Prokofieva (Mendelson), Myra Alexandrovna (1915-1968)–poetess and librettist, S. Prokofiev's second wife.

Richter, Svyatoslav Teofilovich (b. 1915)–Soviet pianist.

Oistrakh, David Fyodorovich (1908-1974)–Soviet violinist and conductor.

Gilels, Emil Grigoryevich (b. 1916)–Soviet pianist.

Milstein, Yakov Isaakovich (b. 1911)–Soviet musicologist.

Rogal-Levitsky, Dmitry Romanovich (1898-1962)—Soviet composer and musicologist.

Pokrovsky, Boris Alexandrovich (b. 1912)—Soviet opera producer.

Ulanova, Galina Sergeyevna (b. 1910)—Soviet ballerina.

Ehrenburg, Ilya Grigoryevich (1891-1967)—Soviet writer and translator.

Botvinnik, Mikhail Moiseyevich (b. 1911)—Soviet chessplayer.

Sergeyev, Konstantin Mikhailovich (b. 1910)—Soviet dancer and ballet-master.

Yermolayev, Alexei Nikolayevich (1910-1975)—Soviet dancer and ballet master.

Yaunzem, Irma Petrovna (1897-1975)—Soviet singer.

1 His *Rhapsody in Blue* is widely known in our country but in the marvellously naive translation as *Blue Rhapsody*. "Blue" means not only blue in colour, but also sad. Hence, the blues—a type of sad fox-trot, usually on the theme "I love you, but you don't love me". Therefore we are dealing here with a rhapsody written on a blues theme, and not with a blue rhapsody. . p. 51

2 *Vinkler, Alexander Adolfovich* (1865-1935)—pianist and composer, professor of piano at the St. Petersburg Conservatoire. Prokofiev studied under him in his early years at the Conservatoire. p. 69

3 *Lemba, Artur Gustavovich* (1885-1963)—pianist and composer. Graduated from the St. Petersburg Conservatoire in 1908. p. 70

4 *Malko, Nikolai Andreyevich* (1883-1961)—conductor. Graduated from the St. Petersburg Conservatoire in 1909. p. 70

5 Opus No. 3 published in 1911 consisted of the piano compositions of 1907-1908: *The Fairy-Tale, Badinage, March, The Phantom.* p. 72

6 *Morolev, Vasily Mitrofanovich* (1880-1949)—a childhood friend of Prokofiev's. A veterinary surgeon by profession. p. 72

7 *Der Ring des Nibelungen*—a cycle of operas by Richard Wagner consisting of *Das Rheingold, Die Walküre, Siegfried* and *"Götterdämmerung"*. p. 73

8 *Zakharov, Boris Stepanovich*—pianist, a conservatoire friend of Prokofiev's. *The Gavotte*, Op. 12, is dedicated to him. p. 73

9 *Cherepnin, Nikolai Nikolayevich* (1873-1945)—composer, conductor and teacher. Prokofiev's tutor in the conducting class. p. 73

10 The collection of piano pieces in question was compiled by N.Y. Myaskovsky in 1927. Piece No. 6 was entitled *Snowy Horror* p. 75

11 *Autumnal Sketch*—a symphonic sketch for small orchestra, Opus 8, 1910. Prokofiev returned to this work twice: it was first revised in 1915, and then in 1934. p. 75

12 *Gury Stravinsky*, the composer's brother, actually died of typhus in 1917 on the Rumanian front. p. 93

REQUEST TO READERS

Progress Publishers would be glad to have your opinion of this book, its translation and design and any suggestions you may have for future publications.

Please send all your comments to 17, Zubovsky Boulevard, Moscow, USSR.

KOSTROVITSKAYA V., PISAREV A.
School of Classical Dance (A manual)

This manual is a methodologically brilliant aid for learning classical ballet over a period of eight years. Drawing on the many years of experience of the Vaganova Choreographic School, the authors have produced a well-ordered system for learning classical ballet.

The present edition has been specially expanded for the foreign reader as compared to the Russian edition. Its detailed descriptions of movement combinations and of final poses in compositions are accompanied by illustrations, thus making the work of both teachers and students much easier while also helping the book's users to penetrate more fully into the "secrets" of the Russian school of ballet.

The book was translated into English by John Barker, director of the New York School of Classical Dance and was edited by the prominent Soviet ballet specialist Natalia Roslavleva.

The book is designed for teachers of choreography and students of classical ballet.

DOLMATOVSKAYA G., SHILOVA I. *Who's
Who in the Soviet Cinema (Seventy Different Portraits)* (Collection)

As the art of film develops headlong, the
Soviet cinema has in recent years produced a
great number of important names. The
masters of different generations are developing Soviet cinema art.

The choice of people included in the book
intends to show in the fullest way possible
the achievements of the Soviet cinema today.
This publication contains literary portraits
of seventy actors and film directors active
in the Soviet cinema.

The book is recommended to both cinema
specialists and the wide circle of readers.